About the Author

Gill Shaddick left Britain aged twenty-one to take up a job in Hong Kong and kept on travelling. She met her husband in a township in Zambia. Together they embarked on a peripatetic journey living in a dozen countries. They counted cotton bollworms in Egypt, Sudan and Iran, tagged eels in New Zealand, owned a fishing business on Lake Kariba in central Africa and ran a rabbit farm in one of Scotland's remotest corners. Their four daughters, each a constant source of joy, amusement and awe, were all born in different countries.

Gill is a distant cousin of Robert Louis Stevenson. His grand-father's clock ticked out the hours as she grew up, which she credits as one reason why, from an early age, she was enchanted by travel and writing.

When she isn't travelling, Gill lives in Sydney. She is currently working on her second memoir. *The Hong Kong Letters* is her first book.

THE
HONG KONG
LETTERS

a travel memoir

GILL SHADDICK

ARCADIA

Author's Note

I have recreated events and conversations from my letters and memories. Some names have been changed in order to maintain anonymity.

© Gill Shaddick 2019

First published 2019 by Arcadia
the general books imprint of
Australian Scholarly Publishing Ltd
7 Lt Lothian St Nth, North Melbourne, Vic 3051

Tel: 03 9329 6963 / Fax: 03 9329 5452
enquiry@scholarly.info / www.scholarly.info

ISBN 978-1-925801-63-7

Cover design: Amelia Walker

For my parents, Sheila and Alan Stevenson

Prologue

It was the stillness that made me wake, adrenalin kicking my eyes open. I bounded up to the deck and found it deserted, the ship gently at anchor, limp in post-typhoon drizzle. Pinpricks of light pierced the blackness and I could see no gap, no way out to sea, as if we'd anchored in a glow-worm cave.

I didn't want to go below deck again so I curled up in a dry spot underneath a lifeboat and waited. The noises that stirred off the water were strange tongues, the fretting of ships' chandlery, foghorns breathing a lament. Through the dawning, soft banks of mist appeared. They furled slowly, stretching and lifting off the water, unshrouding other ships and small craft assembled on the rain-flattened slate sea. The air was wet and salty, weighty with soured cooking oil, fish bones and rot, and macerated with medicinal herbs and liniment; an old, old redolence. Hong Kong pong.

Even now, half a century later, I can still recollect that soggy, foggy dawn when I fell in love with Hong Kong.

It had been a rough voyage all the way. As passengers, we'd been sustained by the bravado of the ship's purser: "That damn lousy typhoon has caused us to change course again, but do not fear, we are not afraid of the Grey Wolf."

When the little Russian ship stole into Hong Kong harbour before dawn we were more than a day overdue and as the storm, Typhoon Wendy, still circled, the port authorities would not let us berth. We queued up and were taken off the ship in a lighter – a flat-bottomed barge – just as my grandfather, Jimmy, had made it to the same shore sixty years before.

Chapter 1

The Hong Kong letters were just as Dad had tied them, thin ribbon crisscrossing a stack of airmail paper. I remembered the ribbon; he used it for bundling medical journals that sat on the bookshelves in his office in Oxford. He must have had a roll of it, dark green, ribbed and thin.

I'd written home almost every day from Hong Kong from the day I arrived in the Colony. Dad had kept all my letters and only returned them to me on condition that I cherished them. So I had toted the bundled package to all the places where I had lived across the world. Astonishingly, they'd survived, a little the worse for wear – dog-eared and foxed, unread for nearly half a century. The sight of the bundle made me feel quite wistful. I badly wanted the company of Mum and Dad but they were long gone. I knew some ceremony was required, so I opened a bottle of wine, raised my glass and sent blessings into the beyond to both of them before I started to unpick the knot. I could not cut the ribbon, it seemed sacrilegious.

Poor dears, it was while sailing in Hong Kong that I'd scared them witless. Dad said the waiting was the worst. "When you were missing I started to have my scotch in a heavy lead-crystal tumbler. I got it into my head that as long as the glass was OK, you were OK, but if I broke the glass I would never see you again. Yet I had to use the glass to keep you alive. I wouldn't let anyone else touch it, I washed and dried it each night and put it away at the back of the cupboard. I knew it to be irrational but the thought dogged me, I was possessed."

Thinking of Dad, I instinctively touched my face. When we hugged, his tweed jacket pricked my cheek and I scented paternal love; a musty, warm mix of English damp and tobacco.

Once I started smoothing out the onion-skin airmail paper and reading the letters, I was quickly beguiled by my own past, and for the next couple of months I transcribed, reading the correspondence out loud; twenty-one again, bashful yet opinionated. Even the between-the-lines stuff was still there; what I didn't tell. Things I'd forgotten or hadn't thought about for years.

And then, in the midst of my nostalgia, that very past walked unexpectedly into my Sydney home, skipping ahead of the narrative.

We'd invited friends over for Boxing Day 2014. One of the guests, Ann, was a bit older than me. She was feisty and forthright, determined to squeeze every last drop out of life. The question she asked was just a friendly catch-up. "So what are you up to now, Gill?"

"I'm writing a memoir about Hong Kong."

"Oh, when were you there?"

"1968 to '70. A long time ago," I replied.

"Goodness, I didn't know that – I was there at the same time."

"Really, what were you doing?" I asked, nodding at another guest.

"Temp jobs mainly. And you?" she said.

"I worked for an advertising agency, but mostly I went sailing," I replied. "Excuse me Ann, I must go and do the rounds. I'll be back, I'd love to talk to you. We must have known someone in common." Ann threw me a quizzical expression.

"Yes, yes, I understand. Go see to your guests, we'll talk later." Then she added, "I did a temp job for an advertising agency where the girl had gone sailing and disappeared. All very dramatic. On the news. Headlines. You might have known her?"

I had already turned away; my hearing is shot so my brain needs extra seconds to put together what is said and my thoughts were interrupted when another guest nudged my arm. "Is the beetroot dish OK for vegans?" The veranda was buzzing, easy laughter, wine flowing. I put one hand on the back of a chair to steady myself, trying to make sense of Ann's words before I turned to her again. "Ann, tell me more. Where was that temp job? What part of town?"

"Oh, it was Hong Kong side, Central. Queen's Road, one of those older office blocks. It was across the road from the Hilton Coffee Shop. I used to go over there for lunch."

I saw it again. The Hilton on the curve. The street. The downstairs lobby of Marina House, a dark, cool sanctuary from sun and heat. The rattling air-conditioner in my office overwhelming the smatterings of Cantonese that drifted in the door. Ann's words had brought it all back. On the day I'd returned to work, Connie, my assistant, had tried to explain. "They didn't know if ... when you'd come back ... there was so much to do, they said." I remembered the hand-over notes on my desk. I hadn't recognised the writing. I remembered, too, my irrational irritation. My chair was not even cold when they had got someone else. And then Connie said she was an Australian girl – awfully nice – which was no help at all.

Ann was already chatting to another guest, but I interrupted.

"Ann, that was me! You stood in for me."

Chapter 2

In the swinging sixties, I was twenty, working in London as a secretary at a Park Lane hotel. I mooched about the city in a long leather coat that swung round my mini-skirt brushing the knee-high, pinot-red, lace-up boots that I regret parting with to this day. In winter, I topped the outfit with a faux-fur Cossack hat.

Siberia had come to Carnaby Street after the film, *Doctor Zhivago*, became a box-office hit in 1965. A collective swoon overtook my final year at school when Lara and Yuri traced ice crystal etchings on the window pane of a desolate snow-clad dacha. We all read Russian literature avidly, weeping en masse at *Anna Karenina*'s spectacular fall from grace and sanity. At night, I shivered under my eiderdown, swept to sleep in snowy blizzards, revelling with high society, dancing polkas, mazurkas and waltzes until dawn. My allegiances were so fickle, now with the revolutionaries, now with the Tsar. Always, it was winter in Siberia.

And it was winter in London when after work one shadowy evening, gusty with sleet, I met up with an old school friend in a Knightsbridge pub; someone I could grumble to comfortably.

"I loathe my job," I said, "but Dad'll blow a fuse if I start looking for another one. He's traumatised that I'm on my third in twelve months and he's convinced it's because I can't spell."

"Well, that's true," said Janet. "You never could!"

"That's not it," I retorted. "I'm bored senseless, but now I'm stuck. I'll have to break a leg or marry or land a job overseas!"

We laughed together and hugged before we parted. I said I had to run for the bus, but it wasn't that. A thought was echoing in my brain and I needed to be alone to catch it before it vanished.

I stood in the bus queue, preoccupied and excited. A job overseas? But where? I stamped my frozen feet – somewhere warm. When a red double-decker kicked up sprays of icy slush and jolted to a stop beside me, I got it. Of course! I knew the answer. I would go East because that was where I had wanted to go from as far back as I could remember.

It had started with my grandfather, Jimmy. He had died on his seventy-ninth birthday in 1954. I was seven. I'd asked my mother if he had opened his birthday presents as his demise would have been doubly tragic had he not. She attached no importance to my question at all; in fact she never even answered me.

I hadn't given Jimmy another thought until I was a young teenager, and his widow, my octogenarian grandmother, came to live with us in Oxford. A thrifty, tall and vitreous stick of a woman, Mamie never seemed pleased to see me and I steered clear of her. But her arrival did resurrect my grandfather, for with Mamie arrived a great many tea chests with *objets d'art* he'd collected on a trip he'd made East in 1908.

My grandfather was a Master brassfounder from a long line of Scottish hammermen. Casting techniques and artisanship fascinated him so many of the souvenirs he purchased were made of brass and its darker sister bronze.

A selection of the treasures soon enlivened our rambling Cotswold house; a Hindu goddess with multiple arms, an intricate brass table top from China, a bronze Buddha, as well as magnificent porcelain, and a panel of exuberant Cantonese embroidery. I was fascinated by the exotica and acquired small curios for my bedroom window sill; tiny bamboo rickshaw drivers who strained in elegant symmetry; ivory elephants, their mahouts laughing in perpetuity; and four miniature porcelain jars from Japan. There was also an intricately carved sandalwood fan with a beaded red tassel that I kept in the drawer of my bedside table. Wafts of fragrant woody perfume permeated my dreamtime. I made a promise to my teenage self that a time would come when I too would go East.

Once the idea was resurrected on that winter's night, it provided the perfect solution. I borrowed a Far East Business Directory from a friend in advertising and wrote to firms listed in Hong Kong where I had no need of work permits or visas as it was still a British Colony.

I didn't say anything to anyone about my letters to Hong Kong which was just as well when weeks ran into months. London acquired a boastful swagger and light sunny evenings stretched, honeyed and restorative. But just as I fell in love with London, I got a job. Mrs Church, proprietor of the Advertising and Publicity Bureau, Marina House, Hong Kong, it just so happened, was looking for an English secretary when my letter arrived on her desk. She arranged for me to be interviewed by a friend of hers in London and soon afterwards, she offered me a two-year contract.

My boss, the hotel's General Manager, said, "Think carefully Gill. You'll soon have a pay rise. Hospitality is a good career; you just need a few years' experience."

Dad too thought the idea was ridiculous. "There were riots in Hong Kong only a few months back. It'll be nothing like you expect and it could be downright dangerous. The Chinese don't want British rule anymore." Mum squeezed my arm. I could feel her suppressing a giggle. "And besides," he added, "you've got no experience because you don't stay in any job long enough to get any." His gruff admonishments didn't fool me; I knew he just didn't want me to go.

If I did falter at all, it was Mum who strengthened my resolve. She told me that somewhere she had the letters that Jimmy, my grandfather, had written on his trip East.

When she found them, she said, "How very strange. He mentions posting letters from Hong Kong but those pages are missing." Our eyes met.

"You'll have to write from Hong Kong instead," she said, laughing. I hugged her tight.

Jimmy's letters were written to my grandmother on thin paper in a spidery hand; each one on a page embossed with the image of a grand hotel or steam ship. I started to read them and charted his journey from the Thames estuary to India, up and down the Irrawaddy River, through the Straits of Malacca to Singapore, China, Hong Kong and Japan.

Every letter was defaced, the first line and the last, scratched out by my grandmother's fountain pen. I tried to think what could have been so racy it had to be expunged for future generations. Maybe a pet name? 'My bonny lass' was all I could muster, my experience of such lexicon limited. Whatever it was, had she left it behind, maybe I could have conjured up an image of her as young and coy, but the scoring entrenched my perception of a prudish and austere woman.

Jimmy's correspondence gave me the sense of a man determined not to miss a thing; up early to be on deck while the ship came into port and keen to go ashore. He cannot envisage any finer building in the world than the Taj Mahal by moonlight. At dawn he goes down to the Ghats to watch ritual ablutions on the sacred River Ganges at Benares. He falls in love – at a distance he hastens to add – with the beautiful girls of Burma, cannot conceive of anything prettier than Penang, finds the Shanghai Chinese to be wonderful people, and in Japan marvels at the bronze work of the Great Buddha of Kamakura.

Jimmy, I decided, would make an excellent mentor. At first I spoke aloud to him. I often spoke out loud; I'd had a somewhat solitary childhood with my brothers shipped off to boarding school, so my own voice was often my only company. He answered back immediately, delighted to hear from me. He had no doubt about it, I should go East.

I accepted the job. I never questioned why Mrs Church could not find staff closer to home, and neither did anyone else think to ask.

I didn't want a breathtaking vault into my new life; I wanted to travel to it. Given my latter-day enchantment with all things Russian, the Trans-Siberian Express was an obvious choice. Reports of hostile encounters at newly opened Soviet border crossings made me keener still, while Dad rolled his eyes and questioned why I did not just fly.

I asked Jimmy why he hadn't gone by train? The Trans-Siberian had not long been commissioned when he made his trip at the turn of the twentieth century. The answer was not long coming. "I am a man of boats and sea, but the train is a marvellous idea." I smiled and wondered about having a conversation in my head with the dead.

The link back to my grandfather may have been tenuous, but once I'd made the decision to go East, he began to arrive unannounced and with increasing frequency.

I left England shortly after my twenty-first birthday. My prospective employer, Mrs Church, had written to say she could not understand why I insisted on going through Russia. I would, she said, meet more than my fill of Communists in Hong Kong. But to me the opportunity to visit Siberia was the most wonderful bonus I could imagine.

The Trans-Siberian Express took a week from Moscow to Russia's eastern seaboard. The Siberia of my dreams was white, a permanent winter underworld of snow and ice where dense fogs and fearfully heavy snowstorms silently enveloped travellers; where winds howled over the permafrost and chilled to unimaginable cold. But looking out from the train that August, there was little sign of my Siberia; just sunny temperate days with occasional showers. But Siberia, like all vast spaces, is imbued with a certain mystique. The empty slowness of the journey and the hypnotic repetition of village, dacha, rail yard and copse of cold-loving spruce was, in turn, both soothing and disquieting. It was a fascinating way to make the transition from Europe to Asia, the faces of passengers boarding the train shifting from predominantly European to Mongolians, Chinese and Koreans. A constant of the journey was illicit vodka available in unlabelled recycled bottles at every wayside stop.

The journey ended at a port south of Vladivostok and there I boarded a little Russian ship, the MS *Baikal*, for the sea voyage to Hong Kong.

Chapter 3

My new employer, Mrs Church, was still in Europe when I arrived in Hong Kong but she had insisted I stay at her house until she returned ten days later. Henry, her chauffeur, collected me from Ocean Terminal on Kowloon side. He was tall and thin; a dignified old Shanghainese. Age had pulled his skin tight back from his cheek bones and I wondered where his wrinkles gathered. He drove carefully onto the car ferry that would take us across the harbour to Hong Kong Island. Salamat, Mrs Church's home, was a spacious old bungalow in Pokfulam, an upmarket hillside residential district. Lined up to greet me were the cook, Ah Tong; the amah and the gardener. I was then introduced to the "children" with exaggerated respect; Pipa, an ancient spaniel, smelly and deaf, Dickie the Dachshund and Lulu the Alsatian.

The house was dark inside, every surface weighed down with knickknacks and photos. All-pervasive was the strong smell of newly applied furniture polish.

I was soon in the garden with a tray of tea and sandwiches. Henry came and pulled up a chair. We talked first about the dogs. "We have to tie Pipa's ears up before she eats so they don't get in the gravy," said Henry.

"What Mrs Church spends on dog food and chockies each month would feed a Chinese family two times," he grumbled. Then he started to grin, straightening out his left knee as if it was necessary to release the chuckle that was building up. "Once we had an amah who thought Dickie would make good eating. Dog meat makes us feel warm in winter. Mrs

Church was going to Europe, so she got a doctor to send the amah to a hospital for crazy people so the amah couldn't eat Dickie!"

Henry laughed out loud and at first I laughed too until I grasped that he meant the amah had been locked up in an asylum and that wasn't funny. Henry, sensing disquiet, went on to tell me the story of how a soft-hearted Mrs Church had rescued Lulu the Alsatian one rainy night at a petrol station, where the stray dog was running around terrified by thunder.

I didn't think Mrs Church's dogs appetising or adorable, though I too, liked Dickie best because on his short coat I could see the fleas.

Fleas were a familiar pest – I'd grown up with dogs at home – but I'd never seen cockroaches in Britain. I met them on my first night in Hong Kong but it was the second night before they joined me in my bed. I freaked out, took to the bath tub with my blankets and slept there blissfully unaware that their most common entry point was through plug holes.

In the morning I told Henry about the roaches. He regarded me with wry amusement, shouted for Ah Tong, who shouted for the gardener, who quartered my room with a pump action spray. I also got him to spread flea powder on the dogs.

I always had to go through Henry. Ah Tong had limited English save a few choice and oft-repeated phrases which, in time I would discover, reflected his mistress's jaundiced view. "England very wet," he said. "England government take all the money," and added with a shake of his head, "too many Communists now in England."

A couple of days after my arrival, three Catholic nuns, friends of Mrs Church, came to stay. The most senior of the trio was Sister Frances, a gentle practical American. Next was a Filipino sister, who laughed constantly and infectiously, and a good-humoured young novice from Tokyo. They'd been uprooted from Shanghai by Chairman Mao's edicts and in Hong Kong they ran a mission hospital and school in the New Territories – the rural hinterland adjoining Kowloon that China had leased to the British in 1898. Ah Tong, without much to do, spent a lot of time with the visitors. They were cheery and lively, dashing off to Chinese opera one day and a course on Buddhism the next, united in their admiration and affection for the Chinese people.

The sisters urged me to join them in the garden on their last night. Ah Tong bought us a tray of iced tea and we sat, serenaded by the crickets, to watch the sun blaze its way down until the sea swallowed it whole. The Filipino sister said she had seen me taking advantage of a change in the weather to do my washing and ironing. "You don't need to do that here, my dear, it is for the amah."

I was stung. "I don't want to propagate a feudal system when I am quite capable of doing my own chores."

The sister looked at me compassionately. "You will upset the amah. By your actions you are saying she is not good enough to wash your clothes, you are not valuing her livelihood."

I was confused. My ethics had so soon been undermined, and I felt a little foolish.

The next morning when we gathered to farewell them, Sister Francis gave me a book to read that she had taken from Mrs Church's bookshelf. It was a slim red hardback, *The Man on Joss Stick Alley,* written by an American missionary priest, Father James Walsh.

"Father Walsh has been in a Communist prison in China for ten years," she said, "held captive by the people he loves. We pray for him every day."

Then, her mood lifting, she smiled broadly and told me Ah Tong had converted to Christianity. Ah Tong was standing behind her and shifted from foot to foot with an embarrassed grin. Henry looked steely. And off the three sisters swept; their black robes flying.

The house was quiet after their departure and I curled up on a sofa with Father Walsh's book. I had my own view on missionaries. I'd attended two high schools, one of which was a convent. The nuns were a mixed bunch. Sister Luke, the School Principal, with a degree in biology, was a pragmatic, yet genuinely spiritual soul. Others were sanctimonious, a few were downright ignorant, and some, gloriously batty. One in particular urged us to be ready for the end of the world. That would happen the day every living person had heard God's word. My instinct for self-preservation was strong and I'd always fervently hoped that a few people would get overlooked, so when I read in Father Walsh's book that the task of reaching China's teeming millions was insurmountable, I found that a comfort.

Although I missed the lively sisters, I had no time to be lonely as other friends of Mrs Church called by to ensure I was comfortable. They were unanimous in their surprise that I had not yet met Mrs Church. "Oh, she's a bit of a character!" the men would say, while the womenfolk focused on her generosity, knowledge and standing in the Colony.

It wasn't long before I picked up that I'd arrived at an in-between time – the space between shock and spectre. The Japanese occupation of the Colony from 1941 to 1945 and Mao Zedong's declaration of the People's Republic of China in 1949 were still raw, while ahead lay the extraordinary notion that when the lease on the New Territories ran out, Hong Kong would return to China in 1997. These events shaped a phenomenal explosion of activity in Hong Kong. Money was the religion and it was a sin not to make it. The Colony had become a conduit for funds from everywhere. Opportunistic émigrés from Shanghai moved over early, bringing with them expertise, skilled tradesmen and even plant and machinery. Demand for Hong Kong manufactured goods soared when the UN slapped trade embargoes on Communist China. Waves of Chinese fleeing from the mainland arrived in Hong Kong with the desperate need to turn a dollar, and with great enterprise and energy set about it, creating thousands of small businesses and providing cheap labour. Some of these refugees arrived penniless, while others brought gold, solid gold, in ingots, in jewellery and hidden in their body cavities. Loans from Western banks added a new-found impetus to Chinese entrepreneurs and there were few restraints; unions couldn't make headway because they were so easily accused of Communist ideology. The clock ticking meant each buck needed to be a quick one.

Great inequity fuelled such unbridled growth; many workers never had a day's respite and worked long hours in poor and polluted conditions. Shanty towns spilled down the mountainsides on the island and hideous tenement blocks were springing up where whole families lived in overcrowded and squalid rooms. It would take a few more years before the Government would be able to invest in improved social services.

Nevertheless, in 1968, Hong Kong had an extraordinary energy and buoyancy and I, already smitten, floated in on a sea of exhilaration. I dawdled in busy streets magnetised by the sight of women hawkers who dodged round me in black pyjamas wearing wide-brimmed straw hats – often with a baby bound tight to their backs. Throngs of chattering Chinese office girls in Cheongsams – the captivating, tight, sleeveless dress with a Mandarin collar that became fashionable in Shanghai in the 1920s – floated past, cool and elegant, contrasting with pale European woman permanently sheened in perspiration. I skirted wizened Chinese men with long poles bent over their shoulders, balancing slopping buckets of indeterminate liquids or touting loads of bricks to be heaved up incredible bamboo scaffolding; I nodded to turbaned Hindu guards who sat at every bank door, leaning on ancient shotguns clutched between their knees; I felt shy when I saw smart young expatriates; I glanced sideways at immaculate Chinese businessmen; and I was amused at old colonials in baggy shorts. I felt conspicuous but the busy, spitting, hawking melee ignored me.

I took the tram up to The Peak, Hong Kong Island's highest mountain, where prominent residents built their houses to catch cool breezes and panoramic views. Jimmy had brought postcards home so I knew he'd been there. At the time of his visit, The Peak was an exclusive reserve of Europeans.

Friends of Mrs Church took me to the Hong Kong Club, a lovely old white colonnaded building, a cool oasis of potted palms and deep leather chesterfields. My grandfather would definitely have been there as well. His father's firm, Steven & Struthers, innovative manufacturers of stern posts, propellers, gun carriages, pumps and gauges, ship's sirens, foghorns, and lighthouse lanterns, had customers world-wide, so at each port of call Jimmy had business connections to foster.

Chapter 4

After a couple of days of sightseeing, Henry took me to the Advertising and Publicity Bureau, known by everyone as the APB. The firm had occupied the same offices for decades. They were right in the centre of the CBD in Marina House; dark, dated and dreary. There was not much for me to do until Mrs Church returned. I was shown around each department. The agency brought British brands to the Chinese market by organising print advertisements for newspapers and magazines, TV commercials and PR campaigns. I was the only European on the staff but I quickly realised I was not the first, just the next, in a succession of English girls who came to work for Mrs Church.

"Our Queen comes home tomorrow," announced Ah Tong.

We all turned out to welcome Mrs Church at the airport; the staff of the APB and the house servants. She arrived beaming, a battleship of a woman in her mid-sixties. She patted heads, dispensed compliments, straightened a tie, chucked a cheek, feigned surprise at such a welcome and swept out of the airport interrogating Henry while Ah Tong, the amah and I staggered after her with the luggage.

When we pulled into the driveway, the dogs unleashed a ruckus of leaping and licking, yelping and yapping. "Oh, my darlings, how I've missed you. Oh, oh, I know you've missed your mumsie so much." I was astonished and felt embarrassed watching Mrs Church fawn over her dogs, but her servants knew what to expect and indulged her, laughing and applauding.

Once inside, Ah Tong fetched tea and Mrs Church sat in her favourite armchair. She was full of beans and full of chat. When she paused to light up a cigarette, I had time to take a good look at her. A strong, Spartan face, her keen eyes hooded by meaty lids. She took great care of her appearance and her exuberance and quick wit repudiated the loosening skin.

After tea, she could not wait to unpack. She called for the amah and then turned to me, her imperious voice scoured from tobacco. "Always shop for fashion in Switzerland, dear, there you can take your pick of French, Swiss and Italian designers. I stop over on the way home every year." In no time, she modelled sixteen new outfits, cast out last year's collection and had the amah and I running in circles, laughing with her, pinning and tucking, discerning hemlines, appraising shoes and handbags.

"Now let's have a gin and tonic, dear, and you can tell me who you know in Hong Kong. I'm sure you must have arrived with lots of contacts."

She settled into her wing-back chair and I perched on the veteran chintz sofa, redolent of dog.

"Well, there is Professor Gibson, he's at the University, he was an usher at my aunt's wedding," I said.

"Oh, Gibby, yes, he fixed my lawnmower. Who else?"

"A Mr Kadoorie – he's a hotelier and a friend of my old boss in London."

"Oh, Horace. I go to him for breakfast every New Year's Day at the Peninsula. They serve eggnog and champagne. I will ring him on Monday. Who else?"

"Mr Eric Marsh – he's a friend of a friend."

"*The* Eric Marsh, Johnson & Johnson?"

I nodded.

"Oh, now that's a very good contact. Who else?"

I was out of names but obviously Eric Marsh had sufficed.

"Eric Marsh, umm" she said, nodding gently.

When we were ready for dinner, Mrs Church reached for a little brass bell that sat beside her place mat. She rang it to summon Ah Tong. The kitchen door swung open and low strains of Chinese music emerged. "Chinese music while I am eating – Ah Tong?" Mrs Church said, arching an eyebrow.

After dinner, she poured us each a scotch and turned on the TV. She chatted during programs but in the ad-breaks, jumped up with surprising agility and turned up the volume. "I made that one!", "That's awful!", "That one must have cost a fortune – wasted money."

When it was time for bed, I thanked Mrs Church for her hospitality and told her I was moving out in a few days, but she dismissed the idea. "No, no dear, you must stay here for at least a couple of months, I insist. There is no question of you going to a hostel. However, I do have rules, you must not spoil the servants – newcomers always do. Also your name is too short. I heard Ah Tong call you Missy Gill. This is no-good. I have told them *they* must call you Miss Aileen from now on."

"I've never been called Aileen in my life; I know it's my first name but I detest it," I protested, but she had already moved on.

The following day the amah announced she had to take her sick mother back to Shanghai. She also seized the opportunity for a final tête-à-tête with Mrs Church to spill harboured grievances. The whole conversation was in Cantonese, but Mrs Church interpreted regularly for me, nodding to the amah and then to me with wry smiles.

I wasn't surprised to learn that Henry and Ah Tong ran the joint, but relegating the gardener to live in the tool shed so they could turn his room into their TV lounge was a step too far. Mrs Church didn't seem surprised either to learn that Ah Tong watered her gin and stole food from the nuns. She turned to me, winked and chortled, "The sisters were probably on their knees asking forgiveness for their gluttony."

Mrs Church patted the amah's knee, but there was more and the amah moved to the edge of her seat as she wound up for the close.

"Oh God, Ah Tong's been selling the steak I buy for the dogs and giving them pet food! My poor darlings, no wonder Pipa looks peaky!" said Mrs Church, swaying back in her chair.

"What will you do?" I asked.

"I'll wait, let him sweat it out, he might suspect the amah is spilling the beans, but he won't be sure, so I'll say nothing yet."

The next day was Sunday and it was barely light when I woke to a soft but insistent knocking at my door. I opened it sleepily in my pyjamas, my hair piled in pink foam rollers. Ah Tong grinned and then jogged up and down, clicking his tongue and whacking his backside with his hand. I had no idea what he meant, but started to mimic him and we were both almost crying with laughter when Mrs Church appeared and said, "What on earth are you doing? Ah Tong? Gill, didn't I tell you, we go to the racing stables every Sunday, early so we are back to get ready for tiffin."

"Tiffin?" I said.

"Curry tiffin – lunch – I'm famous for my Sunday tiffins."

I grabbed up the rollers that had spun from my hair and flew back into my room to get ready.

Henry installed us in the back of the car and loaded the boot with bunches of grass which Mrs Church paid someone to grow for her, packets of sugar lumps and a sack of carrots.

"Has the amah left? Ah Tong doesn't seem to be worried?" I said softly to Mrs Church as we drove to Happy Valley, the racecourse where Jocelyn, her three-year-old racehorse, was liveried.

"She left, but she's not out of reach yet – she will send me a message once she feels safe ..." said Mrs Church.

Henry's neck stiffened almost imperceptibly. I knew he'd heard.

Jocelyn lived in a high-rise stable, loose-boxes slotted in a building similar to a multi-story car park. A Chinese stable-hand walked her down a ramp and around a tiny exercise circle, while the Stable Manager, an Aberdonian vet, praised her form, her potential and her character. Mrs Church's eyes shone with pleasure.

When we got home, the nuns rang to thank Mrs Church and give her the good news about Ah Tong. Mrs Church's eyes widened and she said she must rush. As the phone went down, she roared for Ah Tong. Turning to me she snorted, "Ah Tong's converted to Christianity! He pinches their food and mine, drinks my gin, abuses my dogs and now he thinks he can go to confession and wipe the slate clean ... A Catholic indeed! Phooey! Ahhhhhh Tong!"

Henry appeared and said that Ah Tong had been called away suddenly to the New Territories as his mother was ill. Henry bowed slightly as he left the room walking backwards, deferential – gauging Mrs Church's rage.

She turned to me, speaking loudly for Henry's benefit. "Ah Tong's got no papers – I can have him arrested. And he can't get another job because he's an illegal." Then she blew herself up to shout "Phooey" one last time. When Ah Tong did reappear a week later, Mrs Church was tired of Henry's limited dinner menus and pleased to see him back. She summoned him to the sitting room. I was in the garden and could hear raised voices through the open window. She was angry and certainly scolded him but that was all.

I was completely captivated by Mrs Church. She recounted anecdotes endlessly, praised and punished the servants in equal measure and emitted breathless energy. Visitors called to welcome her home. Fresh supplies of gin arrived and she soon had the house back on track.

Salamat had suffered some minor typhoon damage during her absence and she booked a visit by insurance assessors. When we heard them at the door she said, "Quick, Gill, get out the whisky and the sherry – we'll get much more out of them drunk than sober!" And she did a jig when they left. "It worked, even more than I'd hoped for."

That evening, Mrs Church quizzed me on what I thought of the APB staff. I had little to say other than everyone was very nice. She was disappointed. Mrs Church, I would in time discover, kept her finger on the pulse, gathering information Chinese-style starting at the telephonist, who could listen in to everyone's calls and pay special attention as directed. Cleaners were invaluable; it was surprising what people consigned to waste paper bins. Thus armed, Mrs Church could unsettle and elicit further information from people with a sleight of hand that would take your breath away. She could curtail resignations or hasten them and her wonderful flair for languages meant she could "hear" everything. I disappointed her. I had not picked up nuances and had nothing to add to the fabric she worked on constantly, stitching, threading and designing.

Over the following days and weeks, no matter what took place at the office, after dinner, I was her sweet English companion. Mrs Church poured large drinks. Ah Tong conjured up solid English cooking, and in-between the TV ad-breaks, she recounted her life's tale.

Chapter 5

Mrs Church was born Beatrice Mary Mills, but known as Betty from birth. Her father was a railway engineer from Liverpool. At the end of the 1800s, dividends from Britain's railway system were petering out and investors started to look overseas. At first the Chinese resisted the idea of railways, fearing the iron roads would enable foreign invaders to penetrate the interior too easily. However, investors were not going to be deterred lightly; construction, equipment, locomotives were just the start; the railways would open up trade. Eventually, in 1892, the Chinese government succumbed to the inevitable and the Imperial Railway Administration was set up. British shareholders chose the engineers they wanted to be involved in the projects and Betty's father was one of them. He set off from England with six others.

Betty's father arrived in China during the last years of the reign of the Manchu Empress Dowager Tz'u-hsi, at a time when the Imperial Maritime Customs Service in China was at the height of its influence. Although controlled by the Chinese Government, the Service was run by Europeans. It had expanded from regulating the collection of duties to other areas; collating statistics, improving port facilities, representing China at overseas exhibitions and running the Chinese Post Office. It gave European countries, particularly Britain, enormous influence, tantamount to colonising China.

While on leave in England, Betty's father married and arranged for his wife to follow him back to China. Months later he travelled to Hong Kong to meet her off the ship from Liverpool. He knew his wife was pregnant and the baby was due any day.

Mrs Church lit another cigarette. She kept the gold lighter in her left hand, turning it over and over again slowly with her thumb.

"I was born in a typhoon," she said, pronouncing it *tyfooooon.* "Not just any typhoon, the 1906." The 1906 lived in the memories of an entire generation. *The Hong Kong Daily Press* described it as, "… the most appallingly destructive visitation of the kind that the Colony had ever experienced." About ten thousand lives were lost, and hundreds of sampans, homes to entire families of Chinese, were swept out to sea.

"My poor father came down to meet the boat and heard that my mother had given birth and was terribly ill. She was taken off to the Government Civil Hospital and I was wrapped up in a ragged towel and given into his arms," Mrs Church said. Her mother died two days later.

Young Betty did not enter the privileged life of a child brought up in one of the international settlements in China where foreign traders administered their own laws and several generations of Europeans had been born and called China *home*. Instead, she lived with her father as he travelled the country. "I became a mascot for the other engineers on the railway – far from their own homes and children." She was a precocious child and developed an early self-sufficiency. "I learnt to ride as soon as I could walk – I didn't bother with a saddle, I rode bareback." They camped out as he supervised the laying of tracks and blasting of tunnels at remote outposts, cooking with a kerosene stove under the stars. She listened to the ribald humour of the men and learned the dialects of the Chinese workforce. It was then that she soaked up the codes and cues, rites and rituals of Chinese interaction, observing and imitating as only a child could. Early on, she not only translated for the engineers, but told them what the Chinese were really thinking and saw her viewpoint valued.

Betty and her father adored each other and revelled in their unusual life. They were equally comfortable in the countryside, where itinerant jugglers and Chinese fortune-tellers were their entertainment, or joining friends in the European concessions to go to the races, play tennis and attend concerts. At the age of six, to her chagrin, Betty's father insisted she go to school and during term-time he left her with friends in Shanghai, the most famous of the foreign settlements, which had developed into a great modern city. Each school holiday her father collected her and Betty resumed her nomadic tomboy existence.

When her father went shopping for her clothes at Whiteway & Laidlaw, the Shanghai Department store where foreigners and wealthy Chinese shopped for goods from all over the world, he favoured practicality. "The coats were always too big for me and I looked like something out of a music hall or a comedy show with the pockets down by my thighs." She used the pockets to good effect when her father took her to the clubs which sprung up wherever an expatriate community gathered. "I had a marvellous voice and my father delighted in teaching me silly songs. We'd sing together all the time and at the club he'd say 'There you go Betty, give us a number!' and I'd be off singing *Gilbert the Filbert* or *Goodbye Dolly*. The men would all put a coin in my pocket!"

Ah Tong came in to empty the ashtray and top up the water jug. I looked over at Mrs Church and saw her eyes were moist. She started singing, her voice husky.

> *I'm Gilbert the Filbert, the knut with a k,*
> *The pride of Piccadilly, the blasé roué.*
> *Oh Hades! the Ladies who leave their wooden huts,*
> *For Gilbert the Filbert, the colonel of the knuts, I'm knuts.*

Although she told me a filbert was a hazelnut, the song didn't make any sense to me, but I laughed out loud and felt my heart go out to her. She sang it once more, back among the men, making them chuckle. She stopped, shaking her head as she returned to her panelled dining room from those faraway years.

"Of course," she said, straightening up in her chair, "in Shanghai I was taken to concerts all the time and I adored Beethoven, Chopin and Sibelius. I write my own advertising jingles you know – I'm good at it – I can write the words and compose music for English and Chinese ads; that's how I started in advertising – I could do everything; book space, write the copy, make up the jingles."

She paused, lost in thought. She had a cigarette burning between her fingers and as I watched, a column of ash crashed soundlessly to dust on the carpet. She started singing again, this time the words of *Goodbye Dolly Gray*, another popular song from her days with her father, but she faltered and didn't sing the last verse.

> *Goodbye Dolly I must leave you, though it breaks my heart to go,*
> *Something tells me I am needed at the front to fight the foe,*
> *See – the boys in blue are marching and I can no longer stay,*
> *Hark – I hear the bugle calling, goodbye Dolly Gray.*

In 1914, Betty's father decided it was time to go home. He took Betty back to England just a month before World War I broke out. There was no national conscription at the beginning of the war and joining the British army was entirely voluntary. Betty's father did not hesitate – he immediately enlisted and deposited Betty at a convent in Kent.

It was a closed order and the sisters prided themselves on developing in their pupils a sense of duty and responsibility to God as a prerequisite for every action. "I was a turbulent handful of a child who had lived among men all my young days. I swore like a trooper and did not care for anything or anybody." The strangeness of her home country, entry into a closed religious order and her father's abrupt exit might have subdued some children, but not Betty. The first morning, she picked a fight and when a nun intervened, Betty snatched the wimple off her head. The shocked Sister screamed "You little heathen!" and the Mother Superior was summoned. Fortunately for all, Mother Augustine was a wonderful psychologist and took the ferocious child to her study. She ordered tea and gave Betty time to settle. She recognised the girl before her was used to getting her own way and wisely decided to exploit Betty's strengths. She told Betty that as a born leader she had a responsibility and must set a good example.

It worked for a while, but Betty was irrepressible and Mother Augustine was right; she was a born leader. One weekend when the girls were bored, Betty said, "Let's all pierce our ears, I know how to do it," and her classmates lined up like lambs. She dipped a darning needle in olive oil and shoved it through her ear into a potato held behind and dared the others not to back out. The nuns, hearing crying, found a classroom of girls in tears, ears red and swelling and Betty sitting like a child Dracula brandishing needles dripping with blood. Mother Augustine was out of ideas and threatened her with expulsion; Betty didn't care; she knew they had nowhere to send her.

Mother Superior grew fond of Betty but she found herself sorely tried by the girl's constant challenges. But in late October 1918, her frustration would evaporate. She received news that Betty's father had been killed in action. Either she was trying to clarify the news or simply could not find the right moment to tell Betty and she faltered. On the Front, changes accelerated; Germany began to crumble and the Armistice came three weeks later at 11 am on the eleventh day of the eleventh month. The war was finally over, people were dancing in the streets and celebrating with champagne. It seemed far too cruel to tell Betty at that moment, so more time passed.

Eventually there was no hope left. Mother Augustine called Betty to her study to tell her that her father was never coming to collect her.

When I left Mrs Church that night to go to bed, she was in a sombre mood. I suspected that she had replayed that devastating moment many times in her life. I sat on my bed reflecting on how much I loved my own father and how unimaginable it would be to lose him. I doubted Betty had been given, or took, time to grieve. The war was over, the world was keen to move on and she was one of so many.

Despite the sad note, once I started getting ready for bed, an undeniable sense of elation crept over me. Mrs Church's storytelling had touched me but it was her energy that I connected with. I could scarcely believe my own good fortune that such an amazing woman had chosen me to work for her.

That night, I put the plug firmly in the bathtub to forestall the cockroaches and went to sleep eager to get to my first day at work and make myself useful.

Chapter 6

Mrs Church swept in around noon on Monday, her first day back at work. Gone was the loquacious weekend companion, she was abrupt and business-like. She greeted me coolly, expressed surprise that I had not yet started the dictation she had phoned in half-an-hour before, and sat down at her desk, indicating to me to pull up a chair and listen.

Mr Kwan, the Art Director, and Irene Chan, Head of Media, joined us to bring Mrs Church up to speed on all that had happened in her absence. These two were the pillars of her organisation. Mr Kwan was a formal and dignified figure in late middle-age and Irene, about thirty, had worked her way steadily up the firm's ladder and had an astute head for figures. She was stick-thin and her tailored grey silk cheongsam caught on her angular pelvic bones when she moved. Irene was tight-lipped and I decided she was hesitant to reveal her large teeth, which were out of proportion to her slender frame and dignified appearance. Irene was pleasant enough in a formal way. To her, I was just another flyby.

Other staff were summoned and Mrs Church issued streams of instructions, rapidly switching from English to Cantonese and back. Irene and I shared an office with Mrs Church. Once everyone was dismissed we started to organise ourselves for work and Mrs Church began on a list of telephone calls.

"Good morning, may I speak to Mr Faulkner? What the devil is it to you who's speaking? It's Mr Faulkner I want to speak to, not you, now put me through!"

Her second call was to the British Trade Commissioner in Hong Kong, introducing me to a mantra which would soon become familiar. "I've been promoting British goods in the Colony for forty years and I just don't know what you fellows do all day!"

My desk faced the wall with my back towards Mrs Church. I turned on my electric typewriter. It clicked and buzzed to life. Then I got out my dictionary and placed it on the desk beside me before I settled down to type.

"Can't you spell?" The words thundered, breaking against my shoulders. I swivelled to look at Mrs Church in astonishment. She had pushed back her chair, glaring at me while Irene remained impassive working at her desk. "Why the devil do you need a dictionary? Phooey ..." and Mrs Church returned to her phone calls but within minutes, another blast,

"What have you stopped for?"

And another,

"Can't you read shorthand?"

And so it went on, hour after hour.

"It's better to do it right first time!"

"You waste a lot of time rubbing out!"

"What! Another piece of paper gone! That's my profits you're putting in the bin!"

"Didn't they teach you anything at college?"

I wilted. Surreptitiously I slid spoiled paper beneath my typewriter and took the dictionary in my handbag to the Ladies Room.

"Oh Gawd, have you got the runs; the toilet again?"

When Henry came to collect her mid-afternoon on that first day, it was none too soon for me.

Irene unbent as soon as Mrs Church left and hurried over. "She is always like that. It is just her way. We have a Chinese nick-name for her, *Huloongnu*, it means tiger-fire-dragon."

I was close to tears.

"Wait," said Irene and went out. She came back with Mr Kwan who'd known Betty Church for three decades.

"There is a Chinese proverb which says in these circumstances you need to develop oily wings," he said without empathy, but not unkindly. "Mrs Church is a remarkable woman and we must make allowances for her."

"I know," I said, trying to regain composure, "we have a similar proverb in English – we talk about the need for a thick skin."

I felt so miserable at my catastrophic failure. I wanted both a thick skin and the oily wings. I'd flitted from job to job in the UK, but all my bosses had liked me. And never at work, or indeed ever, had anyone shouted at me in anger.

I was still turning the day over in my mind when I got on the bus to go home. It wasn't quite true that no-one had berated me before. There had been another time; another woman, also in authority and also formidable – similar in age to Mrs Church. I felt my skin flush, perspiration sticking my skirt to the vinyl bus seat as I replayed the schoolgirl scene in my mind.

I'd been twelve when a prefect came to my classroom and asked that I be excused for an appointment with Miss Moller, the headmistress. I had no idea why I'd been summonsed, but my apprehension grew as the tall girl escorted me along the corridors of polished wood, her sixth-form pumps clicking rhythmically.

I remembered the office from the day of the admissions interview which took place just after we'd moved to Oxford less than a year before. The solid door closed soundlessly behind me. I stood in silence on an ocean of blue-grey carpet. Miss Moller continued writing at her desk.

When she put down her pen, she looked over the top of her half-moon glasses.

"Well Aileen," she said (no one ever called me Aileen). "Do you know why you are here?"

"No, Miss Moller," I answered truthfully.

She leant back in her chair, putting her hands upon the desk and pushing off slightly. "You are here because you are a disappointment. A disappointment to me and to the school."

She swung forward to pull some papers towards her.

"I have here your class reports. Your academic record is abysmal; you are undistinguished on the sporting field and no better at art, sewing or music."

I felt my shoulders sag.

"Stand up straight!" she snapped.

The bus stopped with a jolt, releasing Miss Moller's hold on my memories. My legs shook as I climbed down the steps and stood waiting for the bus to move off. I'd never told anyone, not even my parents, about my dialogue with Miss Moller, and if they knew, they never mentioned it. Two years later, I moved schools but perhaps because I'd never shared it, I could never shake Miss Moller's assessment. Achievements thereafter always felt hollow, undeserved – a mistake made by examiners or a fluke. Miss Moller was a school treasure, the kind of Head remembered by grateful school boards when they named gymnasiums and concert halls.

Ten years down the track and on the other side of the world, another cantankerous woman was again laying bare my inadequacies. Panic was rising inside me as I walked over the road and up the driveway to Salamat.

When I reached the house, I crept in the door hoping to skirt round to my room without seeing Mrs Church. "Gill," she called, "is that you, dear? I've poured you a gin, the ice is melting, come in, come in."

It was as if the day had never taken place.

"I'm tired," she said and turned to Ah Tong. "We'll dine in my bedroom."

Numb, I followed her like a lamb. She had donned a voluminous silk dressing gown embroidered with blue dragons breathing sheaths of gold and red flames.

Afterwards, when Ah Tong had removed the dinner trays and moved the drinks table next to her chair, she lit a cigarette and drew in deeply, settling herself back into the story of her life. "Now where was I, where did I get to?" she said, and without waiting for an answer, took up the tale.

She returned to a world of her own and needed little encouragement from me. Nearly an hour passed before she stubbed out her last cigarette and said, "Well, dear girl, I think it's time for bed."

I had wanted to apologise for my disastrous day, but my mortification met with internal rebellion and the words didn't surface. Instead I rose to pick up the glasses, but Ah Tong appeared silently to tidy up. I wondered how he knew the evening had ended, it was all so seamless. Mrs Church seemed quite oblivious that I was in any way out of spirits.

I lay awake for a long time thinking about what she had told me that evening, the contrast between us starkly revealed: her competence and initiative versus my dismal performance. She, too, had sailed for Hong Kong not long after she had finished school in Europe. She became a teacher at a boys' school but wanted more and found a second job at the *Hong Kong Daily Press*. This job, mundane as it was, would profoundly shape her life. She quickly moved on from proof reading to helping clients edit advertising copy and get the best return from their ads. She was quick to learn the technical side of typefaces and column sizes and discovered she was a born salesperson. Her cheeky, lively disposition and attention to detail, combined with a flair for design, endeared her to clients. Ever precocious, she demanded extra recompense. She was confident and, because of her unusual upbringing, comfortable with men, and when she made her outrageous proposition to her first client, it was so plausible that he burst out laughing at her brazen double-dipping, slapped her backside and agreed a fee. "Then I just went to all the others and I was soon raking it in," she said as she laughed out loud.

Betty also started writing for the social pages; she loved theatre and music and was an incorrigible gossip. She attended cocktail parties in high places, lunched with wives of legislators and judges, dined with fashion designers and film directors. Her prodigious energy then, as throughout her life, entranced and captivated as many people as those who found her tiresome and belligerent. Nothing fazed her – she had a devil-may-care attitude and didn't stand on ceremony.

"Once we were promoting a show from Broadway called *A Little Bit of Fluff*. I couldn't get anyone to help put up the posters in time, so I did it myself. Next day a rival newspaper ran a marvellous piece saying that late at night a little piece of fluff was seen sticking up posters for *A Little Bit of Fluff*." Mrs Church laughed and lit another cigarette, drawing in deeply. I imagined her as a flapper with her hair in the latest bob, dashing around Hong Kong streets at night equally amazing to both coolies and colonials.

The Press offered her the chance to travel and sell space in their trade directory. She set off for Shanghai where all her connections were invaluable and then carried on to Japan and Ceylon. The trip was an outstanding success and she made a great deal in commissions.

Then Betty married a lawyer – an impetuous decision – she hardly knew him. They met at a hotel where she took tea each afternoon, not far from the Cricket Club where he played avidly. She had a baby within the year. Her husband often worked from home and with an amah to look after the infant, Betty returned to work at the *Hong Kong Daily Press*, this time in the role of Court Reporter which gave her more sociable hours. She talked easily with the Chinese hawkers who had fallen foul of colonial regulations. She often paid their fines and bought their wares. "I was the only woman reporter in those days and I wrote from the heart and told the stories behind the prosecutions. No-one had done that before – put themselves in a coolie's shoes."

Mrs Church paused; she had come to the end of the evening's reminiscence and she turned to me. "It was all so long ago. I was your age, well, not much more."

I drifted off to sleep once I had convinced myself that my first day was an aberration and the next would be better.

Chapter 7

Irene soon had the office back to an established routine. When Mrs Church came in, the newspapers were on her desk open at the Stock Market Report, with the racing pages earmarked. Her first calls every day were to her broker, her banker and her bookie. Her broker, Mr Mok Ying Kie, was the pre-eminent stockbroker of the Hong Kong Stock Exchange, responsible for about thirty per cent of its daily turnover. He discussed insider trading tips quite openly with the upper echelons of his investors.

Next, Mrs Church issued directions to staff and sometimes she worked herself into such a frenzy that she'd feign a mild swoon, flop back in her chair, her hand to her head, bemoaning the hopelessness of it all, given the staff she had. Revived by tea, she would start on her telephone calls ... and on me.

Whatever I did was wrong. I was either at fault for not having read her personal mail or for having read it; at having taken decisions or not taken decisions.

I watched nervously as she fired staff on a whim and then muttered that she had known all along they were Communists, illegal immigrants, fifth columnists or all three. If they were not Communists before, they possibly could be now, I thought seditiously as yet another packed his desk.

She carried a portmanteau of prescription pills which she would share freely. "You're looking a bit pale, here take one of these." Our assistant accountant, who was twenty-one, came in saying he'd had a splitting headache for five days and was going to the doctor. "Rubbish, it's high blood pressure that causes headaches. I've got pills for that. Go and get yourself a glass of water while I find them." No one was going to the doctor in her time when she had such a pharmacopeia available.

I relaxed a little, realising Mrs Church's ire was quite indiscriminate and, of the twenty or so staff, few were spared. Sometimes her furies were so ostentatious that it was impossible not to laugh. When the hairdresser forgot the red tint in her perm, she arrived back at the office in a terrible state. She stormed in, unnerving even Irene, who leapt to her feet. Mrs Church flung herself into her chair and wailed, "Oh hell, I look just like a Chinese coolie. That damned hairdresser, how could she let me out like this, a coolie, a bloody coolie."

Irene and I said in unison, "Of course, you don't." Yet strangely, with her hair almost black, she did look different and I wondered if the office gossip that her mother was Chinese had some truth to it and the story of her birth was all fabrication.

Volatile and unpredictable as she was, Mrs Church also knew when to pull back. She used Mr Kwan and Irene like canaries in a coal mine, giving early warning that she had stepped too far. When they began to twitch, her censure softened to syrup. An angelic Mrs Church would then walk the offices, patting staff. "Oh, Mr Wong, it is a delight to have such a wonderful employee as you." To Miriam, our PR girl, "I am so lucky that APB has such highly intelligent staff." At my desk she would stand and sigh, "Ah Gill dear, my bright little English protégée." On those days, she'd beam benignly, saying, "Tomorrow is another day," and off she would go home to Salamat and her dog-children.

I lived a dual life, alternating between apprentice and companion. Mrs Church, tai-pan, hellcat, scold in the office, could, at a whim, transform to Betty, fairy godmother, confidant and solicitous hostess.

Mrs Church wasted no time getting back into the social rounds after her return. Her charisma shone brightly at her Sunday tiffins where she entertained a wide and cosmopolitan circle of acquaintances. Race or occupation were no barrier to her friendship, yet she made me cringe when she said, "Oh, he's half wog you know." Such epithets just rolled off her tongue. She saw them as descriptions to aid my comprehension, not as offensive or insulting, and boomed out the words.

One of the regulars at tiffin was a charming old boy. I knew him only as "The Brigadier," a tall, gaunt man in his nineties who'd known Mrs Church for over half a century. "Betty Church has made a mint from nothing, with nothing but the most amazing and persevering gall," he observed.

Another old friend of Mrs Church's was Han Suyin, a well-known author. One evening, I answered the phone to her at Salamat. "I'm ringing dear old Betty to say hello, I hear she's back."

"It's Han Suyin," I said, with my hand over the mouthpiece, "Is that *the* Han Suyin?"

Mrs Church grabbed the phone and launched into animated chatter, switching languages with bursts of laughter. They were two wily women catching up on months of scandal.

Mrs Church was in a good mood after her conversation. She could see I was interested and said, "She's quite scarlet you know!" Han Suyin had a reputation for being "Red," a Communist sympathizer, although I didn't think that was what Mrs Church had meant. She didn't elaborate, but added, "Of course, we've been friends for a very long time. Our fathers were friends on the railways but her mother was Flemish."

I learned more as Han Suyin had recently started publishing an autobiography of China, much of it structured around her own life story. She told of Marguerite, her romantic and headstrong mother, and her father, Yentung, a young Chinese graduate sent from China to study railway engineering in Belgium. Yentung first set eyes on Marguerite in a cheese market in Brussels. "There she was standing on the cobbles, the sun just bouncing off her red-gold hair, a torrent of hair like the muscled water of the Great River." He followed her home. Yentung later told his daughter that he knew undoubtedly it was true love because from that day he could eat cheese which before he had loathed.

Both families were against the match but while Marguerite's family plotted to whisk her off to a convent, she took off and spent time in Paris with Yentung. That settled matters, because some time later she announced she was pregnant.

"Now will you let us get married?"

But poor Marguerite did not arrive in the China that Yentung had left. That China had in any case only existed for the privileged few. She arrived in a period of terrible upheaval. From the start, she endured excruciating ostracism at the hands of both Chinese and Europeans. She was inconsolable when her babies died and alienated herself from the ones who survived. Surrounded by war, famine and pestilence, her relationship with Yentung did not last. Nevertheless, Han Suyin's father confided one day to his daughter that when he was distraught, he could still find comfort in thinking back to the cheese market and the day he fell in love.

When Han Suyin started to write the autobiography, she turned first to read the letters her mother had written from China to her family in Europe. She knew that they had been kept in a big trunk at her brother's house in England, but when Suyin asked for them, she found he had burnt them. "You understand, sister, I never dreamt *you* would need them one day ..."

There was one fragment that had survived, a fragment so potent, the language so devoid of emotion that even although it was only a few lines, it was hard to believe that the writer could bear to write the words: "... the cook has been decapitated. His head is in the garden, so I have shut the window."

At weekends, Mrs Church took me out wherever she went. We visited the Hong Kong Club, its members exclusively European and among the most influential people in the city. I asked Mrs Church about the whiteness of it all and she said there wasn't anything to stop Chinese being members, but no one would be so foolish as to propose one. She greeted everyone by name, the titled and the knighted, government officials, the heads of the major trading firms, lawyers and businessmen. Then she'd take my arm and we'd duck behind the aspidistras where she'd hiss scurrilous titbits of gossip so loudly that I couldn't doubt we were overheard. She passed me off as her "young niece" so I could get temporary membership, and introduced me as her "Dear little Scottish girl from England."

At the office, I soon realised that surviving the morning without major incident was the trick, for at about 11.30 am, she would scan her address book and ask me to ring so and so to see if they would do lunch. Often she'd say, "Gill, you need to come and listen to everything and be my second ears." Afterwards she'd tell me I got it all wrong and that I needed to get my ears syringed.

Usually lunch was at the *Peacock & Pheasant*, the restaurant on the second floor of our office block, where she waged regular warfare with the proprietor because he never had enough fresh vegetables or had run out of the "Chef's Specialty of the Day". She always ordered for us both, so there was little point looking at the menu and, after cocktails and a two-hour lunch, we'd return to work and be flat out until the evening. She was calmer in the afternoons. She'd sink into her chair, take out a big water bottle and mellow as the day wore on.

As a newcomer to the Colony, I found that one of the most surprising things was the overt Communist presence. Red China owned a fifth of the Hong Kong's choicest real estate and ran emporiums, shops and businesses. Communist newspapers circulated freely, daily condemning fascists, lackeys and imperial running dogs – an expression used to describe the USA and other capitalist states and meaning cowardly dogs that did anything for a few scraps. Chinese bookstalls on every major corner sold Mao posters, red-star badges and propaganda.

When Henry, Mrs Church's driver, took me downtown one day on an errand, we were moved on from a parking place outside a Communist store. An angry man in a blue Mao suit came out to berate us for blocking the people's view of a huge picture of Chairman Mao propped up in the shop window. The man had no inhibitions. It mattered not that this was a British Crown Colony, his Chairman needed to be in clear view of passers-by. Henry did not argue and we left.

American servicemen fighting Communism in Vietnam arrived in Hong Kong for R&R and found the posters of Chairman Mao confronting. Even if Ho Chi Minh, the leader of the North Vietnamese, was aligning himself at that time more with Russia than with China, it was still the Reds they were fighting.

About a week after Mrs Church started back at the office, we left work together one evening. The street had undergone a spectacular metamorphosis; an enormous portrait of Chairman Mao covered the whole office block opposite our building. Mao stood, his hand outstretched, his face magnanimous. Workmen swarmed over the nearby Bank of China, covering it in bright red plywood panels. Most passers-by ignored the preparations for the October 1st Anniversary of the founding of the People's Republic of China, but some stood shaking their fists angrily. When I looked up and down the street, whole office blocks were being covered in red fabric undulating gently in the breeze. Yet Mrs Church took the preparations in her stride. "It happens every October," she said. She pointed towards the blushing Bank of China building. "Last year, when we had the riots, the Reds had loudspeakers bellowing propaganda from the top floor, so the Governor ordered our loudspeakers to be set up on top of the Law Courts and played Chinese Opera full blast. You couldn't hear yourself think." She started to chuckle. "Colonel Bogey was played as a finale every evening and so people in the street, Europeans and Chinese, would start skipping along and doing little dances. It cheered us all up!"

The Red presence wasn't ignored. British Intelligence kept a listening watch, but the Hong Kong Government had more sense than to stamp down on blatant Communist puffery and send it underground.

Mrs Church didn't want my opinions on the revolution in China. A flippant comment about it having at least unified China was snapped up by Mrs Church who, not without justification, told me I knew nothing at all about the East and thereafter glared at me whenever any conversation turned to China. "You should have asked the nuns about the real Red China. They'd have told you a thing or two. They beat up and burn Christians and armchair pinkos like you!"

Although Mrs Church continued to berate me at work, I was starting to get the hang of things. Irene and I were surprised to find we rather liked each other. More and more, I managed to get her to break out a wide and delightful toothy grin. Our friendship caught us both by surprise and she coached me until we became an effective working duo.

Chapter 8

Each day had its drama, mostly created by Mrs Church, yet advertising campaigns still came together and clients, stressed to breaking point by her erratic behaviour, were effusive when success followed.

Yardley's new-season's cosmetic campaign cleverly peddled the phenomenon of sixties pop culture to Hong Kong. Jean Shrimpton was the Face of Yardley in the late sixties. She was one of the three most famous models in the world at that time. The others were Twiggy and Veruschka.

It was Jean Shrimpton who caused a worldwide sensation when she turned up hatless and in a mini-skirt to attend the Melbourne Cup in Australia in 1965. Hemlines had been steadily climbing since 1960, but most fashion still hovered discreetly around the knee. It was said that within days of her appearance in Melbourne, hemlines in Australia were on the rise and the mini-skirt was catapulted to international fame.

Yardley's campaign targeted teenagers using colourful packaging and fun advertising. Young Chinese packed venues to listen to pop music and watch a film of *The London Look* which featured Jean Shrimpton touring the British capital. She swung from the platform pole of a red double-decker which obligingly streamed past Buckingham Palace, rounded Trafalgar Square, paraded by Piccadilly Circus and decanted Miss Shrimpton at Carnaby Street into the arms of a gorgeous if guileless gentleman. Together they danced past windows of Mary Quant models, pirouetted in Portobello Road, elegantly caroused at groovy parties and reappeared immaculate for a singsong in a London pub. The film was overlaid with psychedelic swirling pastel rainbows of *The London Look* colour palate.

I gained immediate stature with staff and organisers because I'd been living in London and they wondered why I'd ever left. The pop group Mrs Church had first booked for the campaign fell from grace after a scuffle with police on a drug raid. Mrs Church got straight on the phone to Hong Kong's most famous impresario, Harry Odell. She told me, "Harry will fix it," adding by way of explanation, "he's a Russian-Jew, did a stint as a tap dancer in Japan before he came to Hong Kong in the 1920s." And he did provide the solution, turning up with an achingly polite, smart and scrubbed quartet of young men in *The London Look* ties. Miss Vera Duncan, Yardley's chief beauty consultant, arrived in Hong Kong to complete the campaign. Beaming, her champagne hair curled to perfection, she gave demonstrations of pastel pale make-up to young Chinese girls who gave her a rapturous reception.

After the campaign, Mrs Church asked me to take a small gift up to the Odells who lived on the Mid-Levels, a residential area half-way up The Peak. Harry's wife, Sophie, welcomed me warmly to their Lilliputian house complete with a pocket-handkerchief garden sandwiched between high-rises.

It was where they had lived for decades. The yellowing walls were covered in bric-a-brac – photos, pictures, mirrors and clocks. Patchwork cushions sagged on faded flowery sofas, carpets and rugs overlapped each other haphazardly on the floor, and a lamp made out of a Johnnie Walker whisky bottle vied for space with Ming dynasty porcelain. One wall had completely disappeared behind photographs of the Odells greeting stars of film and stage, some framed in silver, some in plastic, some in wood. There was no attempt at style, it was of their own making – tasteless, startling and yet with an undeniable charm. Although it was mid-morning, Mrs Odell had insisted on giving me breakfast. "Do try the plum jam, dear; a juggler brought it from Bulgaria."

Harry Odell emerged from a bedroom, a cartoonist's delight, with a fat cigar clenched between his teeth, grey curly hair beyond his control, and eyes that were his trademark for they twinkled warmly at everyone. He had to hurry out to wangle visas for a troop of Slovenian dancers and could not stop to join us. Mrs Odell went out to see him off and I was left alone for a few minutes with competing clocks ticking in the memory-filled room. From the jumble of monochrome photos, I was startled to see a young Sophie smiling down at me. I stared at her. When Mrs Odell returned and I looked from the old lady to the gorgeous photo and back again, my young eyes failed to catch the likeness my subconscious had picked out. Oblivious of my bemusement, she chatted kindly and asked me to pass her regards onto Mrs Church and asked if I'd heard any news of Han Suyin.

No sooner had we finished the Yardley's campaign than we were gearing up for the "Montres et Bijou" Exhibition. It was the first time in the Exhibition's long history that it had ever left Europe. The organiser, Chairman of the Swiss Watch Federation, was a short, nervous man who implored Mrs Church to ensure every detail was attended too. Sixty yards of blue velvet ordered through the Chinese Emporium fell through due to the Red Guards playing havoc with mainland industry. Mrs Church had to re-source the velvet through India, which required hours of bellowing into the phone. At one point I heard her yell, "And I don't want to talk to the organ-grinder's monkey!" I giggled and wondered how on earth the Bengali clerk interpreted that. But her savage approach worked, for eventually, the velvet arrived in the nick of time.

Mrs Church had outdone herself, persuading a TV news crew to film the arrival of the Swiss watches and jewels at Kai Tak Airport. She purred in the ear of her friend in the Hong Kong Police, suggesting the risk of a heist was so great it would be a public service to lay on a police launch to ferry the cargo over the harbour. He obliged, adding a motorcycle escort to accompany the shipment from the dockside to the Hong Kong & Shanghai Bank where the priceless pieces would be stored in a vault until the exhibition. "Ah, the Police Commissioner, he is a lovely man and he loves my curry tiffins," said Mrs Church.

On the day, Mrs Church invited me along. "Come Gill, you come too, we'll walk, it's not far." Mrs Church wore tailored jackets with padded shoulders and tight skirts and I marvelled at the way her formidable figure funnelled down to surprisingly well-shaped legs. Like a conical dust devil, her high-heels skittered along while she swayed above. I strained to keep up with her through the press of people. She'd greet Europeans with, "I must dash," and dash she did, intent on reaching the bank, swaying around street vendors and pedestrians and skilfully avoiding old men hawking up phlegm.

As we neared our destination, she called back, "Oh look, over there, it's our security van coming now with the police-outriders, don't they look absolutely marvellous." She gesticulated to the driver and we arrived with them at the bank door to find the film crew already in place. The lead patrolman got off his bike and told the van driver to unload and move on. Guards hopped out and used a mechanical ramp to lower two crates which slid gently onto the pavement. The elderly turbaned Sikh bank guard stood up and, leaning on his shotgun, tried to say something to Mrs Church. "Just wait, can't you see we're filming? You'll get in the show, don't you worry," she said waving on the throng of pedestrians while buttering up the patrolman. When she eventually turned back to the Sikh, she said, "Now, open the doors, my good man. Where are the trollies?"

He was deferential and spoke softly.

"What? Speak up," said Mrs Church, shifting closer.

"Oh gawd!" she gasped, "this door is sealed, we're at the wrong door. We've got to go down the street and round the corner."

The two security guards tugged ineffectually at the crates, but couldn't shift them. The old Sikh was obviously not a candidate. Curious onlookers were knotting around us. "Well, come on, we've got to get them down the street," barked Mrs Church authoritatively to no one in particular.

The patrolman, short of dragooning members of the public, saw there was only one solution and he shouted to the outriders who got off their motorcycles, reluctantly removing their gauntlets and helmets. Using a coil of hessian rope that the Sikh produced, police and guards together started to haul the boxes along the pavement.

Mrs Church, realising that the cameras were still rolling, ran up to the crew shouting, "Stop shooting," which caused consternation among the policemen who were bent double, straining on the ropes, and had the old Sikh scanning the street wildly as pedestrians scattered.

Relief came when we turned the corner. Down the road a bevy of guards with trolleys were looking around anxiously, wondering where the hell the shipment was. On seeing the extraordinary sight, they set off towards us.

The next day, after a screening on Hong Kong TV News of a heavily edited film of the arrival of the crates of jewels and watches at the bank vault, a Hong Kong customs official phoned to say that a condition of the goods being allowed into the Colony without duty was that they were not to be used for advertising and the film on the television appeared to contravene that. It was in such circumstances that Mrs Church's acerbic tongue triumphed. "How can I possibly be held responsible when the shipment was regarded as so newsworthy that it was featured on the TV? Do you think I can control the news? Maybe you'd like me to control the weather tomorrow or the next war? Phooey ..." she blasted and we heard no more about it.

That evening at Salamat we laughed together for a long time. Mrs Church could be downright cantankerous but she was also vivacious and entertaining, disarming me completely with her story-telling and delightful sense of the ridiculous.

Chapter 9

Every day was busy and the learning curve was steep. Business and social activities went hand in hand. Thus neither in the office nor at Salamat could I find a moment to mediate for myself or discuss my performance. I redoubled my efforts to find alternative accommodation, but Mrs Church had me cornered. Not only was it difficult to make calls, but if I did not get to my phone first, Mrs Church would pick it up and I'd hear her say, "It's OK, you can talk to me, what was it you wanted to speak to Miss Stevenson about?"

Each evening, we settled down after dinner and talked about the APB or she continued her life story. I realised she was genuinely worried about the business which was slowing down.

Her hopes were invested in a man called Patrick O'Neil-Dunne, known to all by his initials, which spelt out P-O-D. POD was a World War II flying ace, former Director-in-Chief of Rothmans International, a long-time client of the APB and a very old friend of Mrs Church. He'd retired and needed a tax haven and something to do, so he'd suggested buying half of the business. Mrs Church's enthusiasm for the idea was unbounded.

One evening, she was not her usual self, her hand shaking a little as she poured us each a cognac after dinner. "It's all too much, too much, too too much," she sighed. "No-one has any idea of the effort and sacrifices I've made to promote British interests in the Far East. And now, just as I'm about to get a little support to share the load, this happens …" She showed me a telegram that had arrived at Salamat. It brought news that POD had hurt his back and was in hospital for a delicate operation to fuse his spine. She feared he'd pull out of their arrangement altogether, adding, "He's not just escaping the tax man, you know, he's escaping his wife, but there's no escape from her. She doesn't want him in business with me, so this back thing could just be an excuse."

Mrs Church's spirits lifted when, a week or so later, another telegram announced the arrival of Mr David Dunlop. David was one of POD's protégés from East Africa where they'd worked together in the Rothmans office in Nairobi. His arrival was tangible proof that POD would follow. David had gone out to Kenya in 1952 with British troops to quell the Mau Mau rebellion. He'd stayed on, mesmerised by the beauty of the country, and had become a well-known radio announcer with the Kenya Broadcasting Corporation. He was less enamoured when Kenya gained independence in 1963, and the new regime didn't like him much either. David was deported after he refused to accept the government decree that the name of the country should be pronounced over the air as *Ken-ya* not *Keen-ya*.

When David arrived, he also moved into Salamat. His presence changed the dynamics and I often went to bed laughing at the repartee between him and Mrs Church – witty and sarcastic – as they found the measure of each other.

It was during a dinner at Salamat that I heard a little more about POD – about how he'd broken tobacco industry ranks and been the first tobacco executive to publicly acknowledge the link between smoking and cancer. His announcement stunned a powerful tobacco lobby that had spun cancer research as sensational nonsense with no scientific basis. It even stunned many at Rothmans. After POD's bombshell, PR departments in rival tobacco firms scrambled for traction. Overnight he became the most hated executive in the tobacco business.

"He's so clever. He saw the writing on the wall, and decided to lead the pack," said Mrs Church.

David turned to me to explain. "He knew the cancer evidence was damming and building so he thought he'd use the exposé to steal the market for Rothmans filter tips!"

David lit up another cigarette and said: "'Fun to lead and fun to be followed'. That's a PODism. You'll need to get used to them. 'It's better to meet at a circus than not at all,' is another. His favourite is, 'Remember the O of the O.' That means always be on the lookout for the opposite of the obvious."

David reminisced about his experience when he first met POD. The local Rothmans manager had been wringing his hands as he explained the disappearance of tin-plate advertising signs from the shanty townships that ringed Nairobi.

"Where do they disappear to?" POD had asked.

"Well, Sir, Africans steal them to patch their village huts, seems they are ideal for that."

"Wonderful opportunity! Print more – what a fantastic way to get advertising into the villages. Just where we want it – say we'll give a prize for the best patched hut."

David added, "He's a genius, but never tell him I said that. Everyone at Rothmans has a POD story to tell."

At the office, David grasped Mrs Church's modus operandi and made it plain that he'd been employed by POD, not her, and would await his arrival for further instructions.

David did not mince his words. He told me she was just an old bully and best ignored. Mrs Church did try commandeering him, but he narrowed his eyes, his sunburnt complexion reddening ominously, and walked away talking under his breath.

"Did you call me a silly old bat? Come back here this minute, David."

"No, no, Mrs Church, I simply said I had to get my hat – mid-day sun and all that."

I was speechless, and even deadpan Irene flinched and bowed her head, stifling a smile.

One afternoon when I was alone, David came in, lowered himself into Mrs Church's chair, put his feet up on the desk and reached into the drawer for her water bottle. He uncapped it, sniffed and laughed. "Thought so, she not only promotes Gilbey's, she boosts their sales."

"What do you mean, that's her water bottle," I said lamely.

"No way Jose, that's aqua-gin, Betty's blend."

David's arrival coincided with Mrs Church's favourite time of year, the racing season. On the first day, the three of us were up before dawn in a flurry of excitement. We drove to the races with Mrs Church constantly admonishing Henry for choosing the wrong lane or going too fast or too slow. He was imperturbable, a light smile on his lips, as he concentrated on the road, avoiding the cyclists, rickshaws, throngs of pedestrians and taxis converging on Happy Valley. After a very English breakfast, we watched her horse, Jocelyn, being prepared, and then it was time for the first race. David stood out as a newcomer in the Members' Enclosure of the Hong Kong Jockey Club. He fielded the question of what had brought him to Hong Kong with wry humour. "The Church, actually, I've come to join the Church," and graciously accepted deferential nods.

Before betting began, Mrs Church designated me to list the jockeys' names out of the newspapers, squint at the board to tell her the odds, and read the racing tips. David and I shuttled back and forth placing bets. No sooner were they placed than she changed her mind until just before betting closed when she'd yell out an instruction such as: "Quick Gill, $10 on the nose for Pink Treasure."

"Pink Treasure," I'd repeat to confirm.

"Yes! Will you hurry up!" And so it went on. As each race finished she would shout, "Quick what's it paying? I had money on it."

"No you didn't, Mrs Church."

"Didn't I tell you to ..."

"No!"

"Oh!" in disbelief. And then off we'd go again. If she didn't win, I'd hear her say, "Oh gawd, that damn girl, gone and bought me the wrong tickets – how stupid can you get!"

And if she had a winning ticket, "Where's my ticket? I gave it to you, Gill."

"No, you didn't, Mrs Church!"

"Yes I did, you were standing right there and I gave it to you."

David and I would hunt for the errant ticket and retrieve it from among the papers on the table, her handbag or, on one occasion, on the chair underneath her.

"Phooey, I knew it – where had you put it this time?" And nothing would convince her we'd found it anywhere near her.

At the end of the day, she roared with laughter at herself, told us we were marvellous, what a wonderful day it had been, and switched to berating Henry and his inability to ever be where she wanted him.

David was company for Mrs Church and his presence made it easier for me to leave Salamat. When a room came up at Caritas Hostel I accepted it. I had been staying with Mrs Church for six weeks.

"Oh no dear, you're not really leaving, it makes no sense when you can stay free with me … unless you don't like living with me?" she said.

David stepped in. "Oh, of course she likes living with you but she can't live with you forever, Mrs Church, can she?" He said it with such authority, she asked no more rhetorical questions but added it would be more difficult to introduce me to the cream of Hong Kong society if I was not living with her. Mrs Church had already let me know that I could do well for myself in Hong Kong if I were less opinionated. The portfolio I had was youth and enthusiasm, a short-term currency that could yield financial security if wisely invested in securing a wealthy husband.

I moved out quietly when Mrs Church wasn't around to avoid her posturing disappointment. I left her flowers and a card.

Chapter 10

I'd anticipated how good it would feel to be liberated from Salamat, but the reality was different. The hostel was institutional and I was soon overwhelmed by uncertainty. Loneliness and homesickness manifested with such urgency and dominion that it was all I could do not to book a ticket home to the UK immediately.

My tiny room was high up and had a good view of the harbour and streets with their ceaseless activity far below. So after work, as darkness dropped, I sat alone in my belfry, watching headlights connect the neon signs below and feeling sorry for myself. At the end of a day of relentless criticism, I would sit and eat alone, knowing I had to go back the next morning for more of the same. I hadn't realised the importance of Mrs Church's salve of bonhomie and liquid spirits at sundown each day. I felt friendless in a new city and close to panic. Misery weighed me down each night; I wallowed in it, flopping onto my pillow to weep myself to sleep.

I had never had a problem being alone before. I'd grown up with my brothers away at school, my parents were not socialites and we had few relatives. Summer holidays were spent in Scotland – long weeks in a primitive croft on a bleak peninsula with sheep and seagulls for company. I'd befriended solitude from a young age, but loneliness was a new and terrifying experience; confidence bled out of me and the void filled up with doubts and insuperable problems. I even considered returning to Salamat, remembering the best of times, the jocular moments and the warmth of companionship.

Help came from an unlikely quarter. Petula Clark sang "Downtown" on the radio one night and the words captured my imagination, every line written for me.

When you're alone and life is making you lonely
You can always go – downtown.
When you've got worries all the noise and the hurry
Seems to help
I know – downtown
Just listen to the music of the traffic in the city
Linger on the sidewalk where the neon signs are pretty
How can you lose?

A few days later, I got home from work and after I'd had my ritual sob, I pulled on some jeans and took myself down to the street to mingle with the crowds and *linger on the sidewalk*. I became more confident each night I went out, able to explore further.

I'd walk along Queen's Road Central and take the ladder streets of footpaths and steps which climbed directly up the island's steep hillsides. In the midst of all the development, these ancient byways remained intact, lined on either side with stores, small stalls and workshops. In the evening, oil lamps cast pools of light on families squatting outside to cook, eat and chatter around enamel bowls of steaming white rice and baskets of soy bean curds in a milky brew. Women washed and diced their vegetables, sluicing the earthy water down dirty, sun-warmed stone steps, the slightly brackish scent joining incense and the smell of hot chestnuts, a warm overlay to the quintessential Hong Kong pong which by then was so familiar.

Fortune tellers held cages with birds and for a Hong Kong dollar, the bird would choose a straw for me which, unfurled, would reveal my destiny in Chinese characters, but no-one I could find spoke English so my future remained hidden, rolled up, ready to become someone else's fate.

As I passed by, children shrilled, "Good Evening", the words rising above energetic Cantonese laughter, domestic squabbling, the clatter of mah-jong tiles and the roar of traffic from the street below. I couldn't help smiling. No-one else took any notice except one night an old woman grinned at me, the light of a swaying lantern catching her gold teeth. She gestured to me to have some rice with her family. I could have kissed her and I should have joined them, but I didn't.

Petula's promise that life was going to be alright now that I was downtown was not immediately gratified. When I returned to the hostel I felt even lonelier, a shadow skirting the margins when the rest of Hong Kong connected effortlessly, mingling and fusing. I cried some more.

One solace was writing home. I wrote to my parents, and they to me, nearly every day. My letters didn't reveal the pain; for them I was always positive. I wrote down conversations from the office and described the strangeness of my surroundings. There was plenty to tell. A pattern was set that would continue for many years to come, pouring out my heart, but not my heart, setting the record straight but not straight.

Gradually though, with Petula encouraging my evening sorties, I was not quite so despairing. One night, climbing the ladder street steps again, I bent down to look at some rice bowls for sale between a tiny Chinese alter spiked with joss sticks and a herbalist selling black hen's feet and sliced antlers of young deer. And in that moment, I wasn't alone anymore. I, too, was connected to the world again; the bowls reminded me of dishes we had at home, dishes my grandfather Jimmy had brought from China. I straightened up, my delight spontaneous, and I half turned, expecting to see someone familiar, but there was no one there. I practised my few words of Cantonese on the young girl squatting beside her wares. She smiled and then laughed with me at my terrible pronunciation. My purchases wrapped up in scraps of newspaper, I hurried back, waking up the hostel's night watchman yet again. Suddenly I had clarity. No-one cared a damn about my loneliness, no-one even knew, so how could anyone help me. I was the only one who could do anything about it. Because it was so embarrassingly obvious, my revelation wasn't even something I could tell anyone, yet it seemed such a significant discovery.

As I lay awake that night, I turned back to Jimmy. I told him about buying the china bowls. I told him that I must have crossed his very footsteps in my exploration of Hong Kong.

No longer a lonely belfry, my room was a temporary sky-parlour where I escaped the madding crowd. Gradually over the next few weeks, I pushed myself out of my inertia and melancholia.

I wasn't going home, not yet. I wasn't going to let Mrs Church daunt me. I was going to look up my contacts, find a flat with people I liked, join clubs and make my own life.

Mrs Church did not appear to notice the shift in my poise and confidence. It was subtle; I was still clumsy in confrontation, tongue-tied in contretemps. One afternoon, her parting shot had a snide twist. "Mr O'Neil-Dunne will sort you out my dear, oh yes, POD won't tolerate you, he won't have my patience. You'll have to pick up your game."

I had to talk firmly to my quaking alter-ego that night. I'd written to my old boss at Grosvenor House in London, telling him all my news. He had written back that Mr O'Neil-Dunne of Rothmans was a sometime guest at the hotel. He hadn't liked him at all and described him as a very demanding and overbearing character. He added, "You may be going from the frying pan into the fire. There will always be a job here for you if you do find yourself alight."

I confided my fears to David, who usually made me laugh and feel better about everything. Indeed, he was the only person I could talk to easily. David was still living with Mrs Church at Salamat and told me that waiting around with time on his hands was getting him down. We had time to chat because the office was paralysed by a flurry of cleaning and tidying in preparation for the great man's arrival, which had been delayed for a third time. David didn't do a lot to put my mind at rest. Although he admired POD, when I told him what my old boss had said he admitted the man was not easy to work for.

As we chatted, I realised how thoroughly miserable David felt. He was not filled with self-doubt as I had been – he was convinced his problems were external. He got up and started to pace the floor before he let out a vituperative rant. "It's this place. It stinks. It's bursting at the seams, all neon lights and brothels. And it's full of slant-eyed little bastards and you never know what they're thinking."

I said, "David! Stop …"

He turned towards me and seeing my dismay, he ran his fingers through his thinning hair, his bombastic demeanour draining away. "Sorry, I just want to go back to Africa. I hate cities. This whole place is alien to me."

His tirade renewed my resolve to make my own life outside of work.

POD arrived in mid-October. The first morning after his arrival, he escorted Mrs Church into the office. She grinned from ear to ear, coquettish and playful. He had unruly black eyebrows and a huge nose, yet the sum of it was surprisingly pleasant, the wings of silver hair, keen eyes and relaxed mouth dignifying a blatant bruiser of a face.

POD ambled round the offices greeting staff, for he was well known to most of them. He then came in and pulled up a chair at Mrs Church's desk. They chatted amicably about clients and campaigns, their flow of conversation constantly interrupted by Mrs Church lobbing criticism at me or flicking superfluous instructions to Irene. Mrs Church waved her hand at the stacks of correspondence that sat on her desk. "I can't possibly imagine how I am going to get through the work, just look at it piling up!"

After an hour or so, POD pushed back his chair and said, "Betty, no-one could work under these conditions, we need to make some changes."

Mrs Church concurred, at last she had found someone who understood. She gazed at POD with enormous affection and gratitude, shook out her monogrammed linen handkerchief, dabbed her eyes and left the room.

POD summoned a couple of young men from the art department and moved my desk and Irene's out and had his brought in from the office next door.

A little later when Mrs Church returned, she was alarmed. "Oh Pat, what are you doing? What on earth are you doing?"

He smiled broadly at her. "You and I need to share an office so I can get up to speed. It's important that we can talk confidentially."

He picked up the paper mountain from Mrs Church's desk and said, "Irene, Gill, find a waste paper bin and pull up chairs." We sat with our backs to Mrs Church while he consigned half the mail to the bin, which he said was, "The most important piece of furniture in an office," looking at us over the top of his glasses and sizing up Mrs Church's reaction in the background. He would pause to consult her on some matters, or leave briefly to ask Mr Kwan's advice on others, and then he'd summarise out loud and say, "OK, Betty are you happy with that?" and, without waiting for a response, he'd turn to me. "Do a letter and tell them what I've just said." Forms he passed straight over. "Fill that in Gill, and if you don't understand it, find out, because I don't either." Anything to do with space, bookings and typesetting, he gave to Irene. Within hours of his arrival, he had established a new esprit de corps while Mrs Church, the tiger-fire-dragon, impotently gasped and blew against my oiled wings and thickened skin.

POD dismissed us as Mrs Church was getting to her feet, and Irene and I shot out brimming over with shared excitement. This was going to be bloody good fun. We stifled our laughter to listen at the door.

"Oh Pat, Pat, you simply must listen. You can't do this. This is not how I work."

"Well it's how I work Betty, there's bound to be a few adjustments as we go along."

"You don't understand. For a start, Gill can't spell!"

"Well, doesn't the office have a dictionary? I'll buy one when we're out. Come on Betty, I'm hungry, let's go and find some lunch."

As they walked out to the lift lobby, Mrs Church said loudly, "I've been doing this, Paddy, for forty years ..."

When they returned from lunch, Mrs Church was relaxed and had a rosy glow on her cheeks. She went to her office and pulled out her water bottle while POD ducked off and went round the office picking up trays marked PENDING and tipping the contents into IN trays. He stacked the empty trays in my new office. "There is no such thing as pending," he said, "work is either in or it's out. Send a memo round so the staff understand."

They were going to need that; staff returning to their offices found papers spilled across their desks and were soon huddled in consternation.

The next afternoon POD called Irene and me to the Board Room, a stuffy windowless space panelled with bookcases. He pulled out encyclopaedias, then moved onto business directories and almanacs. Towers of books grew by the main doorway. When Mrs Church emerged to go home she exploded with rage. POD stuck his head out the door. "When did you last consult any of them Betty? It's OK, I've asked Henry to take them all to Salamat, you can store them there." Then he had another thought and shouted after her, "Why do you need encyclopaedias anyway, Betty, I thought you knew everything!" and roared with laughter at his own joke.

POD generated enormous amounts of work and David and I spent long hours and worked weekends trying to keep on top of the tasks he set us. One Sunday, David was stacking film-cases neatly on the floor under a shelf in the sound studio and I was helping him catalogue them when POD came in. "Got to have a system David, no point in putting them in any old how!"

"That's right, Sir, I'm stacking them under brand names: Rothmans, Yardleys, etcetera."

POD had other work for me so within no time he stuck his head back in to see when I would be free. "Come on, no point in spending all day, just pack 'em in," he said irritably and left again.

Then Mrs Church arrived with a picnic basket full of Ah Tong's sandwiches. "Oh dear, we should have washed the floor before you started stacking the films David. We'll have to get Ah Fung to take them all out again."

"Well Mrs Church, I did sweep the floor and we can't stack them on a wet floor can we? So I really don't think we need to get Ah Fung to wash the floor."

POD arrived to hear the last half dozen words that David had spoken and said, "Don't be so dammed stupid David, of course we don't have to get Ah Fung to wash the bloody floor!" before he turned on his heel and strode out.

David gasped for breath, I was doubled over laughing, and Mrs Church beamed, breathing out the words, "He's so dynamic that man," as she followed POD out of the room.

At the end of the second week, POD asked if I could handle working for him and Mrs Church until he got a grip of the business and appointed a secretary of his own. Could he not see I was already his willing slave? Of course he could.

Mrs Church remembered the introduction I had to Eric Marsh of Johnson & Johnson that we talked about on our first night together. She told POD. I had no choice but to pick up the phone and ring Mr Marsh. He invited me to lunch that day. We hit it off and he said he and his wife wanted to entertain me on their boat or invite me to dinner but, if I didn't mind, there was one condition. "On no account bring that heinous woman, Mrs Church, anywhere near me. I can't stand her."

"But her new partner, Mr O'Neil-Dunne's a fresh face," I said lamely.

"He's her good friend, so let's leave him out of it too. OK?"

On my return to the office, Mrs Church and POD pressured me to arrange a further meeting with Mr Marsh to discuss his company's advertising account. I made poor excuses, frustrating them both. That gave Mrs Church an opportunity to highlight my ineptitude. She yelled that I had blown a very good opportunity. POD was puzzled but I didn't know him well enough to confide that Eric Marsh didn't want a bar of either of them.

My office was ideally placed as a listening post and soon I heard POD say my name.

"Well, since she is so useless, let's get you a new secretary and I'll take Gill over."

"Oh, she'd never do for you Pat, she needs a strong hand, and she's far too friendly with the Chinese staff. You've just been taken in by that nice smile she puts on."

"OK, Betty, up to you, but I think you should consider Miriam as your personal assistant, she's bilingual and more mature. Let me know on Monday, Gill or Miriam."

I was horrified; I was being traded like a chattel. As soon as I had a moment with him alone, I tackled POD.

"Gill, calm down, you must give people rope. She won't let me poach you but she'll delight in giving you away," said POD. "Let her make the decision or we will have no peace."

On Monday, Mrs Church chose Miriam.

POD gave me a bear hug and said, "OK, now come, we have lots of work to do."

Mrs Church called me in to say she hoped I was not too disappointed with her decision and that I would still do her personal letters.

I was alarmed, but POD said, "Oh that's nothing Gill, just the odd letter now and then."

From the outset, Mrs Church ignored the spirit of the new arrangement, demanding Ah Fung, the office boy, find her a comfy chair so she could sit in my office. Exasperated at the amount of time she spent dictating to me, POD removed the chair. Undeterred, she stood over me or perched on the corner of my desk. One day, she dictated a letter to the authorities about the indignities Lulu, her Alsatian, had suffered in the dog pound after she had bitten the next door neighbour's cook, who was pinching bamboo sprouts. Just as we got to the piece about the cook being a Communist and an illegal immigrant, POD appeared in the doorway and thundered, "Betty, Gill's time can only be used to write letters relevant to APB. Now finish that letter off and let's get on with the business."

"I'm disappointed, but not surprised Pat, you never were an animal lover," she sniffed and continued to dictate a paragraph about the experiences of a friend's corgi that had died of a broken heart in the same pound.

When Mrs Church knew that POD was safely out of the office on some appointment or errand, she would appear in my office and close the door. "I just want you to write a little note to Mrs O'Neil-Dunne in England." Mrs Church had given thought to these messages and started dictation with each line prepared for maximum disquiet. "I don't think Paddy has told you this, but I thought you should know …" or "ought to know" or "might care to know" and "something you really must know is

… what a simply marvellous time Paddy is having in Hong Kong, kicking up his heels, taken years off him. Loves the social whirl, does our Pat. Just like the old days."

It was true that POD greatly enjoyed socialising – to him it went hand in hand with business. Mrs Church took him along as the new partner in her firm wherever she went to solicit and entertain clients. She was a gambler, and whether in conversation or at the races, she was quick and shrewd, as was POD. But her expansive manner, witty, caustic and scandalous in turn, jarred with POD's approach. When he was seducing new clients with his ideas on marketing, passionately expounding the views of his famous friend, Edward de Bono, on lateral thinking, she constantly interrupted him. Few rooms were big enough for both POD and Mrs Church.

At the office, POD had taken charge of all the day-to-day decisions and campaigns which left Mrs Church with little to do. She walked laps around the office, finding dirt under desks and staff in the tea room past break time. She had aged years since his arrival.

One of POD's first acts was to engage an architect to modernise the offices, and within a week or so, builders and carpenters swarmed in clutching plans. Feng shui experts stalked the corridors with Mr Kwan. New doorways appeared while others disappeared, electrical wiring and telephone systems were replaced, ceilings lowered, modern lighting installed and carpets laid.

POD put up staff salaries, smoothing the differential between Chinese and Western executives. He also took advice on instituting a new retirement fund for the staff.

Mrs Church was very distressed. She had never imagined the end of her empire would be so inglorious. She had changed little since starting the business forty years ago, and protested loudly above the chaos, complaining about the cost and warning the firm would be bankrupted.

"Well, Betty, in that case, perhaps you'd like to repay to the company the thumping great dividend you declared for yourself just before I arrived," he said.

POD and Mrs Church circled each other like old lovers, watching each other's moves, levelling corresponding jibes.

"I told you so."

"If you'd only listened."

"That's what I said in the first place!"

The doors were too thin to mask the storms and tantrums that started to blow between them. Longer and longer lunches were needed to sort out their differences.

The difficulties of working in a building site compounded the rift and Mrs Church was not the only one who was upset. The staff were finding it hard to cope with the speed of change. POD would not accept any excuse for an interruption to work output, and Mrs Church highlighted every inconvenience.

Respite came in November when representatives arrived from Europe to decide on campaigns and advertising budgets for the following year, and POD needed Mrs Church's input again.

Weekend races at Happy Valley Racecourse were also therapeutic, and each Monday morning, POD and Mrs Church arrived at the office arm in arm, all differences put aside, particularly if Jocelyn, Mrs Church's horse, had got a place.

Chapter 11

Mrs Church had planned POD's birthday celebration months before he arrived. Their mutual friends, clients and all the staff were invited to a party at Salamat.

As I ticked off the names of those who'd accepted the invitation, I realised that only one person from the office had declined. His name was Lao. He was one of our artists – a good-looking young man with lovely eyes and talent. Lao had been crippled since birth and used crutches. When he moved around, his limbs took off at all angles.

I remembered that Lao hadn't turned up to the last party, which had been at a Chinese restaurant for David's birthday. At lunchtime I went over to the Art Department and spoke to him. He said the problem was transport. I suggested to the office staff we all put in a dollar and get him a taxi there and back. Nobody wanted to contribute and one even said, "Do we want him there? Why did we employ him anyway, there are lots of artists in Hong Kong who aren't cripples." Our Chinese accountant, a kindly, plump, short-sighted lady, saw I was dumbfounded and offered to bring him.

I had a soft spot for Lao. When his first high school teacher doled out English names for all his pupils, he'd hesitated at Lao and then said, "Bacon". All the names were strange to the boys in the class, but when Lao found bacon defined as shrivelled meat, he refused to answer to the name.

A keen student, Lao had studied for seven GCE subjects, but his parents had six children to educate and could not afford all the exam fees for Lao. He could only take one subject and he chose art. He told me he was grateful for the job but would like to study chemistry and physics again one day.

Lao told me that in his village in the New Territories, people whispered that his parents should have left him outside to die at birth. But he said his parents rebuked the villagers and told Lao that they loved him just as much as his siblings, insisting that he go to school and was not shut away.

The party was held on a beautiful evening and as guests mingled in the garden at Salamat, moonlight caught the ruffled surface of the South China Sea below. Caterers served the food and a musical trio serenaded us. Spitting sparks from braziers rose in concert with operatic shrieks of laughter leaping from the hubbub of animated conversation. Mrs Church and POD made speeches emphasising their long relationship; how happy they were to be reunited in the APB. Mrs Church dabbed her eyes and POD put his arm around her and spoke about the enduring power of friendship and how much he had to learn from such an extraordinary woman. It was all too, too much, as Mrs Church might have said. David and I excluded ourselves and sat looking out to sea while David talked about the way the moon played on his African plains and how God planted the banyan trees upside down. "Go and see Africa, Gill, that's a real country. Until you have watched big game roam the speckled plains of the Serengeti, you haven't lived."

Mrs Church called me into her office during the next week. She said both she and POD had been delighted to see Lao at the birthday party. I knew that was genuine as I had seen her start with surprise when she saw Lao hobbling up the drive and dash forward to welcome him and make sure he got up the steps to where the chairs were arranged. She gave me some rare praise. "Lao told me you organised his transport. I would have done it myself but I was just so busy getting everything ready, so it was a good job you took the initiative this time."

That incident was my first encounter with a traditional attitude some Chinese had towards the disabled. Disability from accident or illness was slightly better tolerated than abnormality from birth, but few bothered to distinguish. The idea of karma, at its most simplistic interpretation, saw disability as a punishment for some heinous deed in a past life. Confucian thinking also regarded disabled baby boys as a break in the links of the ancestral chain. Even the Cultural Revolution in China was carrying on the stigma by promoting the need for strong able-bodied workers, so a disabled child failed not only the family but the country.

It didn't take long for me to realise *the enduring power of friendship* was not enough to cement the business partnership. When I asked POD about his return date after the Christmas holiday, he muttered, "I may not come back!" and left my office. A couple of weeks later he took me to lunch to tell me he had decided that there was no option other than to take over the firm completely and buy the other fifty per cent of Mrs Church's shares. He said she was too difficult to work with. However, he owed it to her to keep her as a figurehead – she would be Life Chairman of the APB but not interfere in the management.

For a while, it seemed that Mrs Church was changing tack. She seemed prepared to step back and support POD's lead. After all, she told the staff, the APB could not have two masters, and she was ready to simply be a guide and pass her beloved firm to POD's safe hands. He was a dynamo of a man and it was she, the doyenne of advertising in Hong Kong, who had brought him from the world stage to our little Colony. There was a twinkle in her eye when she added she had known him *forever,* after all.

POD, too, softened his approach.

One morning, Mrs Church arrived breathless at the office and regaled us with an account of what had just happened at Salamat. After breakfast, she'd played catch in the garden with Lulu, her Alsatian. She threw the small rubber ball and Lulu leapt, twisting her body, ears flying and caught the ball in mid-air. But, to Mrs Church's horror, when Lulu galloped back over the lawn, she saw a round lump in the poor dog's throat. She swore that as Lulu started to shake her head around madly, she could hear the muted ringing of the little bell inside the ball. She prised open Lulu's mouth and quickly poured an Alka-Seltzer down her throat and, after some hair-raising moments, the ball shot out! She shouted for Henry and they tore off to see the vet who said it was an extraordinary reprieve and obviously the best of first aid.

When David and I were having a drink with POD that evening, he said, "Poor Betty. Lulu's getting a bit long in the tooth and we all laughed at that business with the ball this morning but it did give her an awful fright. Betty absolutely adores her dogs. She has no family here and her daughters in England are not close to her. She knows lots of people and they gather round for the fun and partake of her generosity but she's a lonely woman. Her pets are important."

"She has friends to tiffin every week and she sees a lot of Wendy Barnes, the BBC lady," I said, contradicting him. "I was talking with Wendy the other day and she's going to do a radio program about her life."

"Wendy is a transient; she'll befriend Betty for a couple of years and then go home. There are some old stalwarts but they are not close. People are attracted to Betty, I grant you that – like moths around a bright light."

He paused to light another cigarette. "I've made a mistake expecting her to find other interests. Being a figurehead isn't enough for her. I need to find something else to take her mind off the business. I'm going to organise a pedigree German Shepherd puppy to be sent out from England. I've booked a phone call to a kennel in Cambridge. I think she might enjoy breeding dogs, taking them to shows, that sort of thing."

Sure enough, ten days later, David and I were to fetch the puppy from the airport and bring it up to Salamat where POD would orchestrate the surprise.

Mrs Church was overjoyed and named him Prince, but did not take the bait about getting interested in breeding. POD kept up the conversation for some months, frustrated that his ideal solution was ignored.

While trying to keep the peace, POD took me to task too. He said he thought I could be more cooperative. Mrs Church had never accepted my move from her house, Salamat, to the Caritas Hostel. She told POD where I was living was thoroughly unsuitable but that I wouldn't move even though she had found me a much nicer place. She'd used her influence with her friend, the Matron of the Helena May Hostel, which was Europeans-only, and where I would meet decent girls and get bacon and egg for breakfast.

POD suggested I humour Mrs Church in this regard and accept the offer graciously. I just couldn't. "Why would I want to move hostels when I'm looking for a flat to share?" I said, and as an afterthought, "And why would I come to live half-way round the world to get an English breakfast?"

"She's had a very hard life, Gill," he said. "Be patient with her. She has built this business and befriended many poor people. She's a good woman."

"I know, Sir, but she doesn't make it easy to like her."

"You will fit the experiences of a lifetime into your time in Hong Kong. You don't meet people like her every day. Try to see her in a new light. I understand she is difficult, but there is much to admire there too."

I was back to wandering the ladder streets that evening, unsettled and arguing with myself. I didn't feel compassionate towards Mrs Church but I knew POD was right. I had to find understanding. Although I had put the tragedies she had related to me in chronological order, it came to me that such scars couldn't be archived in the past. By definition, they lingered on, always present, biding their time to pervert the future.

I took my mind back to 1925 when Mrs Church, as a young mother, weathered a rash marriage and dwelt in a house too quiet to contain her rambunctious temperament. Her solution had been to throw herself into her new job as a Court Reporter.

Her little baby failed to thrive. A string of European doctors prescribed regimes and medications to strengthen him but to no avail. Betty wanted to ask a Chinese doctor. She accepted alternative modalities, even the arcane, another influence from her strange childhood. Initially, her husband would not consider it, but eventually, in desperation, he relented and Betty dashed out and brought back a well-known Chinese physician. He listened as Betty told him about her beautiful boy, so good he never cried. When the amah came in to change the baby, the physician watched as the infant reached for her hands. He strode across the room and grabbed the woman's wrist. As she writhed and squealed, he called for a toothpick and ran it under her nails, capturing the detritus on a handkerchief. He examined it, even putting a little on his tongue, and turned to the amazed parents. "Opium," he said. "You wanted a peaceful life and your amah knew how. She put opium on her fingertips to quieten your son." The discovery came too late. The amah disappeared and the baby died.

A year or so later, in 1926, Betty fell pregnant again and was expecting twins. She and her husband decided she should go back to England, to the house of her in-laws, to give birth and see the children through infancy. It was never clear what happened to her husband. Mrs Church told me that he had disappeared, leaving behind only what he owed his creditors. On another occasion she said he had died on board the ship on his way to join her in England. Whatever the truth, it had not been a happy marriage and Betty detested her in-laws.

So it was that in 1928, Betty found herself on her own again, now with dependants and debts. She rolled up her sleeves and got to work selling advertising space in London until she was solvent again. She then deposited her twin daughters at her old convent in Kent, and went back to Hong Kong to start her own agency. She was absurdly young but an extraordinary networker. She'd seen an opportunity; agents in Hong Kong were lazy and complacent, simply translating advertisements word for word from English into Chinese characters. To British firms Betty sold a dream; she eulogised the growing markets in China and the opportunities that would follow investment. She created adverts that would appeal to the Chinese, tapping into her knowledge of their culture. And citing China's internal turmoil, she promoted Hong Kong as a secure base, British forever. She was brimming with confidence and enthusiasm and the old honchos that ran the big name brands loved her and, to her enormous credit, were loyal to her for years; Allen and Hanbury's, Yardley's, Oxo Bovril, Bowater Scott, Brand's Essence of Chicken, and Rothmans cigarettes. She used her childhood friendships to cultivate contacts in mainland China and in Hong Kong. She hired expatriate staff, but was more successful at retaining Chinese employees, some of whom stayed with her for decades.

On visits to the UK, she lobbied politicians to support British interests in Hong Kong, establishing herself as a multi-lingual China trade expert. She knew what made a good story and she knew what made money. It was an unbeatable combination; the APB expanded, opening offices in Shanghai and Singapore.

I remember, when she reached that part in the story, she paused, her mind returning to the glory days. A smile played on her lips. "I thought like a man, I could fend for myself and needed no-one, yet men gathered round me like a honeypot."

In 1934, she remarried, an older man, Mr Church, and they had a son, Richard. Five years later when World War II broke out in Europe, Betty brought the girls out from England and they were all together in Singapore when Hong Kong fell to the Japanese in December 1941. A couple of months later, the Japanese were on the tip of the Malay Peninsula and shelling Singapore. True to form, Betty was still going into the office. She had staff to worry about and was filing press stories for overseas newspapers. But the situation was deteriorating fast and Mr Church insisted Betty and the children get ready to evacuate. In the midst of the packing, Richard ran out into the garden to pick his mother fresh gardenias and was killed instantly by a Japanese shell. The distraught mother had little time to grieve; her husband bundled her and the twins onto one of the last boats leaving Singapore two days before it fell. There was still more of an ordeal to come. Japanese bombers hit the ship shortly after it left port. Minutes later an order came over the ship's tannoy: "Abandon Ship".

"I couldn't swim but I had to save my corgis. I jumped in with them and they were so terrified, they bit my ears – look," she said, bending and tilting her head to show me her ear lobes, still scarred and tattered.

"But what about your daughters?" I said, "What about *them?*"

"Oh, I wasn't worried about them, *they could swim!*"

The lookout in the conning tower of a Dutch submarine used a periscope to scan shadows in the inky swell hoping to spot survivors in the light of a waning moon. To his amazement, he heard dogs barking. He relayed the bizarre message down the speaking tube to the control room and guided the sub to the sound. They plucked Mrs Church out of the water. Her ears were running with blood and she had a dog on each shoulder. When she reached Batavia, present-day Jakarta, she got the news that her daughters had been picked up by another boat and eventually mother, children and corgis were all reunited in England.

I was lost for words.

Perhaps she sensed my unspoken incredulity. Mrs Church went on. "Those dogs saved my life. The sub captain told me if they hadn't heard the barking, they would never have found me."

Mr Church was interned in Singapore. He spoke Japanese and this initially was an advantage. But along with many other innocent men, he was implicated in the Double Tenth Incident and arrested on suspicion of involvement in an attack on Japanese ships in Singapore Harbour on 10 October 1943. The men had no knowledge of the raid which was actually carried out by a group of Anglo-Australian commandos who sailed over from Western Australia in an old Japanese fishing boat, the *Krait*. Once near the harbour, the commandos used folding canoes to make a daring raid, attaching limpet mines to the hulls of Japanese ships. The commandos were able to return safely to Australia, but the Japanese military police, the Kempeitai, incarcerated and tortured suspects, including Mr Church, in the old YMCA building in Singapore.

After the war, Mr and Mrs Church returned to the East, re-opened the Hong Kong office of the APB and picked up the threads of colonial life again, but not for long. Mr Church suffered poor health from his treatment at the hands of the Japanese and died in 1951. Mrs Church was overseas and on the phone to him when he collapsed. By the time she told me this part of her story, I knew her a little better and wondered unkindly whether a blazing row had contributed to his demise, but she never had a bad word for him and his death was probably the blow from which she never truly recovered.

Mr Church's body was cremated and flown to London. It was arranged that a pilot would personally deliver the ashes to his widow. Betty Church was alone on the tarmac to watch the plane land. Her daughters had loved their stepfather. The loss nearly overwhelmed her and while she stood upright and composed, inside she ached not just for this loss but for all the others. She waited as the steps were wheeled up to the cockpit door and a young Flight Captain climbed down. He ambled across the stretch of tarmac, pushed his cap back and said, "Are you Mrs Church?"

"Yes, I am Mrs Church," she said, her strong voice flat and formal.

"Well, here's Mr Church." He thrust a brown paper bag into her hands and walked off.

"He never flew again," she told me, "I had him sacked!"

Poor woman; two dead parents, two dead children, two dead husbands and two world wars. I resolved to be more tolerant and amenable to Mrs Church.

The attempts to foster good will were soon forgotten when negotiations over the purchase of the rest of Mrs Church's shares degenerated into a bitter power struggle. The sale price was persuasive but the heartbreak of finally relinquishing her business was gut-wrenching. Mrs Church picked fights over trivial details and changed her mind from hour to hour. She accepted being Life Chairman but she wanted more than a token title; she wanted power. At the office, the air turned blue, especially when Mrs Church caught sight of David or me, for she had decided we had turned POD against her.

POD was terse, thrown by her profanity and frustrated by his inability to nail her down. "Don't answer her back and it's not just you two; don't underestimate her ability to curse and insult in every Chinese dialect. The staff are all suffering too. Mr Kwan is very concerned."

Sometimes I just had to take cover and hid in the sound studio with David. He'd keep the red recording light on to forestall POD and Mrs Church. One time, I'd fled in there in tears and David was consoling me with an enormous hug when Mrs Church burst in. God, did she enjoy that one. The red light took on a whole new meaning.

"Don't be so bloody ridiculous, Betty," hollered POD. The divisions were laid bare now for all the staff, all the clients, and all the world to see.

Mrs Church took to her bed. "She's been to the doctor," said POD to David and me, "and her blood pressure is phenomenal. For God's sake, when she comes back into the office, don't raise it or she will drop dead and be on our consciences for life." POD's blood pressure was rising too. He was crumbling. Each day he seemed a little less flamboyant and came to me more and more often for the codeine I kept in my drawer for everyone's hangovers. David said he had never seen the boss look so ill and muttered that Hong Kong would be the death of us all.

Christmas came to save us. With a mercurial twist, Mrs Church rose from her sickbed and went shopping. Each day she commandeered Ah Fung, the office boy, and they would return hours later laden with parcels. She summoned anyone passing her office door to help her wrap presents, first in paper festooned with holly and reindeer, and then in thick sheets of brown paper ready for posting to clients and acquaintances all over the world. Unfortunately, she also brooded on her choices. Each morning, after a sleepless night, or indeed even after a good lunch, she would peruse her lists and change her mind about who should get what, or want a second look at a purchase perfectly wrapped and addressed. She questioned whether her helpers had followed instructions, insisting the paper be stripped off to check. She sent a traumatised Ah Fung to exchange presents. The poor boy had virtually no chance of a successful sortie, so Mr Kwan had to step in and requisition a staff member to accompany him, disrupting the office work. Mrs Church would telephone the department stores to complain about a purchase and follow it up with a letter about the quality of the item, the staff or the service. Correspondence digressed to how it was when dear old Mr Robinson ran the appliance department or when British goods were sold instead of locally made ones. It was bedlam. POD moved his desk out to the board room and swore at the strands of tinsel and plastic greenery that Mrs Church insisted Ah Fung hang up round the office when he wasn't exchanging presents. Mrs Church turned on the charm, thriving on the maelstrom of frivolous activity. It restored her sense of purpose and her hypertension was forgotten. Even David and I were forgiven. Now it was POD's turn to be short-tempered and bloody-minded. He looked pale, his exhaustion palpable.

She laughed merrily. "Well, at least I've got the Christmas spirit Paddy."

She had her Christmas cards printed with a picture of her and her horse, Jocelyn. Inside she wrote in her bold scrawl: "The old grey mare is still what she used to be!"

Chapter 12

I wasn't the only one who thought it was a loopy idea to keep Mrs Church as Life Chairman of the APB once POD had bought all the shares.

"It doesn't matter that she'll have no executive powers, Pat, the woman is a lunatic," said Freddie Zimmern, POD's lawyer. Freddie and POD had known each other for decades but POD wouldn't listen. Perhaps he could not stomach going back and renegotiating with her. He said that despite the months of all-consuming frustration, he couldn't hurt an old friend and he felt locking Mrs Church out of the business altogether was too harsh when it had been her life's work. Freddie and I shook our heads.

Although I gravitated towards people like Mrs Church and POD, intrigued by their baroque flamboyance, endless yarns and largesse, I related immediately to the grounded and pragmatic Freddie. I'd been curious to meet him. Mrs Church had told me how the three Zimmern brothers had sustained the Colony's social pages when they married three sisters, the daughters of Sir Robert Kotewall, a distinguished and wealthy Eurasian taipan and Hong Kong legislator.

After the meeting, POD told me to take a taxi home but I didn't. Soon I'd move up to the new flat I'd organised to share on the Mid-Levels, and this familiar stroll to my hostel would be just a memory. I enjoyed walking through the busy hubbub, with the soft dark of mid-evening tempering the ferocity of Hong Kong's neon. I was smiling to myself. POD and Freddie had made me laugh; both men playing to my youth. Freddie had assured me that if the APB fell apart, his firm would always have a job for me. It was all in jest, but I felt flattered.

One humid afternoon, POD was sitting in my office working on a campaign report. He tired of the interruptions and asked me to take the phone off the hook. Then he got up, put his head out the door and told Pauline, the receptionist, that we were not to be disturbed. Pushing back his chair a little, he took his glasses off and put them on my desk, rubbed his eyes with his palms and started to talk. He was quietly passionate as he described his vision of a talented team of Chinese and European staff who would transform the APB into a world-class agency able to pitch to Asian and Western clients. There'd be mutual respect and a focus on mentoring Chinese graduates for top management. An office in Singapore, Japan maybe – the whole of Asia our oyster. Expatriate staff would arrive in the New Year to drive the APB forward and allow POD time for his other projects. He wanted to start a food export business to introduce oriental foods to British palates. "Gill, we'll take bean curd to Birmingham, Brixton and Barnstaple," he said, chuckling at his alliteration. He had an idea for a book too; he just wanted time to write it.

The conversation wound down with some small talk, and as POD rose to leave, he asked me how the flat hunting was going. "Fantastic, I'm moving into a new place in a week with two guys and a girl from Japan. They're a bit older than me but really nice." I started to staple some documents on my desk.

There was a moment of deathly quiet. I looked up.

"You can't," he said, sitting down again.

I stared, quizzing him.

"Don't you know about the atrocities in Hong Kong during the Japanese occupation?" His hands gripped the edge of my desk.

I nodded. Chinese and Europeans still paused to recall the barbarity when they drove me round the island. Many of the sites were exquisite landscapes – beaches and verdant hillsides – and it seemed inconceivable that they had hosted wanton massacres twenty-five years earlier.

"It would be insulting to the Governor who gives you protection in this British colony. No employee of APB can share with Nips. Betty and I simply won't have it. You have to make a choice."

I flinched, dumbfounded. What the hell was this about the Governor? Nips? When had my newest hero, my slayer of dragons, morphed into an extraordinary bigot?

"But, Sir, you've just mentioned an office in Japan?"

"That's business, don't confuse the two."

"But Takako, the Japanese girl, is charming and well-educated," I tendered.

"She'll definitely be a spy, then. How could you be so naive Gill?" He shook his head, "She'll have targeted you."

"But I don't know anything," I protested.

"That's how they did it before, fifth columnists; they were everywhere sending information back to Japan, that's how they walked in and took over."

He saw that I was stunned and softened his approach. "Look, you might think it's water under the bridge but people you meet here socially, European and Chinese, were locked up and persecuted by the Japanese. No Geneva Convention for them, Gill. They might not talk about it but it's not forgiven or forgotten. And surely you know Betty's story? And Freddie Zimmern, who's not only my lawyer but is on our Board; two of his four brothers were killed when the Japanese invaded. And Harry Odell, the impresario, I know you've met him – he was interned at Stanley prison camp. How could you have contemplated this?"

I sighed. "Well, before I found this flat, I did try to find a room with a Chinese family because I thought that'd be interesting ..."

"Oh good God, Gill, knowing you, they'd be Communists. Just stick with your own kind," and he got up and walked out.

The next morning, Mrs Church took me aside. "As for me, dear, I was just so happy to hear that you had found a nice flat on the Mid-Levels. It doesn't matter to me who you share with, but we must all listen to POD now, mustn't we?" She went off smiling and humming to herself.

Soon afterwards, I heard Mrs Church ringing her friend, the Matron at the Helena May Club for women. "Yes, yes, she's got herself mixed up with some Japanese triad, the Yakuza, it'll be drugs they're running," she boomed. "Even POD's tearing his hair out about her this time. She hasn't a clue, so we need to step in."

When POD next came into my office, he said Betty had organised a room for me at the Helena May. I stared at him, unable to trust how my voice would sound or indeed what I might say. "OK," he said, "I knew that was a long shot. I will explain it to Betty but we're going to help you find somewhere else." I said nothing except to get to my feet and pick up my handbag.

I walked down the stairs instead of taking the lift. The walls were peeling and the vacant shabbiness matched my mood, my heels clicking against the concrete. I had never quite understood why there was such outrage about the adept way the Japanese had gathered information before World War II. British soldiers and officers had unwittingly patronised restaurants, brothels and hairdressing saloons that had been set up in Hong Kong by Japanese agents. Every snippet of information gleaned by the agents was sent to Tokyo to map a comprehensive picture of Hong Kong's key communication and transport hubs. In contrast, the British had relied on feeble bureaucratic intelligence reports that portrayed the Japanese as bad shots, incapable of fighting after dark.

The Japanese hadn't *walked* into Hong Kong as POD said. China and Japan had been at war for a decade. Tens of thousands of Japanese troops were on the Chinese mainland and Hong Kong was extremely difficult to defend. World War I British officers, using trench warfare mind-sets, had built a string of "pill boxes", marvellously named "The Gin Drinkers' Line", with ventilation shafts that proved an ideal fit for Japanese grenades. The attack came on the same morning as Pearl Harbour; before Japan had even declared war on Britain. Commonwealth troops and Hong Kong Volunteers fought valiantly. During the battle, the Japanese troops massacred POWs and civilians without any regard for the conventions of war, and after the surrender, terrible atrocities took place that would remain etched into the collective memory of the Colony for generations.

I took myself over to the Hilton coffee shop and sat in front of the shiny chrome expresso machine and ordered a green tea. I knew animosity lingered after the war. Dad refused to buy a Japanese or a German car and my mother loathed chrysanthemums, but I never felt obliged to own their post-war prejudices. My mother had instilled an *accident of birth* philosophy, our arrival and station on earth being a lottery. What was it all to do with me? The war hadn't been my experience. Did I bear a generational responsibility to be wronged, nevertheless? It had all happened more than a quarter of a century before, before I was even born.

I glanced at the other tables. American servicemen, another war, this time in Vietnam. And a sea of faces from every corner of South-East Asia. I looked at my watch. It was nearly lunch time. Perhaps they would get the message that I was angry and upset. I also felt vulnerable. I wondered if Mrs Church was phoning the agencies to see if there was another English girl to take my place. Maybe I should just find somewhere with "people of my own kind". But who were they? POD meant people who looked like me, white and middle-class, yet I often felt a misfit with my own kind. Maybe I should stay at the hostel until the New Year and start looking for accommodation again after Christmas, I thought. How would I tell Takako? Ring her up or ask her out for a coffee? What would I say? I'd ordered a sandwich but pushed it away untouched. I put my elbows on the table, cupped my chin in my hands and stared blankly at the bank buildings over the road. After a few minutes, I sat back, straightening up. I couldn't summon white lies to spin to Takako and I couldn't hurt her with the truth, so my choice was made. I paid the bill, went back to the office and got down to the pile of work that had appeared on my desk.

That evening in my sky-palace, the events of the day were still going round in my head. I thought back on Jimmy's letters from his trip East. My grandfather had enjoyed his visit to Japan in 1908, admired their industry and peaceful philosophy. That was before its rulers had so blotted the twentieth century copybook of history, taking war to Korea,

China and the Pacific. What was it about island nations and their need for empire?

I wrote home. My letters mirrored my hesitations, knowing full well that despite all their tolerance, my parents too might have wondered why I'd choose to live with the enemy of their war.

Without a word to anyone else, I moved in with the Japanese. I'd hoped to get away with it. POD was leaving in ten days to go home for Christmas. He'd not brought the subject up again and with luck he'd be too busy to revisit my private life. It was not to be.

"Look here, Gill, I'd really like to know for sure that you've secured a flat before I go. In the papers today there's a good place in Kowloon. I've spoken to Betty, you can borrow Henry to take you over and have a look," said POD full of bonhomie.

"It's OK, Sir, don't worry, I moved into a place last weekend."

His face changed ominously. "You moved in with the Nips didn't you?"

I nodded.

"You want to be independent? So be it, but don't ever expect us to rescue you. Your reputation will be ruined. Don't make things worse broadcasting this to our clients." He stormed out to lunch, propelling Mrs Church by the arm. I'd united them for the first time in weeks. It seemed, however, I'd kept my job.

Mrs Church had her say too. She'd forgotten her earlier enthusiasm for my choice of accommodation and she smirked. "Tut, tut, dear. Bad decision; some people will shun you for this you know."

"In that case, Mrs Church, they are not people I need to know," I answered primly.

She laughed. "Oh you, you have a great deal you need to know, my dear." Off she went and I heard her relay the conversation to POD, pleased with her repartee. "I did tell you Pat, she's a silly little thing, can't see what Mrs Wentworth saw in her at the interview."

I tried to shrug it off. Dad had replied to my letter. He wrote, "The world can't progress if the sins of the fathers are visited on the children."

Chapter 13

Mixed feelings ambushed me when I packed up my hostel room for the move to the flat on Mid-Levels. I was strangely sad to leave. Cocooned inside those four walls, I'd challenged despair and climbed out of the abyss. POD's arrival was providential; nevertheless some paradigm shift had taken place inside me even before his appearance on the scene.

I gathered together the few breakables I'd acquired, carefully wrapping the rice bowls I'd bought on the ladder street. I looked out the window; walls of low cloud boxed me in. Was any decision the right one? With a sigh, I picked up my bags and went down to find a taxi.

Hong Kong taxis were problematic. During the 1967 riots, the majority of drivers were labelled Communist sympathisers and lost their jobs. A year on, the new cabbies had little English and even less hang of the geography of Hong Kong Island. When a European got into their cab, they headed on a colonial circuit, Hilton Hotel, Hong Kong Club and so forth. So I sat in the front seat and directed the driver up The Peak to MacDonnell Road. As we drove up the mountainside, the fog cleared and the sun scratched through the haze. The taxi driver helped me up the stairs and the amah opened the door wide, curious to see the new Missy.

My new flat had no grand view, just a tantalising glimpse of blue harbour threaded between other apartment blocks on the lower side of the road. Neither had it any opportunity for solitude for I would share a bedroom.

Instead it had Takako. She was a little older than me, a bustling chatterbox whose laugh rippled easily round the large flat. A lock of recalcitrant black hair constantly brushed her eyelid. She flicked it back every few moments and I was dying to get a pair of scissors and snip it off. Takako introduced me to her flatmates. The oldest Japanese boy was always polite but I didn't see much of him and all I remember is that his brother had *failed* as a kamikaze pilot – he'd returned to base in the last days of the war.

Ochida, the other boy, was closer to my age and, like Takako, loved good food. And it was a focus on food that united the three of us in those early days, easing my assimilation. Ochida volunteered packets of fermented beans, jellied fish and dried seaweed while Takako experimented in the tiny kitchen, incurring the amah's displeasure. We also ate out together at the smallest excuse, for enjoyment of food came only second to making money in Hong Kong. Tanks of fish, snakes in baskets and caged birds awaiting despatch were too gruesome for me. Street stalls sold octopus by length, vendors tumbled plump dumplings from sizzling woks and sliced glistening Peking ducks. The influx of refugees from the mainland had diversified Chinese cooking. Spicy, heavy or light, you could take your pick. Our favourite was a Buddhist restaurant where soft-footed monks served vegetarian food. It was right next to the laundry we frequented when it was wet or the amah was on holiday.

Because we shared a twin-bedded room, Takako and I often talked together after we put the lights out. At the time, I didn't appreciate what a complex and unconventional person she was, but I loved hearing her stories. And they helped me to understand that though she bubbled cheerfully along, below was a solid bedrock of caution. She was tidy, prudent with our housekeeping purse, and mindful of our wellbeing and of our reputations.

Her father had been a Japanese diplomat in Europe before World War II. Takako was born in Paris and spent her early years in Warsaw, where her father became terminally ill. He converted to Catholicism four days before he died. While his widow made preparations to take her three small daughters back to Japan, the Polish Archbishop organised a papal audience at the Vatican. Takako didn't remember meeting the Pope but it had become part of her family folklore. On her return to Japan, Takako's mother became a lady-in-waiting to the Empress Nagako, consort to Emperor Hirohito.

Once Takako reached marriageable age, her mother started looking for suitors. The process would examine blood lines, look for evidence of any diseases, physical or mental, and note the education and occupations of relatives. Takako dodged the first few candidates until her mother settled on a tax inspector. Takako was not in a strong position to refuse. After all, she was without a father, and Japan was still in post-war turmoil, but Takako had decided the life of a tax inspector's wife was not for her. It was the early 1950s and Air France was recruiting air hostesses for the new Polar Route, which would connect Tokyo to Paris via Anchorage. The publicity posters featured a Japanese hostess demure in a pink kimono. Takako signed on, knowing that such a career choice alone would forever exclude her from her echelon of Japanese society and would also save her from the tax inspector.

It took me a little longer to realise that Takako, despite distancing herself deliberately from her family, was still supporting them financially. Her sister was ill and the medical bills were crippling. Takako was doing all she could, taking on translation jobs and working at weekends, but it was never enough.

Takako told me more about her situation. A few years before, she'd read a newspaper article about a spiritual healer who'd had good results restoring physical and mental health. Takako thought if she could help her sister recover, it would ease the situation for the whole family. She made an appointment with the healer. He listened carefully. He did not offer help but advised Takako to go to India and visit Sai Baba, an Indian guru and holy man. So she did. Sai Baba was candid and sincere. He could not help Takako's sister, but he could teach Takako how to accept her own situation and alleviate her personal suffering. Takako made several more visits to India to take teachings and Sai Baba introduced her to many other devotees and spiritual practitioners. She had only recently returned from a visit to India when I moved into the flat with her.

One night as we lay in the dark, Takako asked me about my spiritual belief. Mine was bequeathed dogma – a cultural label that I'd never questioned. I said I was a Christian and tolerant of all religions. As I spoke I could hear how patronising that sounded.

My family was Presbyterian, but Mum had her own brand. After my brother returned from his first time at Sunday school in Belfast terrorised by tales of fire, brimstone and eternal damnation, none of us ever had to go to Sunday school again.

After I arrived in Hong Kong, I'd done a course on Buddhism. I took a distant, unconnected view, as if I was learning about some archaic culture, but the idea of consequences and taking personal responsibility watered a dormant seed in my mind.

My father had told me that he envied the comfort religion brought to believers. He also told me that when, as a young doctor, he'd delivered babies, he'd found it hard not to believe in miracles. However, he couldn't really embrace religion himself and said that at times his reticence had upset his mother and sisters. If I was going to be a believer, he didn't want to put me off, so he bottled up things he wanted to say about faith until they just had to come out – usually at odd times and places. He told me there was only one thought that really resonated with him in the whole of the Bible and that was that the Kingdom of Heaven was within us. We didn't need to go looking for fulfilment anywhere else but inside of us. He tried to explain more but I didn't really understand. He left me with a sense that while fulfilment was within us, it was an elusive encounter that we had to keep searching for. The conversation was uneasy for both of us. Dad wasn't comfortable talking about God, or rather no God, and he didn't want to enter into a discussion. In a way that was good because the intensity of his delivery ensured it was unforgettable.

Takako said it sounded as if my father was quite enlightened. I smiled. That wasn't an epithet that would have sat easily with him.

One evening, Takako announced that one of her friends from India was coming to stay for a few nights. I really liked Takako's eclectic circle of friends; a photographer for *Life Magazine*, an American doctor, and a Japanese fashion designer, and I looked forward to meeting the next one. He was Swedish and travelled the world teaching meditation.

I was dismayed when Erik arrived. He was dressed in a long white shirt. He looked like a tall, Nordic Gandhi with dreadlocks. I was polite but excused myself to read in the bedroom where I fumed quietly. I'd read all about transcendental hippies and here was one in the flesh. Surely Takako couldn't be so naive. He'd be filling her head with a search for utopia and probably belonged to a cult. Did he do drugs, I wondered?

A new wave of interest in Eastern religions had swept England earlier that year when the Beatles had flown off to India to practise Transcendental Meditation at a Hindu ashram. I sided with the conservative backlash in vogue – to ridicule Maharishi Mahesh Yogi.

Fortunately, Erik stayed for several days and I relaxed a little. I could not help but be drawn into conversation. He wouldn't argue and despite myself I liked his voice, soft but well-modulated, and there was nothing he said that I could really dispute.

When he left, I was surprisingly sad to see him go. He was only the first of a succession of strange men who came to stay; hairy men in dhotis and kurtas who chanted and stood on their heads. I realised these were no new age hippies, they were yogis and sages that Takako had befriended in ashrams she had visited in India.

Takako enjoyed discussing philosophy with them and was obviously knowledgeable. Sometimes she seemed so conventional, yet she was confident being curious, broad-minded and discerning. She opened chinks in my bourgeois armour.

Chapter 14

It was POD's idea to honour Mrs Church by hanging a larger than life photograph of her, proud and uncompromising, in the Board Room. Beneath it a plaque read, 'Betty Church, Life Chairman and Founder of the APB.' I told POD the image reminded me of a remark Mrs Church made one evening at Salamat. "At school I took the nickname Boadicea."

It was also POD's idea to make it a surprise. He wanted to spring it on her the evening he left to spend Christmas with his family in England.

He had a surprise for me, too, that morning. "I've engaged a young amah to help my wife at home. You haven't seen our house in Cambridge, but it is huge and Biddy needs more help. The agency's mucked up the paperwork and I can't get her on my flight. I didn't want to involve you but now you'll need to sort it all out."

While I had accepted having an amah in Hong Kong, the idea of sending a young girl to England smacked of exploitation. I looked at him askance. He knew me well enough to understand exactly how I felt.

"It's a marvellous opportunity. Her family's dirt poor, mother's a coolie on a building site, father's a seaman. Her name is Tai and you'll like her. She'll be a companion for Pik-Yuk too."

With Mrs Church's help, Pik-Yuk had been adopted by POD and his wife from a Hong Kong orphanage when she was a baby. She was now a teenager.

POD said, "You'll need to get onto it right away. Tai will be here any minute."

Tai was stocky with a wide and open face, her thick black hair cut in a bob. She spoke hardly any English, but had an attractive earnestness about her and I sensed humour too. POD had underestimated the amount of bureaucracy we had to surmount. We circled the immigration department for her visa, the labour office for her agreement, the airline office, the recruitment agency, and last-minute medicals. I pulled strings, called in favours, berated and cajoled.

When I got back to the office late in the day, POD grabbed my arm as I came through reception, gave me a huge wink and whispered, "Perfect timing … Boadicea's hung. I'll get the champagne out of the fridge. You go and get Betty to join us in the board room."

Mrs Church was a canny, astute old bird who never had much difficulty seeing through me. She followed me, hawkish and suspicious. POD mistook her intake of breath for pleasure and was too busy popping the cork to read her better.

"Take it down Paddy. You should have asked me."

"Oh come on Betty, I thought you'd be delighted. It's a very handsome portrait, almost regal," said POD, turning to look at it again.

"Get rid of it."

Neither of us said a word until the clack of her court-heeled shoes was inaudible.

POD looked briefly at the ceiling. "She'll get over it. Women are never happy with their portraits."

"I'm not sure vanity is the problem, Sir, she likes that photo."

"You know, Gill, men are such simple beings and women are so bloody complicated. We love them, but we'll never understand them. Women play a game without rules, shifting, unpredictable, convoluted hoopla. Where's the fun?"

I was the last to leave the offices because I had waited until the taxi arrived to take POD to the airport. When I switched off the lights in the lobby, I stood for a moment staring at the spinning dust motes caught in the blood-red neon light flooding through the window, streaking the polished floor. I picked up my jacket and pulled the door shut behind me listening for the lock to snap into place.

By the time I got to work the next morning, the portrait was gone. Mrs Church had come into the office very early.

"I couldn't sleep all night," she said. "He wants me in my grave."

"He meant well, Mrs Church, he wasn't trying to upset you," I said.

"You don't know anything. But he knows. Oh, he knows. In China, you put up pictures like that when people are dead. Dead."

I couldn't worry too much about Mrs Church as I was still trying to get all the paperwork done for Tai, POD's amah, and had to meet her at Kai Tak Airport in the early evening. She was waiting at the check-in desk when I got there. She was immaculate in a black and white check suit and knee-high socks, surrounded by well-wishers and a mountain of luggage. I kicked myself. I'd expected she'd have few possessions. I explained three suitcases would have to go by sea and took her to a quiet corner to repack. Mother, aunties, uncles, cousins and friends followed. All of them inspected, commented and offered advice. Her bulging suitcases gave up tinned food, bamboo shoots in plastic bags, dried mushrooms, scrolls, handbags in four colours, clothing – so much clothing, shoes, makeup, paper, brushes and ink for calligraphy, shrimp paste, noodles, bed socks and umbrellas.

Someone suggested she wear more and they dressed her, jacket upon jacket, two overcoats and all the pockets filled. She was practically circular and carried her airline bag, a handbag, a huge paper carry-bag full of last-minute presents, an enormous envelope with her X-rays, as required by British immigration, and a folder with passport and tickets.

A pit hollowed out my stomach as I watched the clock, the preparations and the dozens of well-wishers. Tai had been buoyant but when her flight was called she broke down. I took all her papers and bags and the younger relatives brought her mother through the throng with reverence and gentleness. Her mother was old, wizened and vital. She spoke no English and read no Chinese.

Tai was taller and broader than her mother, their embrace a juxtaposition. We all stared and I could not bear to separate them. There was another announcement in English and in Cantonese. Tai pulled away and I handed her back her bags. She had no hand left to wipe away the tears streaking down her face. She sucked in air, her tongue flicking away the salty drops. Her mother keened and turned flailing to clutch me, burying her head in my chest. I too blubbered, my tears landing on her balding scalp and I hugged her, my bare arms scratching on the rough fabric of her jacket. Tai's father was not there; he was away at sea and knew nothing. Tai had planned it that way so he could not stop her. It would be her mother who would break the news to him.

When they all left, I found a place where I could sit. I could not leave the airport until I knew the plane had taken off. I bent my head to regain composure. Why had I agreed to be part of this? I tried to reason that Tai going to England was just like me coming to Hong Kong. But, I knew it wasn't; it was very different. I felt as if I had conspired in some grubbiness. The plane was delayed and it was quite dark by the time I left the airport. I was glad to get on the Star Ferry and feel the wind in my hair. I looked around at the sea of Chinese faces. How was I to judge? Maybe it was a great opportunity for Tai or maybe it wasn't. One thing I knew, she was courageous. I hoped the old adage was true that fortune favoured the bold.

The next morning Mrs Church bounded into the office and made a resounding announcement to all the staff that she'd had a change of mind; she was not selling out the APB to Mr O'Neil-Dunne after all. David disappeared into his studio and switched on the "Recording" light. Mr Kwan smiled, inclined his head and shrank into the fur coat that he wore indoors and out during the winter months. But other than rhetoric, Mrs Church made no real attempt to take control again. It was not the firm she wanted back but POD, back the way she'd dreamt he would be.

On Christmas Eve, Mrs Church gave last minute errands to virtually the whole staff. She even had David so busy wrapping presents that it wasn't until 4.30 pm that he realised he must leave.

"Mrs Church, I really have to go now and get my wife a Christmas present or there'll be hell to pay," he said firmly.

"Don't worry, David, I've got her something."

David turned red. "I'm going now, Mrs Church, see you this evening."

"Well if you must, you must. But just a box of chocolates or a few roses, David. You can't afford to go blowing the hard-earned money I give you on gifts. POD's spent it all anyway, so there'll be no pay rises in the New Year."

That evening, David drove me and his wife Anne to Mrs Church's Christmas party. David parked the car on the road outside Salamat facing the city. "So we can make a quick getaway if we need to," he said, before we walked together up the driveway. Residual irritation faded at the sight of the huge fir tree in the garden decked in fairy lights. The lighted windows of the house beckoned and inside Mrs Church had created a scene worthy of Norman Rockwell's paintbrush. A Christmas tree ringed with presents. A large Italian plaster nativity scene filled one corner. Swarthy shepherds stared astonished at a robust, pearly baby, its arms and legs forever extended in newborn startle reflex. The mahogany table shone in the candlelight of an enormous silver candelabrum. Salamat had seen it all before, but it was no less magic or less generous for all that.

Chapter 15

Although I kept my mouth shut about my choice of accommodation, it was not long before Mrs Church demanded to know why I had not invited her to see my new flat. She didn't give me a chance to answer.

"I know why," she said. "It's because you live in a slum."

I was still feeling irritated that evening as we ate dinner so I told Takako and Ochida about Mrs Church's outburst. Ochida was alarmed, but Takako responded. "Please invite her and then she will see this is a perfectly respectable establishment."

I doubled up laughing. "That makes it sound like a brothel Takako; she'll pick you for a madam or Ochida for our pimp." I never did invite Mrs Church.

Some nights, Takako and I would meet up after work and buy food in the street stalls before we visited her friend and admirer, Leon Comber. He was the Far East Manager of Heinemann, the publishers. We'd sit on his floor eating bean curd wraps and dumplings surrounded by the proofs of the latest book he was editing, or chat as he typed up his broadcast for *Pick of the Paperbacks* on weekly radio. Leon was amused that I'd read *The World of Suzie Wong,* an improbable fifties romance between a penniless artist and a bar girl which painted Hong Kong as the quintessential oriental fleshpot destination. He said nothing when I told him about the other love story I'd read, *A Many-Splendored Thing*, by Han Suyin, Mrs Church's old friend.

Leon was English and had come East in World War II. He was in his early twenties when he'd fought the Japanese in Burma. He said, "Every allied serviceman wanted to save his own skin. Fighting men inoculated with the Bushido code, who were genuinely unafraid to die, was quite terrifying."

After Burma, Leon sailed to Japanese-occupied Malaya with a British invasion force, Operation Zipper. Shortly before they made landfall, the Americans dropped atomic bombs on Hiroshima and Nagasaki and the Japanese in Malaya capitulated. Leon's role changed to restoring order. He fell in love with the country and its peoples, stayed on after the war and joined the local police force. He soon found himself gathering intelligence on ethnic Chinese Communists during the Malayan Emergency, a civil war, in all but name.

Leon was suave and wonderfully literate, a scholarly man. His face was open, his lizard-lidded eyes unflinching, yet behind was a deep reserve. He was twice my age and took me on board kindly as Takako's flatmate, teasing me in a paternal way. Each time he brought Takako gifts from his frequent trips abroad, he made sure I had something too, a cocktail stirrer from Thailand, a book mark from Singapore. He loved to tell me he and I were gweilos, the name Chinese gave all Europeans; hairy, red-faced, smelly and inferior. He wanted me to understand perspectives – the Chinese and Europeans both traded insults, both felt themselves superior – and it was these matching native eccentricities that made for healthy Anglo-Chinese relationships.

One night, Takako told me she was invited to a special dinner and Leon had suggested she wear her kimono. "Can you get home a little early and help me dress?" she asked me, "It's a ceremonial kimono. It's hard work and it needs two people."

Although it was a complicated practice, Takako was confident in the fine art of kimono dressing. It reminded me of her heritage, yet each wrap of the formal cloth seemed at odds with her vibrant personality. Each fold took her back into the culture she had eluded.

When Leon knocked at the door, and the amah opened it, Takako was uncharacteristically stiff yet resplendent in her kimono. Taking small mincing steps, she turned, her bright eyes shining, and bowed to me. Unexpected pleasure shivered up my spine.

That night I waited up until Takako returned. We sat on the bed and she told me about the party and how tiring it was to be dignified all night long for it was impossible to relax in a kimono. She said some of the guests were friends of Han Suyin, Leon's first wife, and she had felt a little awkward.

"Leon was married *before*? To Han Suyin, the author?" I said.

Takako nodded.

"Mrs Church is a good friend of Han Suyin," I added.

Takako looked concerned. "Oh, Leon doesn't like to talk to anyone about Han Suyin. I wouldn't want you to say anything to Mrs Church."

"Takako, of course, I won't. Leon's a dark horse! He never said anything even when he knew I'd read her book. But word about you must have got back to Han Suyin already – Hong Kong's so small!"

Leon's romance with Han Suyin had started when she was working in a Hong Kong hospital. They married in 1952, the year she published her best-seller, *A Many-Splendored Thing*.

The book, thinly veiled as fiction, was a cathartic homage to Han Suyin's love affair with a married Australian journalist who'd died reporting the Korean War. The backdrop to the affair was her cultural dilemma, torn between her love for a European and her desire to work as a doctor in Communist China. She hoped the Red Revolution might offer her people a chance of unity and peace.

A furore followed the publication of the book. The shock in the British press that she, a Eurasian, wrote openly of her sexual liaison with one of their own, turned to outrage as the book divulged her lover's infidelity to his unsuspecting wife and grieving family. Han Suyin, who had achieved her medical degree through a British scholarship and helped Allies in the war effort, was branded as anti-establishment and a thoroughly ungrateful, selfish woman. The book and the melodramatic film that followed – *Love Is a Many-Splendored Thing* – would also bring Han Suyin further pain from another quarter. It flushed out the Australian journalist had had other lovers in other ports.

"Leon comforted her and supported her against her critics," Takako said. "After they married, Leon took Suyin back to Malaya."

There Han Suyin practised as a rural doctor and many of her patients were Malay Chinese. From them she heard disquieting rumours. Once more her loyalties were split and she was torn between the plight of her people and her love for a European on the side of the establishment.

In her next book, *And the Rain My Drink*, fiction once again mirrored reality. It was a tale of Chinese struggle and British injustice and ineptitude in Malaya. Small incidents and characters glowed with authenticity, collected from the company she kept with Leon. Leon's colleagues saw themselves identified and felt betrayed. Han Suyin was again labelled unpatriotic. Gerald Templer, the British High Commissioner in Malaya, not only side-lined Leon's career, he tried to have an embargo placed on the book. Leon was embarrassed and irritated by the book's revelations, but he knew what his wife had written was not treasonable and he could not stomach attempts to silence her. He walked away from his beloved Malaya and soon afterwards from Han Suyin, who'd found a new lover.

Leon had moved on but his past lingered, too exotic to shed. His silence fuelled the mystery. Takako and I had plenty to whisper about after we put out the lights.

Takako told me that our amah had announced she was leaving to go back to China to care for a sick relative. At that time, the newspapers were full of articles about the shortage of amahs in Hong Kong because there was plenty of work around in factories. I said I would go to an agency and we would just pay the extra fee and get someone through them. I think I also had in mind that I might recruit an amah who was less aggressive than the one who was leaving. She was a hazard for any casual visitors. Once when I'd been writing home, sitting at the dining table, there'd been a knock at the door. When the amah opened it, I glimpsed a European man and heard him ask for Takako.

"She not in," said the amah and slammed the door with incredible force.

I rushed over to open the door, imagining the poor man might be out stone cold in the hallway. He was rubbing his nose.

I told Takako when she came home thinking she might reprimand the amah, but she laughed it off and said it was a sign we had a very capable Cantonese amah. "It's a good idea not to step forward when any amah opens the door. You need to know that she's been specifically told to expect you at a certain time, or that's what she'll do – slam the door in your face!"

There was another incident with the amah that had unnerved me. When the two Japanese boys or Takako's friends visited Macau, a Portuguese colonial enclave across the Pearl River delta from Hong Kong, they always bought us back a bamboo basket of live crabs and gave them to the amah. With her chopper she'd take off the claws and leave the poor things to scrabble about until she'd boiled the water to cook them. One night I went to get a drink of water from the kitchen tap. It was dark and when I turned on the light, the crabs were still on the loose, wandering the kitchen confused and dismembered.

I had high hopes for my new recruit who came from the agency with very good references. She arrived, took one look at Takako, turned to me and said, "You no tell me Nippon Missy," and she was gone. As I closed the door behind her I thought, yes, you are right, it's an easy mistake, I no tell you because I no think about it.

Takako found a replacement, one who could speak a little Japanese but no English. Leon was over having dinner with us and chatting to her in Cantonese when he laughed out loud and glanced at me. "What is it?" I said.

"Nothing … just the amah has given you a nickname."

"And …?"

"Young fresh face. That's the closest I can translate," said Leon. "It just amused me because when I told my assistant I was coming here tonight, he said if you see the girl with the cute baby face, give her my regards."

By this time Takako was laughing too.

I turned to look at her, raising my eyebrow.

She said, "Ochida says you are beautiful, like his sister's American doll, with a round face, curly blond hair and rosy cheeks." I was mortified. Was it not enough that every amah referred to me as the "big missy" because I towered above Takako. I didn't want to look silly, so I pushed back my chair and pretended I thought it was funny too. Leon resumed chatting to the amah and Takako started to help her clear the table.

I sighed inwardly. I wanted to blend in, not be a caricature white girl. I got up to carry dishes into the kitchen. The amah shooed me out but not before I'd caught sight of her little statue of a laughing Buddha clutching his round tummy. He seemed to be looking right at me. I knew too that I was larger and my face rounder than when I had arrived in Hong Kong – all the good food was beginning to show. The next day I rang the Squash Club and asked them to send me enrolment forms. I knew I needed to get fit and lose weight.

Leon visited more and more frequently. Late into the night with Takako neatly cross-legged on her bed and I sprawled across mine, we charted their relationship. It was a formal courtship and would not be an intimate one until cemented by marriage. I had no experience of relationships, let alone cross-cultural ones, to contribute much.

One night, we were both feeling restless and as we sat chatting, we convinced each other that Hong Kong, for all its beauty, was claustrophobic. Takako also felt she needed to show Leon that matters between them were not settled yet. She was independent and he was slow popping the question. We giggled, fantasising we were abandoned damsels, moated in, sitting on a castle rock. "Well," said Takako, "I have an idea, let's catch the ferry tomorrow after work and go to Macau."

"Are you serious?"

"Why not?"

Takako's spontaneity was galvanising. The following evening I met her at the ferry terminal. We were as excited as schoolgirls playing truant. Passports, tickets, money. We'd leave Hong Kong with its tall angular stiffnecked buildings, transistors, cheap plastic frippery and frenetic energy and catch the ferry to Macau, with its crumbling Portuguese architecture of arches and colonnades, flowery hand-painted pottery from the Algarve, rounded flasks of Mateus Rosé and Mediterranean lassitude.

Macau was the Monte Carlo of the East, a casino kingdom. We weren't going for gambling. We both had good books and we just wanted to take time out, relax and read. Of course, Takako knew of a good Portuguese restaurant we had to try and we went out to dinner on the Saturday evening. On the way home, I wanted to return to the hotel through the back streets, but Takako refused. "I don't want to walk in the dark, let's get a taxi back."

"OK," I said, taken by surprise. Takako was not petulant, just pragmatic. She flicked back her hair. "You are only a gweilo, but I am a Nippon monkey and of the two enemies, the Chinese dislike me more."

I burst out laughing and so did Takako. Fresh-faced baby doll hugged Nippon monkey and together hailed a taxi.

Chapter 16

POD stayed in England with his family until well into the New Year. I kept my head down and got on with my work keeping to the small routines. On Fridays, pay-day, I went for lunch at a yum cha restaurant with the girls from the office. There was one on the top floor of almost every high rise in the CBD. Brightly lit, utilitarian spaces that pulsed with noise, the din of dishes and chopsticks clattering on Formica-topped tables, waiters crying a bill of fare and the sing-song of animated Cantonese intercourse. Trollies trundled the aisles stacked with bamboo baskets of steamed dumplings, brilliant green vegetables, chicken feet, spare ribs and sticky rice balls. Gossip was grist for the sisterhood.

There was always plenty to laugh about when I joined the girls for yum cha. One day I told them how I'd bought an ice cream cone when I was out for lunch. Because I didn't want to meet anyone I knew while I was licking ice cream, I ducked down an alleyway and strolled along glancing at the newspaper I held up with the other hand. The headline was about the astounding rise in the Hong Kong Brewery share price after they'd received a take-over offer from Carlings. Seeing it, I knew why POD had recently bought so many Brewery shares. Absorbed in the thought, I tripped and my scoop of raspberry ice cream disengaged and shot forward, hitting the back of a smart Chinese businessman who was walking in front of me. I was left holding the cone. My first reaction was to dump it and look innocent, but the man turned and putting his hand on his back realised he'd been *got*. It might have been an alley way but I was not alone. Hawkers and tradesmen were gobsmacked until I stepped up and apologised profusely. The onlookers roared with laughter. Someone produced a cloth, helped the man take off his jacket and wiped off the ice cream. I was mortified but the Chinese gentleman insisted that it was a small thing and took great pains to make sure that I did not feel embarrassed. His impeccable manners and immaculately tailored suit made me feel very clumsy, as if I took up too much space in that narrow passageway.

Other times, my lunches with the girls gave me the opportunity for insights into things that happened at the office that I didn't understand. Once when POD was in his office working on something brilliant, or so he claimed, an old woman dressed in grubby rags walked up to my desk and shoved an envelope at me as she gabbled away in Cantonese. All the Chinese staff were having lunch so I went to the canteen and got one of the girls, and when we came back the woman was squatting in a corner of the reception area and refused to budge. Two more staff came to help while the others watched, gesticulating with their chopsticks from the security of the lunchroom. The office boy resolved it. He took the envelope, examined it, and talking kindly, helped her up and out the door into the lift lobby. Then he did a quick turn, flew back into our offices, locked the door and pretended to hold it shut with his back to it. I had not a clue what was going on but just loved watching the expressions of the junior staff who were often quite formal with me. They all burst out laughing, unrestrained and playful.

POD heard the noise and shouted for everyone to get back to work and said he needed me. He was in no mood for my story, so I wasn't able to find out what it was all about until the next day at yum cha. The old woman had found an envelope in the street and made for the first office that she could find with an open door. She demanded money for returning it to us. The letter was not addressed to us and in any case the woman could not read. The office boy had told her she had come to the wrong office and the one she wanted was over the corridor. I felt a bit sorry then. I would probably have given her a few dollars if I had been quicker to work out what was going on.

Also over yum cha, my friends revealed aspects of their characters that were not on display in the office. Miriam, reserved and professional at work, did a very good impersonation of Mrs Church:

"Why are there no messages on my desk – do I have to come and ask you for messages?"

"There are no messages for you Mrs Church."

"Don't be ridiculous, of course I have messages."

I couldn't avoid Mrs Church altogether in POD's absence. She tried to reassert her authority over me and I had to be polite, but she easily rattled me. Mrs Church knew of every small lapse of mine, the phone call I'd forgotten to return, a deadline I'd stretched or any day I was late from lunch. She exaggerated every misstep, never resisting the opportunity to drop a comment or a knowing hint. I knew it was the Chinese staff who sustained her, like workers feeding a plump queen bee.

I went home from the office feeling frustrated. I enjoyed the company of my Chinese friends and felt, especially since joining them each week for yum cha, that we had a good rapport, so it was galling to think they went to Mrs Church behind my back. I sat down at the dining table to write to my parents. Takako was biting the end of her pencil, adding up the household accounts in a little notebook. Leon arrived and settled down to read the paper while the amah prepared dinner. My irritation was building as I scratched at the thin blue airmail paper until I pushed my correspondence aside and turned to Leon, unloading my exasperation.

Folding the newspaper on his lap, he listened patiently, then said, "Gill, you are a gweilo. Your mind is too rigid."

"Leon, it's bloody deceitful for the Chinese staff to go round telling tales all the time. And they have no sense of loyalty – as soon as POD is gone, they switch their allegiance back to the old bat and tell her every little thing that goes on."

"Such over-simplification. You are categorising and focused on correctness," counselled Leon. "You are dealing with an oriental mind, one that is tolerant of contradictions because the world is ambiguous."

"Leon, talking in riddles isn't helping me. What do I do?"

Leon leant forward, putting his palms together between his knees, pursing his lips a little. He was looking for a way to try and succinctly explain thousands of years of Chinese cultural behaviour. Generations of Europeans had lived in the Orient and yet the divide remained. Leon lamented the Western inability to grasp the richness that a little understanding would deliver.

"So much complexity needs compromise, so the problem becomes a puzzle, with many possible moves to reach a solution. You, too, need to perceive obstacles in the same way. Think of it as a game."

"A game! This is deadly serious. If Mrs Church keeps interfering she will destroy the whole business. It's not right that they keep aiding and abetting her."

"You're not listening. They, your Chinese staff, are faced with a fluid and difficult situation, and are finding the middle way." He paused, reaching over to pour us both more tea. "Truth isn't an absolute, Gill. And what you see as 'right' might be simply what suits you."

Leon was too erudite for me to absorb all of what he had to say. Takako got up to turn on the light and pulled up a chair so she could put her hand on my knee. I felt clumsy and opinionated. Leon frustrated me, I wanted concrete solutions.

That night I lay awake long after Takako's breathing was regular and I knew she was asleep. I was miserable and remembered the early words of Mr Kwan; *in this situation, develop oily wings.* Oily wings were not enough.

I thought more about what Leon had said. The only solutions I could think of were firing all the staff or murdering Mrs Church. I was tired, too tired to think. Maybe, I thought, there was something in what Leon had said. I should see the situation as a childish game of Chinese whispers and then try to laugh at its distortions.

Gradually I became more conscious of my exchanges with the girls at yum cha and was not such a greenhorn. It was indeed a game, and once I started to understand the rules, I knew I could play too. I began to know what would go back to Mrs Church and what would remain between us. I was almost as observant in the office as they were and once I made that known, the playing field levelled out.

I followed up on the resolution I'd made to get fit and booked my first game at the Squash Club on Ladies Night in January. It was there I met Greta. Greta befriended all newcomers as a matter of civic duty and at first I was just another new face. She was Scots and it was important to me that she understood our kinship since I was London-born, raised in Belfast and Oxford and had a plummy English accent.

My mother was not given to hyperbole, but made my Scots lineage clear. "You have not a drop of English blood in your veins."

It always made me giggle.

I told Greta about my childhood holidays in our croft on the west coast of Scotland: solitary days with gulls wheeling overhead and the constantly changing sea and sky. Greta had grown up in a small village north of Aberdeen. The gales that swept the coast made work for her father, who mended roofs, replacing slates and tiles. Her mother was a nurse with a strong moral compass and instilled in Greta many of her own values, not puritan or prudish, but those of human kindness.

Perhaps it was our shared experience of the storm-swept Scottish landscapes that joined us so easily. Something special cemented our friendship – it was an unlikely alliance as Greta was several years older than me and we were still young enough for that to matter. We soon developed a weightless, undemanding affinity.

Greta was practical and purposeful; a primary school teacher in a government school on a three-year contract. She had an energetic Scottish face that easily switched between moods of jest, empathy and curiosity.

Every meeting with Greta was an exploration because she had an insatiable quest for knowledge and a principled approach to time. Time was a gift not to be wasted. It did not take long for me to find out she was also daft. Daft in the Scots sense; merry, frolicsome and loveable, easily unravelled by a flying cockroach and downright bad-tempered if woken from deep slumber. In a short time Greta and I were inseparable. Greta's government flat was in the block opposite mine and Greta and Takako liked each other immediately, which made a close-knit sorority.

Greta and I partied together all over the colony, on ships and on beaches, in clubs and discotheques, in flats and mansions, spontaneous get-togethers and meticulously organised soirees. Since that amount of partying required wardrobes we could not afford, Greta's solution was that we made our own. Around Tuesday we would decide what patterns we'd run up for the weekend. Each evening, we'd cut, tack, sew and chat, finishing each other's hems as we headed out. Often, we would be responding to several invitations in one evening; cocktails, a dinner and dancing into the night. We could not fit it all into weekends, so socialising spread into week nights where it contended with squash games, language lessons, cultural classes, sewing and everything domestic. This was way before social media or mobile phones. Our complicated, interrelated and oft-changing arrangements relied on notes and messages, patience and planning. It required a fiendish amount of energy to handle it all.

Some days I felt bad that I was so happy when there was so much discord in the office. David had not settled into Hong Kong. He remained isolated, irritable with the culture, the Chinese, and the situation at the office. Even the arrival of Anne, his wife, hadn't helped; neither of them was happy. While his dark humour made me laugh, his rants wickedly funny, they were all at the expense of everything Chinese.

I decided I needed to alleviate my good-fortune guilt. I wasn't up to collecting orphans or closing opium dens, but some token atonement was required. I put my hand up for some office work with Legal Aid. I worked with a couple of bright young Chinese girls who were lawyers helping the very poor. The issues were mostly around domestic violence or the arrests of women forced into sheltering triad members.

One day, one of the lawyers walked me through a shack with old and emaciated men lying in three-tier bunks on either side of a corridor, smoking opium. A young girl was preparing the pipes and she was the Legal Aid client – she was threatened with eviction. Another time we chatted to the prostitutes and bar-girls in Wan Chai, the red-light district. I had been told by Irene that the local girls resented the Hong Kong expats and European residents visiting their waterfront establishments in Wan Chai. She said many Chinese office girls made a bit of extra money in Wan Chai, not necessarily as prostitutes, but simply keeping visiting sailors company, and it was horribly embarrassing for them if they were recognised and word got back to their employers. Although I was accepted, the conversations among the lawyers were in Cantonese and I felt I was prying where I did not belong. I did some typing for Legal Aid but it was pretty dry stuff and they really needed someone who was bi-lingual.

Each morning the office boy, Ah Fung, brought me green tea and dropped the *South China Morning Post* on my desk. If I was in the mood, I'd quickly flick the pages, scanning the advertisements we'd placed, or be ghoulish and read about yet another chopper murder – domestic violence in Hong Kong almost always involved a meat cleaver. One day a modest headline caught my eye about an organisation that taught English and martial arts to young factory workers in a resettlement area. A line of bold type at the end said they were looking for an English mother-tongue volunteer for conversation classes and gave a telephone number.

I made the call and a week later I took the Star Ferry over the harbour after work, holding a piece of card on which Irene had written in Chinese characters; "This person is to get off one stop before the terminal". She told me to get the No. 2 bus from Kowloon. It was dark by the time the driver waved me off at a stop towered over by four matching tenement blocks. I looked up, every window ablaze with light. Thickets of TV aerials and wooden rods slung with laundry whiskered the buildings. Chinese signboards stuck out from the buildings one behind the other up a street jam-packed with people and traffic. Transistor radios blared either pop music or Chinese opera. I walked past tea-rooms, cheap restaurants and shops packed with plastic and electrical goods. A redolence of burning cooking oil drifted from the sizzling woks of the food stalls hung with strangled Peking ducks, red-brown and shiny, turning slowly by the neck. There was not another European face in sight. I followed the directions I had been given and found Hannah To waiting for me at the Youth Centre. Hannah was the girl I had spoken to on the phone. She was one of the organisation's founders. The Centre was an oasis of space and relative quiet.

Hannah introduced me to my class, mostly youths in their late teens and early twenties. I sensed they were all as nervous as I was. After the introductions and a couple of stilted forays into conversation, it all stalled. Perspiration prickled down my back, the silence so heavy I could hardly breathe. I could not think of a single thing to say. Their faces were so eager and hopeful, checking out the gweilo. I was unequal to the scrutiny; without doubt I was ungainly, red of skin and offensive of odour; out of place and out of words. I wanted to run but the lesson was only half over. Out of ideas, I started again with their names. This time, I said, I would write them down.

"Wong Kwok Keung."

"Tong Yiu Chung."

The third boy said "Henry". The class burst out laughing and the first two decided they also wanted English names. Back to the start.

"William."

"Hugh."

"Henry."

Then a pause. I looked up. The next boy could not think of an English name. Soon the class was raining suggestions, which he ignored. He was struggling to bring something forth. I could tell it was coming. I willed him to speak. We stared at each other.

He blurted it out. "Friar Tuck."

I was so taken by surprise, my mouth dropped open. Worse still, he was the only plump boy in the class. No-one else seemed to think it strange, so I wrote it down and moved on.

On the bus home I relived what had gone wrong. I was used to being out in the streets at night on Hong Kong Island but the resettlement area was different. It was still raw. The lesson hadn't been a success; it all seemed a waste of time for them and for me. I wasn't cut out for this. The bus took over an hour to get back to the ferry. I thought about the worst of it. How could those moments of silence have shaken me witless? How was it that I hadn't been able to think of a single thing to say? I took a crumpled piece of paper from my bag and smoothed it out on my knee. I started to write down some ideas about ordinary things like family, school and work. Nothing else came. Then I tried the alphabet. Abacus and abalone. Bamboo and Buddhist purgatory. Calligraphy and colonies. My mind was racing now. Mah-jong and mandarins. Typhoons and tigers – one had been spotted in the New Territories quite recently. By the time we arrived at the Kowloon stop, my piece of paper was covered with scribbled words and I knew I would go back the following week. I hurried over to the Star Ferry – catching it had become so commonplace I didn't even bother travelling first class on the upper deck as it was often quicker to get off from the lower deck. As the motors churned the water and we were underway, I knew the resettlement area would soon become as familiar as the Star Ferry.

The next week on my way out to the Youth Centre, I worried about Friar Tuck. I couldn't let him go out into the wider world with that moniker. Why hadn't I had the sense to say something straight away? Poor bugger, I could just imagine a bigoted gweilo teasing him about Robin Hood.

I need not have worried for they had all changed their minds and William became Raymond and Hugh became Eddie, Henry now David and Friar Tuck was Robert. I found the shifting names perplexing yet it was a much more successful class. After the lesson, I went round to the tea room to find the Chinese teachers. They laughed at my bewilderment. "You have to keep up with the news," said one. "They read the newspapers and you'll find next week's names all there. The week Nixon comes to power, they are all Richard; the Governor hits the headlines and they are all David." Another said, "They don't need English names in the factory so they don't think about them until you come back again and by then they don't even remember the one they last gave you."

By the third week Hannah had to chase us out of the classroom. We had carried on talking long after the lesson had finished and she wanted to lock the doors. From then on at the end of each class we'd move onto the streets into a haze of oil-lamps and cooking oil. We'd hover round the food stalls buying noodles and rice, the faces of my students animated and natural, not straining to hear or comprehend. This was their time to teach me. They took me to the bus stop and waited with me, calling to the driver to take me safely to the ferry. The next week, they were there when I arrived. Some afternoons, when it was pouring, and I was snug in the office, I wanted to make an excuse not to go to class but I thought of them standing at the bus stop in the neon-washed rain. Waiting. Waiting for me. I had to go.

Takako worried about my safety and waited up for me on my teaching nights. She knew all about the latest crime syndicates, police corruption, triads, opium dens, muggers and thieves. It was enough to make anyone nervous, yet each week I felt more comfortable. When I was pick-pocketed, it was while I stood waiting at the ferry terminal.

The wizened old man was ham-fisted – I nearly grabbed his wrist – but he escaped, surprisingly fleet of foot. A Chinese man saw what happened and noted my consternation. He stepped forward and bought me a ferry ticket – a first-class ticket for a second-class gweilo.

Chapter 17

The morning after POD returned from his English holiday, he rang early and asked me to meet him at the Hilton coffee shop for breakfast. I hurried over. As soon as I saw him sitting in a corner scribbling away in his notebook, I knew he'd returned with new energy and vigour. He gave me a bear hug.

"I've spoken to Freddie and he says you did well while I was away. I know Betty was changing her mind all the time, but the contract of sale is agreed now and it's all ready to sign."

I interrupted him so I could order coffee and a croissant.

"I've had a brainwave Gill. Once Betty signs the agreement, I am going to give our lifetime chairman a thank you present. In fact it's a present for all of us," he said with a laugh.

"What kind of present?"

"A world cruise – first-class ticket – four months. She deserves it. She built up this agency and she hasn't had a proper holiday for years. It'll be a wrench I know," he said chuckling. "We'll have to do without her around, but dammit, it's her due."

I burst out laughing.

"Think Gill, four months without Betty. Before she goes I can pick her brains, get all the old clients settled and she'll have plenty of time to figure out her wardrobe for the trip." He paused. "It also means I can go home for the summer and know that she is not causing havoc here. And another thing Gill, I want you to go home in the summer too for a holiday."

"What! Me go home, why?"

"You deserve it Gill. I couldn't have managed without you and David told me how miserable you were. He said you had cried on his shoulder."

"Oh, but Sir, everything's changed, Sir, I'd love to go home of course, but I don't need to, I'm happy now, so much has happened ... I've met a Scots girl, Greta and I volunteered ..."

"Well, that's even better, then you'll be happy to go and happy to come back."

We finished our breakfast and walked back to the office. Once outside I felt choked with emotion. I could hardly believe it and I could not wait to telegram the news home.

POD did pull it off, the contract was signed and he bought all the shares in the APB. Mrs Church was sceptical when POD presented her with the cruise ticket but the Chinese staff clapped almost as loudly as we did and eventually she came round to the idea and her upcoming trip was soon the talk at curry tiffin.

It was a tremendous relief to have everything settled. Even David seemed to be enjoying his work. He'd recovered from a very ugly office incident days before POD's return. David was an artist and spent countless hours perfecting the drawing of a white and fluffy Persian cat for a new ad for Bowater toilet rolls. It took Mr Yi, the Art Director, who didn't like David, seconds to sink his ink pen into the delicately etched original. "It needs stronger outline to make it more reproducible," he said.

David bristled with indignation and glared at the diminutive Mr Yi, threatening that if he ever touched his artwork again, *he* would need to be reproducible. Mr Yi looked confused, but held his ground. He was the Art Director and his intuition told him he'd be there long after David was forgotten.

POD didn't want to hear about the cat. "David, I've built you a sound studio. If I'd wanted you to be an artist, I'd have built you a bloody art studio."

POD had visited potential accounts in England and sought ties with major agencies in London.

A new manager joined us, poached from the Rothmans Hong Kong office, a 26-year-old bachelor. Mrs Church knew the family. "Old Hong Kong family, good stock."

"Got local knowledge," said POD.

Diffident and nervous, Edward was nevertheless well-spoken and not bad looking either.

Shortly afterwards, another young man was due to fly in, the son of an old colleague of POD's. POD asked me to meet him at the airport. I protested. I had a party to go to that night and was meeting Greta straight after work. "Surely, Sir, the guy is capable of getting himself from the airport to the hotel?"

"No, Gill, you have to go, it's important that people feel wanted when they arrive in a new place – it's a long flight from Johannesburg."

"Oh no. Not someone else from Africa. Look at David, he climbs Kilimanjaro every night in his dreams and I don't think he'll ever be happy until he's back there."

"You wait, Gill. One day you will go to Africa and then you will understand. But tonight, where you'll go is the airport."

With little grace, I went home with Greta and got dressed for the party. It was impossibly hot and humid. To get ready to go out, Greta and I would take it in turns to stand in front of a pedestal fan to get our faces dry enough to apply make-up and then stand there a bit longer to set it. I told Greta I'd catch up with her at the party. I knew it was a battle lost before it was begun. By the time I'd made the ten-minute crossing on the Star Ferry, my hair and make-up were redone by the elements.

I arrived at the airport and stood leaning against a bollard, bored and irritable, holding up a cardboard sign. I watched the arrivals come through the gate and move off, the Europeans tall among the mass of Chinese. One was impossibly handsome, several passable, I mused, and the rest mundane. Silly idiot probably missed the flight, I thought.

"Gill, you must be Gill? POD said you'd be here."

I was startled, ambushed. Close-up, he was even more good-looking. Blue eyes looking into mine, mouth smiling at me, a natural charm flowing easily as he relieved me of the piece of cardboard and lifted my sweaty hand in his cool dry one and bent to kiss it. I squeaked redundantly. "You must be Pierre."

The next morning, an Irish secretary Mrs Church had engaged for a couple of months flew into my office. "Gill, you've got to meet the new guy! He's drop-dead gorgeous."

Pierre's head appeared round my office door. He laughed oh so effortlessly, and said, "It's OK, we've met. I took Gill for a drink last night."

It was true. I did get to my party, but quite late – the urgency had gone right out of my evening arrangements.

With two young bachelors at the office and David, who was older and married but always protective of me, the office became a social hub. For a couple of months, they flirted and so did I. But working together was a fast track to uncovering their idiosyncrasies. Edward was incapable of making a decision to save his life and Pierre was hopelessly disorganised. Once impatience set in, romance was out of the question.

With the new staff on board, POD indulged his passion for training and set up regular staff sessions on management and marketing. "Fun to lead and fun to be followed," the battle cry his old staff remembered fondly. He liked young people. Youth were the future in any organisation he said. He enjoyed motivating us all and we were swept along by his infectious enthusiasm.

POD wrote the copy for a new glossy brochure promoting the APB and promising a market with a future. He assured prospective clients that the people of Hong Kong "... know the Union Jack will always fly over Hong Kong island, and as for the New Territories which are leased from China, well, twenty-nine years is a long, long way away. Who knows what is going to happen in 1998 – in the United Kingdom, the United States, Europe, Asia ... or Hong Kong? The course of history can well change in twenty-nine years just as events twenty-nine years ago changed the course of world history."

The small fortune POD had invested in the APB needed to show dividends. POD lectured us on the need for economy but diluted the message by frequently taking us all out to dinner at expensive restaurants. He insisted on ordering the most bizarre dishes with the excuse that he needed to sophisticate my palate.

My work was changing. I was sorting out the company records for the APB going back decades and setting up investment companies for POD, so I had my head down working hard. I was confident now. Freddie had allotted a young solicitor in his firm to help me and I had my own secretary, Connie Tang, a very young, very clever lass. POD left me paperwork with margin notes, "Gill, can you fix it?" Each time it was a challenge. If he ever doubted me, he never let on. He told me once that he'd been impressed by George Patton, a famous US General, whose advice was: tell people what you want done, not how to do it.

We worked long hours alongside POD and in the evening he liked nothing better than to open the drinks cabinet, get in front of the piano and try out David's latest advertising jingle.

"We've nailed it! Come on, once more. And David, record it this time."

It sounded good, but in the morning, we'd listen to the taped rendition which usually needed "more work."

POD produced proposals, reports, graphs and predictions and the clients loved it. We were presenting to new accounts and winning.

Even Mrs Church was caught up in the spirit of the new order. One of her oldest clients said, "My God, Betty, what's happened? Your firm's turned professional overnight. I don't think I've ever been more impressed with an ad agency visit in my life."

POD dashed into my office with a huge boy grin to tell me the news.

Mrs Church offered to help canvas new business.

"Sir, do you think it's wise?" I said.

"Why not, it's her forte; after all, as she never lets us forget, she's been doing this for forty years. It's important Gill that we carry her along with us as the organisation grows."

It didn't take long.

Mrs Church picked up the phone. "Yes, yes, I do know your current Advertising Manager, and in my opinion, he's a snotty-nosed newcomer who knows nothing about China or the market. Now as I was saying … what? How dare you, I'm completely British and I've lived in this colony for forty-one years! Phooey …", and she slammed the receiver down.

We heard it together because POD was standing at my desk, the door to their office open, yet he couldn't believe his ears. "Betty, that wasn't Mr Dowling of the new account we discussed, was it?"

"Yes, Pat and he's as green as his Advertising Manager. These people should stay in England and let people like us, who know the Chinese, do the work here. Quite pinko some of them."

POD went over and grabbed the paperwork he had given her. "You can't talk to clients like that Betty."

"I'll talk to whoever I like, however I like," she snorted.

He slammed the door shut and an almighty row ensued. When he wrenched the door open again, he didn't even glance at me, but muttered, "Don't say a word," as he strode out of my office.

POD let off steam to Freddie Zimmern, his lawyer, and took me with him. The meeting turned into lunch. "We are not going to ruin our digestive systems so we will not mention Betty," said Freddie, laying down the rules, and we readily agreed.

Freddie looked at me and said, "By the way, you are starting to get to know people. I really need to find a Japanese girl who might do some translation for me."

I was taken aback, so though I replied to Freddie, I looked straight at POD and said, "Well I do know someone as a matter of fact. I share a flat with a lovely Japanese girl who does translations."

POD choked on his soup, grabbing his serviette.

"Are you OK, what's up Pat?" said Freddie, looking concerned.

I knew what was up; but the surprise to me was that POD wasn't choking, he was laughing, the tears running down his face.

"Nothing, nothing, Freddie, my wonton went down the wrong way," said POD when he had recovered and dried his eyes.

The introduction was a success and Freddie and Takako immediately hit it off. A couple of weeks later Freddie said he was surprised POD hadn't met my flat mate and so had invited Takako to lunch. POD was gracious, Freddie engaging, Takako vivacious, and I jubilant. When we left the restaurant, Takako and Freddie walked ahead deep in some discussion and POD hung back a little so he could talk to me without being overheard. "Gill, she's a damned nice girl."

"I hope you don't mean the 'damned', Sir."

"Oh, it's a figure of speech, I mean Gill, you made a good choice, she's quite something."

"Something?"

"Women! You've become a woman Gill, as difficult as all the rest of them," and he chuckled, shaking his head and linking his arm through mine.

I was most grateful to Freddie. Ever since we had first met, he and his wife Doris were constant cohorts, inviting me to dinners at their home, taking me out on trips and introducing me to their relatives.

Much of my social life still revolved around the friends of Mrs Church and POD. Many invites stemmed from the ebullient Mr Mok Ying Kie, Hong Kong's premier stockbroker. Mr Mok ignored me when Mrs Church first introduced me as her new secretary, but once I was elevated by POD, it was, "Call me Mickey". He was the consummate host, his guests an eclectic mix of clients, financiers, youthful Chinese stockbrokers fresh from Oxford or Harvard, bankers from the USA and economists from Europe.

There were frequent outings with Mickey and once, when I was with POD, he sneaked us into the Hong Kong Stock Exchange on the top floor of Edinburgh House before trading started – only members were allowed on the Floor. It was full of blackboards and Chinese clerks and runners who sat on tall stools sitting behind high desks with big black telephones. The whole atmosphere was Dickensian, with a touch of Charlie Chaplin. Trading hadn't started for the day so the phones were not yet buzzing. What I didn't see was the ex-British Army officer who managed the exchange. Mickey Mok told me he inspected the exchange at 9 am every day with a swagger stick under his arm checking that the cleaners had properly mopped the teak floor.

There was a great deal of snobbery around the exchange. An "entrance fee" equivalent to the amount a client might pay for a good apartment or townhouse was a prerequisite to signing up with a stockbroker.

After formal dinner parties at Mickey and Mrs Mok's elegant Repulse Bay mansion, he'd tap the shoulders of his elite singles and off we'd go to the newest nightclub or to a floorshow.

It was Mickey who took me on my first boat trip in Hong Kong on the *Deri-Vica*.

Everyone on the rich list had a boat but few were sailors. Whether it was a motor launch or a junk, the marine varnish gleamed; uniformed Chinese crew cast off and liveried staff served cocktails and sumptuous buffets.

On that first boat trip, I detached myself from the party. The talk about some new share set to soar bored me. I could hear POD's voice above the others; he was in his element. I sat on the prow, hugging my knees, cooled now and then by small showers shearing off sparkling bow-waves. I contemplated the coastline, indistinct, sketched in watercolour, while a master of oils had painted the seascape jotted with the sails of Chinese junks.

To my surprise Mickey came to find me. He pointed and said, "Look up, Gill, see my flag is red with a gold M on it. What do you think it stands for, Mok or Mao?"

"You tell me," I said laughing.

He answered obliquely, "No Chinese junk will quarrel with us even if we stray into Chinese waters."

He sat beside me pointing out the islands and identifying where the Chinese vessels came from by the set of their sails. "Come on," he said, "We need to go and join the party, we are going to land at Ma Wan Island to see its thermos factory."

The little island relied on shrimp fishing and the family-run factory. The blowing of the glass was mechanised, but each flask had to be twisted off and finished by hand. The inner and outer flasks were separated by small asbestos disks and these were the responsibility of a very old woman who sat outside straddling a huge tree stump covered in grey dust. She had a sheet of asbestos and moved around it with her punch and hammer cutting out each disc one by one. Children ran happily between the tree stump, the factory and the packaging shed, moving materials and finished flasks around.

I walked round the island with Mickey through an undertow of dogs, cats, chickens and small children. Outside each small house was a rack of fish hanging up to dry. We walked past rice paddies and vegetable gardens, past homes made from old sampans raised up on stilts, mended and extended with planks from wooden packing crates disporting foreign brand names and logos.

When I thanked Mickey for such a fantastic day, he was visibly pleased and said, "I will take you and POD to Aberdeen Harbour at Chinese New Year." Aberdeen was a town on the southwest of Hong Kong Island named after a British aristocrat – the 4th Earl of Aberdeen. It was said to be the original "fragrant harbour'" of Hong Kong folklore where foreign sailors experienced an exotic landfall, the warm air scented by incense trees and spices.

Chapter 18

Virtually every month there was a festival, but Chinese New Year was the big one. Paradoxically, in colonial Hong Kong, Chinese cultural rituals played on, while in real China they were being stamped out by successive revolutions.

I knew that my grandfather Jimmy had landed in Hong Kong at Chinese New Year time because his letter from Singapore had mentioned that he was looking forward to the celebrations when he reached Hong Kong.

The exact date changes with the lunar calendar, but Chinese New Year always arrives in springtime – not a nice season in Hong Kong; winter's end leaves the colony mantled with tepid mist. Clothing, bed-linen, towels and books sopped up the moisture, swelling with heavy damp. I often dreamt I stood immured in mist, mesmerised by the stillness, aghast at the multiplying mildew. I'd wake, my skin crawling, coated with the sheen of perspiration.

Mickey Mok was as good as his word and took POD and me to Aberdeen at Chinese New Year.

Aberdeen Harbour was home to the Tanka people, sea-gypsies who, according to legend, were pushed out by the Han Chinese, took to their boats and ever since had lived by or on the sea along the southeast Chinese coast.

At Chinese New Year everything afloat was feathered with red and gold paper bunting fluttering in concert with the throb of the harbour. The constant wash of the water, boats bumping, sucking and pulling at anchor, gave a rhythmical backing track to the boisterous Cantonese exchanges floating across the bay. Barking dogs, bawling children, the rattle of ice being tipped over barrels of fish waiting for market, the flap and crack of laundry in the wind and the slap of rope and sail added chorus to the ensemble.

In the shallows, rafts of boats bobbed on the harbour swell. They would never go out to sea again and were banded together with a tangled snare of washing lines, ropes and nets and a heaving scaffold of planks and gangways which children learned to navigate from birth, swinging on the backs of their mothers and very young siblings.

In the deeper waters, massive wide-beamed fishing junks swung at anchor, and all around were smaller craft. Tiny sampans threaded through narrow passages shadowed by overhanging decks and choked with floating debris. Impertinent little market junks plied their trade, crammed to the gunwales with colourful plastic household goods or fresh vegetables. A weather-beaten woman in black pyjamas, or a slip of a boy or girl, propelled and steered the craft with great dexterity using a single oar arcing a swirl of water, calling out for passengers or hawking their wares.

Everywhere there were licks of flame as preparations for feasting were in full swing; even the smallest sampan home had a little coal fire burning in a tin tray at one end, and a multi-generation family perched around rolled-up beds and pot plants. Bigger boats had whole pigs spreadeagled on deck, ready for roasting. Children and adults were caught up in raucous celebration and waved to us, laughing, pointing and inviting us to join the fun as we floated past in the *Deri-Vica*.

Chinese New Year was also time for huge flower markets in Victoria Park. Irene joined Greta, Takako and me for a visit and we bought white narcissi, lucky orange trees in pots and branches of pink cherry blossom. Brightly coloured feather dusters were on sale everywhere and Takako said it was because Chinese New Year is the time for a spring clean. "It's exactly the same in Scotland – we clean before Hogmanay," said Greta.

It was Irene who told me that 1969 was the Year of the Rooster. She said it would boost my confidence and I should look after valuables. She'd worked out I had been born in a Pig year. I listened, amused and sceptical. The traits of the Pig were conflicting. It seemed I was easy-going or easy to anger. I tended to give in to strong personalities but I could be a leader. I could be stubborn and was definitely naïve. I encountered problems with equanimity, but I was easily deflated by criticism. Not good at managing money, but lucky.

I was lucky. While Hong Kong celebrated Chinese New Year, cat burglars scaled the flats at Mid-Levels. I went home to find the bars of the amah's window were sheared off and Takako's jewellery gone. That morning as I left the flat, I'd thrown my jewellery box in the dirty linen basket because Takako had told me that there were lots of thefts at that time of year. Poor Takako, she'd warned me but left her own jewellery in her drawer. No insurance money could replace her mother's ring; she had lost a touchstone to the past.

Irene's warning that the Pig was ever naïve didn't sink in. I missed the cues, took conversations at face value and was genuinely surprised time and time again.

When Mickey Mok invited me to dinner at a popular Chinese restaurant, I arrived expecting a party, but it was just a table for two. It wasn't long before his hand was on my bare knee. Small talk ran frivolously while my brain scrolled. It could be the hand had simply strayed; the affectionate gesture of an old man to a daughter or dear young friend. Maybe he had just forgotten himself and the hand would shortly disappear. As long as it stayed motionless, I felt weighted down, unable to make a move, but as soon as the fingers started to explore, shifting inquisitively to my thigh, I had no excuses left for him. I tried not to stand up too quickly. "Please do excuse me," I said and disappeared to the Ladies Room. When I returned I swung my chair out of reach and we finished our meal pleasantly, an understanding reached. It would take the publication of a book about the Hong Kong Stock Exchange decades later for me to learn

Mickey was a well-known philanderer with "an insatiable appetite for the ladies of the night".

With Mickey I was more careful after that. But I was still not wise. Greta and I would meet men when we were out on the town, or at parties, and often move on to night clubs with a live band and dance floor. I loved dancing and if afterwards my newfound companion suggested we go back to his hotel to have a drink "for the road", I would readily agree, a nice finish to a great evening. The hotel rooms inevitably commanded a captivating view. I'd stand gazing out at the harbour, a sight I never tired of, and it seemed in no time at all, my host would reappear in a bathrobe and proffer a lot more than a cognac. That was my cue to give a quick peck on the cheek, hastily grab my bag and take off.

I'd wake up Takako when I got home. We'd drink tea and sit giggling. Takako would be horrified that I could be so stupid more than once, but I just laughed it off. Takako thought my reputation was at stake. I could hear the disapproval in her voice so I said, "It matters what you do, Takako, not what people think you do."

"No, Gill, it's what people think you do. Of course what you do is important but it's all for nothing if people think you do something else."

The Ching Ming Festival, "tomb-sweeping day", fell not long after Chinese New Year. Greta said we should visit the cemetery at Aberdeen on the day after the festival as she didn't want us to disturb family gatherings.

Aberdeen cemetery was huge and covered a whole hillside overlooking the harbour. Chinese culture deemed it auspicious to be buried on a hillside.

I felt the Chinese had a much better take than the West on such a quintessential part of life. Ching Ming combines honouring ancestors with a celebration of Spring's perennial promise of renewal. Tombs are swept clean. Offerings are made of food and flowers. Candles and joss sticks are lit and relatives burn paper money, cardboard effigies of houses, cars and material possessions, symbolising that they continue to care for their relatives in the hereafter. Finally, the family has a reunion with the ancestors and feast at the gravesite or nearby.

I warmed to the idea that the worlds of the living and the dead interacted with one another forever. It reassured me and made my dialogue with Jimmy, the grandfather I had never really known, feel legitimate.

There were so many delightful facets to my social life in Hong Kong. James and Christian Gibson were Scots, old friends of my aunt, and James had once been a colleague of my father at Queen's University in Belfast. Joining them felt like going home. James was Professor of Pathology at Hong Kong University. A good day for him was either at his microscope or walking Hong Kong's hill trails and the Prof made sure he seldom had a bad day. Every weekend in all weathers, James and his wife Christian set off with a cheerful bunch of medics and I often joined them. The nine hills of the Dragon's Back that separated Kowloon from the New Territories were his favourite. The undulating and windswept trail ran along the crests where our boots crushed sage and wild myrtle far above the concrete citadel of Hong Kong. Other days we'd walk along the border overlooking red China, where Communist slogans were scored out in English on the hillsides. Once a remote path was blocked by two purple-black bull buffalos, rain sheeting off their broad rumps.

Christian whispered, "I've read they hate the smell of white people and are very dangerous."

The Prof armed us with heavy bamboo canes and we crept past, bent double. The huge beasts looked on benignly at the rain bouncing off our rumps.

At the end of a day's hiking, the Prof and Christian would take me to their modest government flat and he would pour ample sherries while she rustled up a roast dinner and pudding.

I'd told them that I wanted to do some community work. Christian was involved in charity organisations and she heard that the Duke of Edinburgh's Award Scheme needed someone to help with a hiking assessment for a girls' school.

When I explained to POD why I needed the Saturday free, I quipped, "Training Chinese fifth columnists for guerrilla warfare, Sir."

"It's important to know when the battle is won, Gill," he said, looking over the top of his bifocals without a smile.

My engagement with the Duke's Scheme was short-lived; I assisted an army Major on a Bronze Level test. Ostensibly all we had to do was man the checkpoints. We met up at the Outlying Islands Ferry Pier on Hong Kong Island. Lively, neat, brightly dressed, chattering loudly, the girls arrived, wearing smooth-soled sneakers and carrying airline shoulder bags. The Major and I were in full hike regalia with back packs. He was twice my age. "Oh God, this lot looks set for a St Trinian's picnic," he said. We disembarked on Lantau Island and set off for Silver Mine Beach. At the beginning of that lovely strand of sand, the Major gave an introductory talk. He finished with, "How will you find your way if you get lost?"

"We will follow our sense of direction," one brave soul volunteered and was backed up by a titter of approval.

"Can anybody think of a brighter suggestion?" said the Major.

"No," was the quick and unanimous reply.

The Major was unamused. He separated the girls into three groups and set them off at ten-minute intervals. We stood watching as the first group of girls walked a little way and stopped to wait for the next two groups. Then they all set off – a cheerful, chattering gaggle. We watched them miss the correct path. The Major couldn't stand it. He bellowed, "Are you sure you're on the right track? Keep looking at your maps."

His voice was carried away on the wind. The figures turned, raised their hands in greeting and walked on.

We followed at a distance until the group slowed, bunching up on the narrow paths banked between rice paddies, slipping and giggling. As we caught up, an angry farmer berated them. The Major navigated his way to the front of the girls, apologised in Mandarin, which the Cantonese farmer barely understood, but he nodded and grinned as he waved us off his land. We herded the girls back to the beach, spread the maps out on the sand and pointed out the right path.

"We should fail this lot right now," the Major said through gritted teeth. "Right Miss Stevenson, we will make one group and we will accompany them rather than just see them through the checkpoints. Remember, our job is not to guide but we need to keep track of them or we'll end up having to call in a bloody search party."

The first checkpoint was at the top of a waterfall. The path led along the side of the valley. Some of the girls spied water through the scrub and moments later they left the path en masse, took off for the river, and began walking up its edge towards the falls. In no time several girls slipped, falling over on the slippery smooth stones. "Regroup, retrace now," commanded the Major while I helped them wipe mud and slime off their clothes.

We took the girls back to the path and walked with them the rest of the way to the top of the waterfall. After that the path took us along a ridge for a while and then dived down a long and very, very steep slope. They looked over the edge with trepidation. I led off, picking my way down the path gingerly, sliding on my bottom on the steepest bits. The girls followed, doing the same. The Major barked, "Come on, what are you sitting down for? Stand-up, look ahead, run 1, 2, 3, 4." And to my amazement, he flew past me in exactly that manner shouting, "1, 2, 3, 4, heads up, 1, 2, 3, 4." Incredibly, we all did what we were told; stood up and shot down that hill as agile and quick as mountain goats. We piled breathless into one another at the bottom, dizzying terror giving way to exhilaration, but the Major was already mounting another hillside nearly as steep as the one we had descended. "Bring up the rear, Miss Stevenson," he shouted.

We scrambled uphill, scattering lizards and startling enormous green grasshoppers that flew sideways. I relieved one tearful girl of her shoulder bag which was the signal for a general abandonment of paraphernalia, and I laboured up the slope collecting bags, hats and jumpers. Right at the top there was a steep rocky step. When I got to it the girls were waiting and reached down for their bags so they could get out their sandwiches for lunch. I had to make another two trips to recover everything. When I eventually clambered up and made my appearance, the Major came over from where he had been standing in the shade and said, "Humph, there you are – took a bit of a rest, did you? Didn't see how you could have got lost, it was just straight up."

He didn't wait for me to answer but walked off. In any case, I was speechless.

All that was left was the gentle descent to the coast. We followed the girls down to the road whereupon the leader turned round with a grin from ear to ear and said, "Major and Miss Stevenson, this is our destination."

The Major got out the map to show them they had not arrived at their destination which was still half a mile up the coast.

"You're having a joke with us, Sir."

He turned a little purple and force-marched us to the ferry terminal. We missed the ferry, which was just pulling out as we got there, so we settled down to wait for the next one. Clouds of dust and noise preceded a cavalcade of vehicles which came over the hill road and down to the little dock. Camouflaged Land Rovers flying pennants and open trucks full of soldiers pulled up in a row. A young Captain climbed out of the lead vehicle. It took him a few minutes to recognise the Major licking a mango ice cream, surrounded by Chinese girls sitting rubbing their feet.

"Oh, um, can we give you a lift back, Major?" he said.

"Not unless you take my Chinese children, too."

About ten minutes later, launches arrived to take the troops back to the mainland. The Captain negotiated with the coxswains. Although the men were hot and tired after their war games, they were good-natured and squashed up to make room for us. We set off in formation, landing craft on either side. The Major and I sat on the gunwales and after a shout of warning from the Captain, our launch accelerated and we powered across the Lamma Channel to Hong Kong, the girls shrilling with excitement and even the Major grinning.

Once on land, the girls asked me, "Did we pass, Miss Stevenson?"

I laughed. "You'll have to ask the Major." When we turned around he was gone.

"Never mind, Miss Stevenson, you come with us next time."

On the following Monday, POD, Connie and I shared morning tea at my desk. POD asked me how the weekend had gone and I made him laugh. He got up. "When you've finished your tea, Gill, meet me in the Board Room, I want a private word."

I wondered what on earth was up now, trying to think if I'd done anything wrong and, clutching my shorthand pad, I knocked on the door.

"Come in … you don't need a notebook, there is just something I wanted to say to you. Don't look so worried."

I sat down.

"Don't ask me any more about it Gill, but maybe you are due an explanation. I had a brother who was taken prisoner and tortured by the Japanese during the war. A lot of terrible things happen in war. It seemed to me that some were unnecessarily terrible."

I opened my mouth to try to respond, but he put his head down and waved me away.

Chapter 19

The APB landed an airline account. POD saw it as a turning point, the fruition of all the work he had put in. He and Pierre set off for Taiwan to sign the agreement. POD dictated last-minute instructions as we waited by the lift for Pierre. He arrived, impossibly handsome, impossibly disorganised, coat tails flying, briefcase bulging, "I'm sure I've forgotten something."

POD retorted, "Well, you'll get hell from me if you have and you haven't time to do anything about it!"

When they were back a couple of days later, POD said, "That boy does nothing but sleep – incapable of doing anything without twelve hours in bed – he's got worms."

"I'll put it on my to-do list Sir, 'Worm Pierre'."

POD looked up at me sharply; he wasn't in the mood for back-chat.

Anyone pale or peaky, sad or surly, POD pronounced "Riddled with worms". He thought I tore around too much in the office and told me not to dash everywhere. One day, I was rushing and slipped, landing on the floor. "Worms," said POD looking down at me and extending a hand, "It's the only explanation."

I called in to see Greta on the way home. I did so almost every day unless we were meeting out. We'd have a cup of tea or sew together and catch up on each other's news. We laughed about POD's worm obsession, but she had a solution for my excess energy which sounded more appealing than worming powder. "Come sailing with me," she said. "That'll slow you down."

I knew that every Saturday Greta went sailing.

"I'd have to ask for time off," I said. "I work Saturdays … and I've never sailed before, but I would love to try." I paused before I added, "One thing though: I can't swim. Would that matter?"

"You are joking, aren't you?"

I felt embarrassed. "A few strokes maybe, but not out of my depth."

I told Greta about how I hated swimming lessons at school. The pool was surrounded by a high wooden fence to exclude prying eyes, but it also shut out the tepid English sunlight so that the crystal clear water had an icy chill, even in mid-summer. Mum gave me excuse notes to say it was "my time of the month". Eventually, Miss Howarth, my sports mistress, summoned me to the staff room door and suggested I needed a physician. "You are beginning to remind me of the woman in the Bible with the issue of blood," she said to drive her point home.

I got up to pour Greta some more tea and said, "I've tried since school but I just sink. I can't put my head under water."

"Well," said Greta, "you'll just have to learn."

It seemed like an extraordinarily novel idea.

"We can go to the beach on Saturday and I'll teach you."

It was nearly dark when I began to walk back to my flat. I paused to look out over the harbour. The nightly metamorphosis was underway. Barges and lighters no longer wallowed ungainly across the water but skittered like fantastical illuminated insects. On the foreshore, a kindling of lights in the dusk triggered a blaze of coloured neon, a magnificent funfair of firework colours reflecting at the water's edge.

The night was clear and there was magic in the air. Anything was possible I thought; even learning to swim. "Touché!" said some inner voice, "about time too," heralding the most exciting and rewarding part of my Hong Kong sojourn.

The club where Greta sailed was at Stanley, a fishing village on the south side of Hong Kong Island, a drive over the mountains, picturesque and green. On the way down to St Stephen's Beach, Greta pointed out the Fort high up on the peninsula. It was a military base, she said, "Home to the Duke of Wellington's, a Yorkshire Regiment. They run the sailing club."

In Stanley Bay, Chinese fishing junks were at anchor and the water was dotted with sailing dinghies and yachts. A water ski boat was doing wide laps, disappearing to just a slow moving ball of spray and then coming closer until we could make out the crew and skier.

My tuition began. Takako had come along too and she spread out a towel, amused at my initiation. She assured me swimming was easy. I wasn't at all sure she knew. Greta quickly gave up on style; my sideways breaststroke would have to do. She didn't even force the point about putting my head under so I swam ungainly, head up. I made progress, learned to float and tread water. Greta and I were back at the beach the next morning. Together we made it to the diving platform moored some way out and Greta challenged me to swim back to shore on my own. I did it. I was ecstatic and swam out again immediately.

Greta took me over to the sailing club to introduce me to the army boys. Just a handful sailed regularly. I met John, the joker; Twiggy, the practical gentleman; Len, the dependable ballast, and Gerry, the dark horse. They were all privates and all a year or so younger than I was at the time.

John was in charge at the beach; his army duty was to turn up every day in his swimming trunks. He taught sailing, skiing and managed the boats. It was a dream job, fit for an army recruitment poster.

"Jump in at the end of the pier and swim to shore, just so I know you can swim," he said, but didn't watch closely. I reached the shore, which was enough. Greta winked and took me out for my first sail.

I fell asleep that night with a smile on my face. I thought back to those childhood holidays in Scotland. Cumbersome in yellow oil-skins, I'd helped my brothers heave a wooden row boat, heavy with layers of tar, down to the shore where the chill North Sea froze my ankles. I'd enjoyed my childhood boating but a two-man sailing dinghy, a bikini and warm water put a totally different slant on seafaring.

I was smitten. I morphed into an enthusiastic, curly-headed, water puppy. I just couldn't keep out of the water.

I badgered Greta to take me with her whenever she went to the "club". The small shed, some well-used dinghies and a run-down 40 hp ski-boat didn't do justice to the grand name: the Hindoostan Sailing Club. The name immortalised battles won in India by the Regiment more than a century before. And the club's burgee – a red swallow-tailed flag – was printed with an insignia granted by the royal decree of George III; a yellow elephant with a howdah. I found it incongruous – British India was long gone – but that didn't worry the army.

I had to prove myself in order to get a chance to crew so I volunteered for every job. I rubbed down boats, washed sails, varnished centreboards, fetched coffee, no job too little or too large. Ah Loong, the old boatman, watched me with a toothless grin. He lived with his extended family next door to the club in a rude shack, its roof an upturned sampan waterproofed by layers of black bitumen that melted in the sun, soft gobbets of tar dropping to the sand. He leaned on its half-door, his face wreathed in smiles, while his grandchildren played on the shore and he kept an eye on the boats, which earned him a retainer from the army. When winter came, he closed the doors and smoke curled up from a piece of tin pipe set at a jaunty angle. When a typhoon signal went up, Ah Loong came into his own. I knew exactly what was up if I reached the beach and found Ah Loong, eyes bright, swinging his arms, shouting "Woosh Woosh". His relatives would appear from the village and, giggling and laughing, help haul boats onto trucks to go up to the shelter of the fort in sharp contrast to the surly troops sent down by the army to do the job. Once the beach was deserted and everything tied down against the typhoon winds, Ah Loong gathered his family into the hovel he'd positioned close to the steep verdant hillside that sheltered it from the elements.

Hong Kong was the premier peace-time assignment for British troops. Short stints on border duty and practising crowd control left plenty of off-duty time to enjoy what Hong Kong had on offer. Mostly that meant Wan Chai, Hong Kong's red-light district. Western servicemen didn't invent prostitution in South-East Asia, but in the sixties, the British Forces in Hong Kong, with some serious competition from the Americans, certainly fuelled the demand. Not that the Yanks arrived sex-starved from Vietnam; Saigon had been turned into one big brothel, but there was more choice in Hong Kong: Filipinos, Eurasians, Indians and White Russians.

The sailing club was their alternative to Wan Chai, or so the boys said.

Because it was an army club, my application had to be approved by Major Hoppe, the Duke's officer responsible for the club. When Greta approached him about my membership, he waved his hand and I was in. He liked Greta, and he had a soft spot for John. I didn't know John well at that time, but I had already realised that he ran the club on the beach with a maturity beyond his years. Skinny, with tousled sun-bleached hair, a permanent grin and irrepressible cheek, John's buffoonery made us all laugh. His CO and senior officers indulged him, but younger officers were not so sure about John. He was cleverer than most of them and, despite his youth, a better and more experienced sailor. Down at the beach, it was John in charge and some found that hard to take. Although John could not intervene when officers dragged newly painted boats over the sand or left equipment out in the open; he had ways of making them uncomfortable. He used his wit and humour like a rapier. Was what he said in jest or was it insubordination? Officers did not always know what to think.

POD had been overseas for Easter when I started sailing. Although I heaved a sigh of relief when he left the Colony, because he was a demanding and exacting boss, I idolised him. When he was in the office I juggled all my tasks, working long hours regardless of which day of the week it was, squeezing my burgeoning social life in around him.

On POD's return, I tried to continue as before, but he quickly smelt a rat.

"Are you in love?" he asked me abruptly.

"No, Sir, what made you think that?"

"I sense a change, Gill."

I told him about the water, my addiction, about how I had been going down to the beach after work almost every day. I assured him I would come in early and be there whenever he needed me. We both knew it was a lie; I was no longer his devoted protégée.

The next day he called me in. "Throughout my working life I've seen young secretaries with more brains and competence than their male counterparts who enter on a management trajectory. I've never liked it. I've made you Company Secretary but you need to formalise your career path. Without a piece of paper, you'll always be exploited."

POD went on. "I have ordered the prospectus of the Chartered Institute of Secretaries. Passing their exams equates to an honours degree, probably more."

I felt nervous and flustered. Exams. Miss Moller, my old headmistress, gave me a nudge. I said my thanks and got up to go.

"Gill, I haven't finished, don't jump up like that. You came to work for Betty for peanuts. Don't do that again. You are still underpaid. It's difficult at the moment as the APB isn't generating enough revenue, but I have put your pay up."

"Crikey, Sir, again?" It was the fourth pay rise I'd had in a year.

"Extra peanuts, Gill."

I used the pay rise to buy myself a little car but I hadn't time to study as well as work and play. I got a reprieve when the prospectus came in and I found I needed 'A' Levels which I didn't have.

"Rubbish," said POD and recommended me to the Institute in such glowing terms they waived the entrance requirements and I received a letter advising that I was enrolled as a student. It would be some years before I would make good on POD's determination.

My little cream Mini soon knew the road to the beach so well, it practically drove itself.

John worked at the beach whether he was on duty or had time off. He was always cheerful, friendly and uncomplicated. My swimming improved. I would never be a strong swimmer but I felt safe. I knew I wouldn't drown on John's watch but I did suffer innumerable dunkings. I would open my mouth to tell John that I couldn't put my head under water, but he never took any notice. The therapy worked, I lost my fear.

John taught me to sail. Deciding I was not listening to his instruction, he lay down and feigned sleep. He would not move to balance the dinghy. He simply opened one eye and told me to do it with the rudder and sails.

He had tactics with teaching water-skiing as well. I was a slow learner, happy enough to be towed around, showered with sparkling spray, ploughed under in the smooth shiny softness beneath sun and sky. John leaned over the edge of the ski-boat to pull me in one evening. "Over there," he said, gesturing to the far side of the bay, "there are some of the biggest jellyfish I have ever seen. We've been towing them out to sea with the ski boat all week. Next lesson, if they are still there, I am going to take you over and drop you in with them. That'll get you up." I'd seen them when I'd been crewing on the ski-boat, floating swarms of Lion's Mane as they were called, squishy and white with tentacles that could stretch ten yards or more. Next time I got up.

I jumped at every chance to crew for John in the ski-boat when he was towing skiers and when it was used as the rescue boat. Every outing was an adventure for me and we laughed together so much my sides hurt.

One day an officer from another regiment capsized near some rocks. John asked me to crew when he took out the speed boat to rescue him. The officer was a rude bugger who did not even greet us when we reached him. Instead, he shouted orders at John from the water and refused all John's advice. Each time he got in the dinghy, he capsized it again. The weather was coming in, the rocks dark and dangerous. Eventually, John told the officer to stay in the water and hold the transom to keep the waterlogged boat balanced and he'd tow him in. The officer kept up his tirade. His words were whipped away in the wind but when he got too voluble, John would gently apply a little more throttle, increasing the wash that spouted behind the dinghy to silence him. The man was half-drowned by the time we got back and while John had to be careful and solicitous helping him ashore, I was delighted at the man's discomfort.

Major Hoppe, John's officer in charge of the sailing club, was liked by his men and nick-named "Punchy", for he'd been an army boxing champion. He was the only officer of the Duke's who sailed with us. He had a dogged approach, never up with the winners but determined to sail.

No one ever volunteered to crew for Major Hoppe so he designated Cliff, an amiable, dozy lance-corporal, as his crew. It was an entertaining partnership. I was in the safety boat on a rough and windy day when John went to help the Major and Cliff who were making heavy weather of a capsize. As we neared, the Major was standing on the centreboard bringing the dinghy upright. Before we reached them, the Major broke off what he was doing and, with a holler, he grabbed a paddle and tried to thump Cliff who swam expeditiously round the hull to get out of range. The Major swam after him, roaring abuse, the paddle missing its target and smacking the water. Cliff bellowed, "I only offered, Sir." On dry land, John asked, "What was all that about?"

Cliff said, "I just told Hoppe since we'd been over four times, he might let me helm."

Other days, in calm weather, John and I had plenty of time to chat as I crewed while he towed skiers round the bay. I'd also give him lifts up to the Fort or drive him round to pick up boat spares. We explored the hinterland of Stanley, visiting the war graves, headstones marching down the hill in serried ranks, so peaceful and so sad. On a walk through the undergrowth between two beaches we came across the graves of two seamen killed by pirates. We imagined their shipmates stealing ashore to bury them. John picked flowers and put them on each grave.

John didn't wear his heart on his sleeve but he told me his story bit by bit. He'd been brought up in a children's home and was briefly and disastrously reunited with his family in his early teens when his father came to take him home. John was thrilled until he realised the invitation had been extended because he was of an age to earn and contribute. There was little else in the exchange. John ran back to the home he knew and the house-parents he loved, a dedicated couple who had no children of their own. When he came of age, John changed his surname by deed poll and adopted the couple. The larrikin we all knew and loved hid the hurt well by making sure he didn't give anyone else the opportunity to shaft him.

Although I hung out with John, he was too experienced a helm for me. Twiggy took me sailing too. He was another of the core of army boys who spent every spare moment at the beach. Twiggy was skinny, with straight, spiky hair that shot out over his forehead.

He'd joined the army on the same day as John. They had met as boy soldiers.

Twiggy was nicknamed as a raw recruit, the year that his namesake and compatriot, a stick-thin supermodel with a boyish haircut, was named "The Face of 1966".

"You could count my ribs at a hundred paces when I joined the regiment," he told me.

Twiggy sailed with Len. They made a good pair as Twiggy weighed nothing and Len was solid and capable.

I was teamed up with Gerry. Gerry had joined the army from school in York where he'd grown up. He'd been born in India before the family emigrated to England. He hadn't started sailing until he got to Hong Kong and John had taught him as well.

Gerry and I were the weakest helm and crew in the club, but we soon made up for it with outrageous enthusiasm. We might have been the clowns and we were certainly the capsize kings. We might not have won races, but did we care? Not a jot. We went sailing in all weathers just for the hell of it. We'd sail to get our coffee, sail to set out the buoys for racing, sail to look for a lost water ski. Any excuse was a good one. We became competent by default.

Gerry started to take racing seriously and when he asked me to be his regular crew, I was thrilled.

There was one more attraction at Stanley. A kindly benefactor had lent the club his yacht, a 27-foot sloop called *Peta Ann* for the army to use or charter out for income. When she was hired out, John captained the *Peta Ann* with two or three of the boys for crew. Major Hoppe turned a blind eye when Greta and I joined the charters as extra hands.

After dropping off passengers at a secluded island beach, John would sail *Peta Ann* round to the next bay and anchor, giving us the whole day to just fool around, exploring the island, snorkelling in solitude or practising Tarzan swings with long ropes from *Peta Ann*'s mast. We held competitions for climbing the mast and diving off the cabin; no prank was too silly, there was no limit to the immersions.

At the end of the day, we'd take *Peta Ann* back to her moorings, clean her up and as the sun finally settled, slip into the silky warm water to swim ashore.

Sunset after sunset, the islands to the south turned deep purple against a backdrop softening to pink and mauve. In the west, fishing junks and sampans were silhouetted against a sky of gold streaked with red fingers. We sat and chatted on sand that still held the day's heat until stars stabbed through a canopy of indigo and then we'd swim, splashing the water so the phosphorescence arched and sparkled in the moonlight.

I bought a small BBQ to carry in the boot of my car with a bag of charcoal so we could have supper on the beach. When I got into the car to drive home, I'd drape my bikini over the back of the seat ready for the next day.

On Monday mornings I'd be stiff and red, my hair sun-bleached and salt-frizzled from my weekend on the water. Unwittingly acquired bruises would bloom purple, green and gold. Once, after a particularly energetic weekend, POD surveyed my bared arms and legs said, "You look as if you are going bad."

Greta and I separated the beach from the other parts of our life in Hong Kong. We called the soldiers "the boys". They were men of course, but boys were fun like brothers, yet they looked out for you; men were a different game. We didn't mix our worlds.

Chapter 20

POD kept me busy, too, with social invitations that he didn't want to fulfil. Once, it was to take an aristocrat neighbour of his shopping. He told me to first take her to lunch at the Hong Kong Club and to have as many gins as I wanted for I would need them. Next it was coffee with a young family friend, Caroline. She brought along her boyfriend, Ian Winton-Bell. Seldom had anyone irritated me as much as Ian Winton-Bell.

He was a parody of English aristocracy. The word *blimp* came to mind. He was namedropper fantastic, bluff-book reader and utter English bore, and thought himself God's gift to women. He invited us to visit him to see his home movies. I declined, but to my horror, when I got to the office the next day, POD said that Caroline had phoned and asked that I go with her. POD said she felt uncertain and didn't want to go to his house alone. No amount of protest was going to wash with POD. "The man's harmless, just go and keep her company."

Ian Winton-Bell's home movies were terrible.

A week or so later, Ian appeared at the office to say, "Howdo" to me. He was having great difficulty finding a job in Hong Kong to suit his station in life, but that did not matter because all his life he'd been looking for nice girls and had suddenly found two at once, Caroline and me. He said he felt that he and I had a particular affinity and that we should see each other again. I dissembled. I was very busy, I had no spare time. He leaned over the desk and breathed, "But we need to get to know each other better; a lot better. I find you very attractive. Not many come up to my standards you know. You are one lucky girl." I swiped my hand away as his pudgy one tried to pat it and leapt up, saying I really had to go … I had some art blocks that had to reach the print shop. I managed to get out the door without so much as a peck on the cheek because I was bloody fast on my feet.

Several times, he rang the office again, "Does my name ring a bell – it's Ian Winton-Bell."

A month or so later, Caroline rang up in tears. She had lost her job and was uncertain in love – she was not sure if Winton-Bell was the man for her. Could I have coffee with her? I'd had enough. I passed her on to POD. He roared into the phone, "Ditch that useless man and go home." He offered to pay her fare.

I took POD to task. Although I made him laugh when I recounted my experiences with Ian Winton-Bell, I vowed that I'd never ever help him out again with his social obligations.

I told him truthfully that I simply did not have time. Greta continued to throw out new challenges. She had completed her Stage 1 scuba-diving training and she wanted me to do the course so we could go diving together.

The first part of the scuba training was a swimming test – several laps of the pool. I could swim the distance easily but the test was with a weight belt and that was a stroke too far for me. Each time I failed, my instructor, a stocky New Zealander called Ashley, said to continue training and do it the next time. So I learned to hold my breath, clear my mask, share air with my buddy, sit on the bottom of the pool and take off all my scuba gear and put it on again. But I kept failing the basic test.

I had no confidence when my last chance came. As before, on the final length my strength gave out and I struck out to grab the side of the pool. A shout took me unawares and a wooden pole pushed me out to the middle of the pool.

"Swim you bugger," swore Ashley.

I sank, spluttering and panicked. I tried to grab the pole but it was gone. I was sinking fast but echoing through the water, the words came again, as did the pole.

"Swim, swim you little bugger."

You couldn't call it swimming, that desperate gasping and striking water. But it was enough, I reached the end of the pool and Ashley ticked the box.

After that, when Greta and I were not at Stanley at weekends, we were scuba diving over at Hebe Haven, a harbour on the eastern coast of Hong Kong mainland where Ashley and his new wife Maureen kept their dive boat. They were generous hosts, organising expeditions and magical barbeques on isolated beaches. Greta and I would often miss the last ferry and catch a walla walla, a motorboat that operated as a water taxi, over to Hong Kong island, arriving home exhausted, salted and happy.

We bought our own scuba tanks and added equipment as we could afford it. We went together to have wet-suits tailor-made and the Chinese shop owner asked if he could take photographs to put in his shop window. We felt quite cute, but the photos made us look butch and chubby, perspiring under the studio lights. We comforted each other that no-one we knew would set eyes on them.

It took about a week before someone on Stanley Beach said he'd been in the depths of Kowloon and was so surprised to see our faces in a shop window …

Chapter 21

The summer exodus was approaching, and I'd booked my flight home. Greta had a trip planned to South-East Asia. POD would spend the summer at Brantwych, his beloved Cambridgeshire manor house. It was being featured in the *Ideal Home* magazine and he wanted to be home to enjoy the kudos. Mrs Church was preparing for her ocean voyage, and was leaving earlier than the rest of us. She didn't want Ah Tong to repeat the disappearing dog steak fiasco, so rallied friends and staff of the APB to make impromptu inspections of canine tucker.

At a staff meeting a couple of weeks before Mrs Church's departure, Pauline Lo the receptionist came into the Board Room and whispered in my ear that there was someone in the reception to see me.

POD overheard. "Who is it?"

"He won't give any name, Sir," said Pauline.

"Well, tell him to get lost," grumped POD.

I went out to investigate and there was Freddie Zimmern. He was practically apoplectic, grabbed my arm and towed me out to the lift lobby.

"Get POD over to my office immediately."

"What's happened?"

"We've got a letter from Betty's lawyers to say she signed the sale agreement under duress. She's starting legal action. She's reneging."

I wrote a note and passed it to POD. He asked us all to leave the room as he needed to have a private word with Mrs Church. That didn't take long. Twenty minutes later, POD and I were sitting in Freddie's office.

"I've asked Betty to resign as Life Chairman. The situation is untenable now she's initiated legal action," said POD.

"Not a chance. She won't resign, Paddy, not that old girl," said Freddie.

"Well, in that case, start another company and we'll sell the business to the new entity. That'll get rid of her."

"Paddy, you know she has first option. You'll have to offer the APB back to her and she won't buy it but she'll string you along. You overpaid her and she knows it."

Both men looked glum. Freddie said, "It's my guess, Paddy, that she will try starting another agency. She's got a lot of good will with overseas clients."

"But that's in the contract too, she can't."

"In theory, but think about who we are dealing with. She will go ahead regardless. You'd have to sue her, she'd tie us up in court for years and the bad publicity would destroy you. She's an institution in the colony. She has friends in high places and while a lot of them detest her, she's one of them, while you're the new kid on the block, Paddy."

POD had thought that with new blood, systems and goals, the agency would fly. He'd enjoy the company of old friends, tweak the ad business now and then and have time left-over for a food export business and writing his book.

POD had no choice but to instigate his own legal proceedings. Each day another writ, another subpoena, another statement. Slander, defamation, damages, third parties, clients, staff, court hearings – sapping energy, disrupting the ground, rattling everyone.

Once it started, no space was too small for a stoush. When Mrs Church met David and me in the lift, she shouted she'd see us both out and swung her handbag at me over the head of a diminutive Chinese businessman. We jumped out when the doors opened even though it wasn't the right floor. I took to using the Ladies Room two floors above … and I used the stairs to get there.

The old guard, Mr Kwan and Mr Yi the Art Director, were confounded by the visceral rivalry. They had somehow deftly managed the volatile proprietor of the APB for decades, maintaining a respectful and cordial relationship. They admired her audacity; she was more comprehensible to them than other more stitched up members of the European community. Mr Kwan was aghast to see the younger Chinese staff beginning to ridicule Mrs Church, careless about keeping one foot in each camp until the way became clear. It was a complex campaign, and anyone could win.

The wrangling was hurting POD financially. He had told me soon after his arrival that it was easy to make money in Hong Kong, but that was changing too. A bunch of extremely well-educated, Chinese multi-millionaires were challenging the way Mickey Mok and his cronies controlled the Hong Kong Stock Exchange. Unable to achieve a compromise, the newcomers proposed a rival Exchange to open up the market to small investors.

"Hong Kong has a stock market! It's been here since 1841," said Mickey Mok, who was clearly overwrought and agitated by the developments.

His outrage briefly reunited Mrs Church and POD, for the changes would sweep away the privileges they had long enjoyed.

"It is an absolute nonsense," said Mrs Church.

"I agree, they'll never get away with it," said POD.

But they did. A new exchange opened that year and another would follow. Suddenly, everyone in Hong Kong, even amahs and street-cleaners, were able to bet on something even more profitable than the Happy Valley Racecourse.

POD had his problems on the domestic front too. His wife was bored in England, and felt neglected. She had made a brief visit earlier in the year to trial living in the Colony. Mrs Church had viewed her arrival with ill-concealed malevolence. POD did everything he could to keep the peace and make the visit a success, but it was fraught and Hong Kong's humidity had not agreed with Mrs O'Neil-Dunne; she ended up in hospital with pneumonia. The morning after her admission, I got a call from Mrs Church.

"I'm very ill and I have to tell someone. POD is completely preoccupied with that wife of his. She can never get enough attention. A little cough and she calls the ambulance. Phooey ... It's me who's sick and the doctor wants me to go to hospital. But you are not to tell anyone. When POD asks, say I've gone to visit friends in Macau."

"What does the doctor say is wrong Mrs Church? Which hospital?" I asked.

"I'm sick, I just told you. Never mind which hospital. Henry's taking me now," and she rang off. I rang back and Henry whispered what I needed to know.

I told POD Mrs Church's version first.

"What? She doesn't have any friends in Macau that I know of and she hasn't gone gambling there for years. Why would she take off without a word? Doesn't make sense. What's the old girl up to now?"

"I agree, it doesn't make sense because that's not where she is. I'm breaking her confidence, but in fact she is in hospital. The same hospital as your wife."

"Good God, just as well Biddy's in a private room – imagine if they'd ended up in a ward together." He chuckled at the thought and then said, "I'd better go and visit."

POD returned at lunchtime. "Gill, you got your wires crossed. Betty's not in the hospital. You should have checked before sending me on a wild goose chase." He was irritated; yet another work day disrupted.

I smarted but not for long because shortly thereafter I heard Pauline, the receptionist, put a call through to POD's phone.

"What? When? Is she all right? Good God. I'll be there right away."

I flew into his office, "What's happened?"

"Betty's just attacked Biddy in the hospital."

Mrs Church had used an assumed name, pleading with the staff that she had to remain incognito as POD was stalking her. Wearing her silk dressing gown with dragons, she located Biddy O'Neil-Dunne and told her to get up and stop malingering. Biddy was a petite woman and very unwell; she quailed in the blast, shrinking under the covers. That only infuriated Boadicea. Mrs Church dragged her out of bed. The nurses heard shrieks and rushed to the room to find both women entangled in bed sheets on the floor.

Mrs O'Neil-Dunne had departed the Colony as soon as she was able in a wheel-chair. She found it increasingly difficult to understand why POD was in Hong Kong at all. She resented being left at home coping with their children who, she said, were in the throes of adolescence and making her life hell. POD was bemused by his misjudgement. He'd avoided home with his career as an excuse and now, in retirement, he was doing the same thing. Long-distance parenting wasn't his forte and it wasn't getting any easier. The memos he wrote his children, bullet-point instructions, were increasingly ignored.

The litigation that had started had no chance of resolution before Mrs Church left the Colony on her cruise which would deliver her, well-rested, right to the front, to the offices of her dear old clientele in London.

POD left shortly after Mrs Church and a hiatus followed as it did every time he went back to UK. The pace flagged, decisions hung in the air. No-one could fill his shoes, certainly not the expatriate staff he had recruited. He couldn't keep up motivation from afar. Letters took a week or ten days to turn around, phone calls had to be booked days in advance and telegrams were only for a few terse words. Mr Kwan, who had maintained the business in Mrs Church's annual absences, stood back, inscrutable, watching POD's young men. Watching them flounder.

POD's young men also took the opportunity when he was gone to party hard. I didn't socialise much out of the office with them, but the colony was small and sometimes we would meet by chance in nightclubs or bars. Each time I met Edward he had a different girl on his arm, but a couple of times it was Eva, a Chinese model. She and I sometimes bumped into each other at the market near Causeway Bay. If she was with friends, she'd introduce me by saying that I worked for her boyfriend Edward. I was irritated that Edward, who could not make a decision to save his life, was seen as my boss so I tackled him in the office. He looked dismayed and denied even having a Chinese girlfriend. He ran his fingers through his hair. It was just, he said, that when we met socially, he had to explain who I was.

"Well, next time, tell whoever it is I'm your boss!"

I had a long letter from POD. When he started visiting our clients, he found Mrs Church had pre-empted him, paying calls on all our accounts, old and new. Life Chairman still, she explained, but cheated out of her business, diddled by her dearest friend, left penniless, she said. Her real concern, the reason for her visit, she simply had to let them know, was that Mr O'Neil-Dunne did not understand China. "I, on the other hand, have more than forty years' experience," she said. POD telegrammed Freddie who engaged London lawyers, costly and futile.

Greta was leaving for her holiday too. She had a berth on a battered cargo vessel delayed in port when Hong Kong Police recovered a record haul of heroin. The boys from the sailing club and many other friends wanted to give her a good send off. We took her out to the ship in a walla walla and after a few rounds of drinks, we romped round inspecting the ship, terrifying the crew who thought a new drug raid was in progress.

I left Hong Kong last and returned first. My family took me back briefly as their own. My letters told everything I was prepared to tell. We did homecomings well in our family. It was a time when Dad could show emotion unabashed and Mum cooked wonderful dinners and took me on long walks with the dogs.

When POD returned, he said it was a clean slate. Whatever Mrs Church was up to, she was far away and we should forget about her. She would not darken our doors again. And in the autumn when Mrs Church did return to Hong Kong, it wasn't to the APB offices. Instead, she held court at Salamat, resplendent in her new wardrobe from European designers. She entertained clients to tiffin and frequented the Hong Kong Club and the races at Happy Valley and talked of the new business she intended to start up.

Chapter 22

Mrs Church's departure was never really final. POD took a full-page advertisement in the *South China Morning Post* announcing his purchase of the business and her retirement. However, soon everyone knew her new mantra, that she would see us all out and sink Paddy O'Neil-Dunne once and for all.

Fate seemed to be on her side. Two unexpected departures would change things both for the APB and for me. Both were unsettling and permanent. Both made me sad.

The first was my sailing friend, John. John had bought himself a scooter and a puppy, but coming down the hill to the beach one day, with Gerry on pillion and the puppy at his feet, John failed to take a bend and flew off, breaking his leg very badly. Gerry and the puppy were unscathed.

Greta was one of John's first visitors at the British Military Hospital and found him in terrible pain. Long weeks later, the break wasn't healing and it was decided John must be sent home to UK. There was talk of a medical discharge. John was devastated; the army was his extended family and he'd made Stanley Beach his domain.

I was at the hospital at dawn to say goodbye to him. The nursing sister told me they had never had a more popular patient and people from all walks of life had turned up at his bedside. Early morning in Hong Kong is rather lovely, for surprisingly it wakes up much later than other big cities. Rickshaw drivers, newspaper sellers and hawkers work into the night and are slow to greet the day. It was a sad farewell and I wished the wind would drop and the harbour not look quite so beautiful. It was hard for John to leave on such a grand day. I wrote home to Dad and asked him to contact John in hospital and make sure he was OK.

The second departure wasn't an accident but was almost as sudden. It was from the office this time.

Edward passed by my desk. "How lovely is the bird-song today?"

I thought it strange, since all I could hear was the rattle of the air-conditioner and voices filtering through from the outer office. I didn't take much notice. I had little time for my gweilo colleagues. When I was at the office I worked flat out in order to be able to leave in daylight in time for the beach, so I simply nodded. A few minutes later, Pierre arrived looking nonplussed but as dashing as ever. "Have you seen Edward?"

"Yes, he just walked through here."

"Did he speak to you?"

"No ... Well, he said something about birds," I said irritably.

"Christ," said Pierre. "Were they singing?"

I straightened up and stopped what I was doing. "Pierre, have you gone bonkers?"

"No, not me, but I think Edward has – I mean it – he has completely flipped, seems to think he is in an English garden, birds and flowers." Pierre sat down and sighed. "He's hearing birdsong wherever he goes."

Pierre had my attention now. He and Edward were flatmates. "When did this happen?" I said.

"He's been under a lot of stress, a lot of stress."

We traced Edward to the Accounts Department. He did believe, he said, he'd heard a thrush that morning. The bookkeeping staff looked confused, the clicking of their abaci silent. Strange gweilo.

POD came in and found all three of us in his office with the doors shut. "What the hell's going on?" Pierre and I both started talking at once but stopped when Ah Fung came in with tea and put the *China Mail* down on POD's desk. Pierre visibly blanched and sat on it. POD and I stared at him.

"Has everyone gone raving mad?" said POD.

"No, just Edward," whispered poor Pierre.

"Well get *your* bottom off *my* desk then."

Pierre stood up and revealed the front page of the newspaper. The headline ran: "JILTED MODEL TAKES PILLS." Beneath was a picture of a girl, teary but elegantly posed.

I stared. I recognised her. It was Eva, Edward's Chinese girlfriend. Underneath the headline ran the story. She'd taken sleeping pills after a fight with her European boyfriend who had found a new love. She could not face life without him. Her boyfriend and his flat-mate had taken her to hospital.

I looked at Edward, who was oblivious, standing by the window with his head cocked listening for the birds. Pierre was shrivelling under POD's glare.

"That's Edward's girlfriend isn't it?" I said, looking at Pierre.

POD picked up the newspaper, piecing it together.

Edward took a step over and stared at the photograph. "She put a spell on me ..." Then he sat down and put his head in his hands.

"I'm going to have to bite the bullet and call Betty," POD said. "She knows the family."

"I always knew that lot had turns," Mrs Church snorted, "I would never have taken him on."

"This is a little more than a turn Betty. The boy has looped the loop."

The idea of Edward going to the Castle Peak Mental Hospital was vetoed. It was important that the whole business was kept quiet until the family worked out what to do. A Catholic nursing home with locks on the doors was the answer and Edward was dispatched there.

POD spent a long time with Pierre in the Board Room and when he came out, he said, "Gill, you wouldn't believe the half of it. Debauchery and decadence in Shanghai in my youth are beginning to feel quite tame. Pity you didn't take Edward and Pierre sailing."

"They're not the sailing types," I said, "but whatever they were up to, I thought Shanghai was *the* 'Sin City'?"

"Gill, Shanghai was 'The Paris of the East, the New York of the West.' It had style. It was seductive and glamorous."

He sat down by my desk and took out his cigarettes. "The European bordellos were run by American women." He smiled. "Gracie this and Lucy that. Then came the White Russians. They flooded into Shanghai, fleeing from the Bolsheviks – some from the Imperial Court ... princesses and countesses. And there were *the voluptuous vampires from Vladivostok*." He laughed, grinning as if a particular memory came back to him. "The Russian ladies had an enormous penchant for very expensive French champagne!" He drew on his cigarette and deliberately blew a smoke ring, tilting his head to watch the vapour drift up into the ceiling fans. "It was cosmopolitan, lavish and luxurious. Cabaret, taxi-dancers and gin slings in the moonlight – opulence you can only dream about young lady." He paused, shaking his head a little. "These boys," he said with a wave of his hand towards Edward and Pierre's offices, "have just no idea. A crummy apartment, a bunch of bar girls, cheap booze and pills to pop. No idea at all."

I grabbed Pierre and we went out to lunch, but he was rueful and didn't want to tell me whatever it was he had divulged to POD. So instead I probed him about Edward.

"When did you realise Edward was unravelling?" I asked.

"Well, he was juggling three girlfriends and he just couldn't keep up. The guy was exhausted."

I giggled.

"Then last week he set his bed on fire with a late night cigarette." Pierre was trying to keep his face straight. "I woke up with him shouting. He'd opened all the windows and was fanning the flames and leaping up and down yelling 'Yippee, a fire'."

"Christ, what did you do?"

"I got a bucket of water and smothered it, but the whole place stank, so I manhandled Edward into the lift and we went to an all-night club."

POD rang the editor of the newspaper that had run the story and threatened to withdraw our advertising if they published any more about the incident. Pierre was then despatched to ask Eva, who had made a full recovery, if she would like a holiday in Singapore.

After a week or so with the nuns, Edward was bored. He fished his address book out of his pocket, called a few old flames and tricked a young novice into letting him out. David and Pierre eventually tracked him down to the Cricket Club Bar and joined him for a few pints before they rolled up the hill to the convent to deliver Edward back to his keepers. Mother Superior phoned POD the next day to complain that the three of them were inebriated. POD swore under his breath. If the good sisters had not let Edward out in the first place, he would not have had to send the rest of his staff scouring the town looking for him. POD went off to the convent to read the riot act to the nuns and consult with the psychiatrist. That was where he was when the police arrived at the APB.

Pauline shot into my office to tell me and I followed her out to her reception desk in the lobby. The three constables were very young and shiny. "We have a warrant for the arrest of a Mr David Dunlop, Sound and Vision Manager of the Advertising & Publicity Bureau Limited."

"What on earth for?" I said.

"Please tell us where Mr Dunlop is."

I asked them to step into my office but they said they would wait in the lobby. I went to get David. David's temper was legendary, so I had to weather the explosion first.

The police constable formally identified him, and announced, "Mr David Dunlop, you are under arrest. You are not obliged to say anything unless you wish to do so, but what you say may be put into writing and used in evidence."

"But what is all this about?" David and I said in unison.

It was an unpaid parking fine. David had stuck a few HK$ notes in an envelope and sent it back at the time. He binned the subsequent warnings and threats of summons.

David was ignominiously bundled into a paddy wagon.

"I'll phone Freddie," I called.

"And call Anne ... no, on second thoughts, don't call Anne," he shouted back.

When POD came in, I said, "I think you'd better sit down, Sir."

He listened to the latest news and lent back, running his hands through his silvering hair.

"Gill, remind me we are running an advertising agency. Isn't that what we are supposed to be doing? My wife is threatening divorce, my daughter is about to elope with a croupier from the Playboy Club. Edward is in an asylum under a spell, David in a police cell and Betty's starting a new agency. Tell me, do you have plans? Something you might like to share with me rather than making it a surprise?"

It was decided that Edward had to go to the UK for treatment. It was not the first time his mental health had broken down. There had been a previous incident when he had been extricated from the cockpit of a Boeing 707 at Heathrow Airport. No one was quite sure how he'd got there. It wasn't until he requested clearance for take-off that the Control Tower alerted security.

Someone had to fly back to England with Edward and Dr Vincent, his psychiatrist, was happy to take up the offer of a free ticket. Scandal surrounded Dr Vincent – he was on his fourth wife and a Chinese one had hanged herself. He was also reputed to be seldom sober. The nuns had rung POD to say that the doctor had forgotten to instruct them what drugs to give Edward and he hadn't had any medication for twenty-four hours.

"Oh God, Gill. Be prepared to find him off the planet," said POD as he saw me off to the airport with Edward's passport and papers.

I was delighted to find Edward was his old self. He leaned close and whispered, "I don't know if I'm looking after the good doctor or vice versa – if I'm a little bonkers now, I'll be all the way by the time I've sat beside him for twenty hours."

Chapter 23

From time to time Greta and I had to take enforced leave of absence from sailing and diving when we contracted Hong Kong ear, the name given to infections we picked up swimming in the warm waters of Hong Kong which were often clouded with silt from the Pearl River.

One weekend when we were both afflicted, Greta suggested a walk on Aberdeen Island, also called Ap Lei Chau. The island lay at the mouth of Aberdeen Harbour warding off ocean swells. On the walk we encountered the worst poverty either of us had seen in Hong Kong. The squatter huts were abject and dismal, and we felt guilty, but relieved, to climb up to the highest point and discover the seaward side of the island, bare and deserted, except for wild dogs. We crossed a steep slope of scree and very crumbly rock. Had either of us slipped, there would have been little to halt our slide to the jagged rocks that barricaded the shoreline.

Ap Lei Chau island had been the launching point for one of the most daring escapes of World War II. The drama unfolded on Christmas Day 1941 as Hong Kong fell to the Japanese when five Royal Navy torpedo boats collected from the island sixty naval men, a handful of civilians and Chan Chak, a one-legged Chinese Admiral. The Admiral was a very senior figure in the Chinese nationalist movement, allies of the British. He was an old adversary of Japan and the torpedo boats secreted in outlying islands had received instructions to wait for him, but not to leave until Hong Kong had surrendered.

When the single word "Go" crackled through the radio, the torpedo boats cautiously approached the seaward shore of Ap Lei Chau under cover of darkness and miraculously made contact with the boarding party sliding down the scree. They'd swum to the island dodging Lions Mane jellyfish and bullets after their boat was shot out from underneath them by Japanese artillery. The Admiral had had to abandon his artificial leg to swim which was a double blow as it was stuffed with money. The skippers navigated their boats away from Ap Lei Chau, sailing to the south of the Po Toi Islands, eastwards past Waglan Lighthouse, before they turned north and headed towards Mirs Bay. There they landed in China and were spirited through the Japanese lines to freedom by the Chinese.

Little did I realise as I stood on the island's crest, scanning the scattered islands out to sea, that soon I too would sail past Waglan Lighthouse to Mirs Bay on my own adventure.

Greta and I made our way back down in the late afternoon to a path along the shore that wound through a maze of miserable piggeries and hovels. We were glad we did not have to wait long at the small jetty. An old woman in black picked us up in her sampan to take us back to Aberdeen.

I had become a member of the Hong Kong Enterprise Association – Enterprise being the class of dinghy the army sailed at Stanley. It was in early December, after one of the Association meetings at the YMCA on Kowloon-side, that Major Hoppe took the boys and me for a few drinks. The conversation quickly turned to the upcoming regatta at Taipo, in the New Territories. The Taipo Club had invited us and said we could borrow their sailing dinghies. All we had to do was get ourselves there. It didn't take long before we hatched a plan to sail *Peta Ann* over and camp on the Saturday night. Major Hoppe agreed on condition that Mick and Jim went with us so they could take responsibility for the boat. They were both twenty-six and had sailing experience from postings in Cyprus. I knew Mick slightly but I hardly knew Jim at all. Twiggy, Greta and Gerry were going too, nearly the whole gang.

By the time the weekend arrived, both Gerry and Greta had pulled out saying they had too many other things to do.

I worked like crazy the week before so I could get off early. It was never easy getting away from the office at weekends when POD was in Hong Kong, but once I'd taken up sailing, I was keen to edge out the door early each Saturday. Around midday I'd appear at POD's desk in my sailing shorts and bright yellow anorak, clutching a folded jib sheet I'd collected from the sailmakers or a tin of marine paint. He'd look up at me over the top of his glasses, taking in the scenario, and say, "Did you have plans for today Gill?" Usually, but not always, after looking very stern for a few seconds, we'd both laugh and I'd be out of there.

The day I was going to Taipo, I called good-bye to Pierre and David as I left, knowing they'd unwillingly be in the office all day. Pierre mouthed to me, "How do you do it?" I laughed and waved but I couldn't really tell them POD's verdict. "The guys just screw everything in sight and drink themselves stupid, so they might as well be working, but sailing, now that's different."

I ran to my car, praying the boys hadn't left without me. I concentrated hard, driving my Mini fast along the winding roads from Hong Kong's CBD to Stanley through brilliant sunshine, revelling at the magnificent views over the blue sea and islands. At the end of the pier, *Peta Ann* was rigged, her sails flapping. The boys lost no time unpacking my car and I raced up the pier, throwing kisses to other friends on the beach.

When we were in open water, Twiggy commented on the white caps out to sea and Mick said the guy at the Met Office had warned of a falling barometer.

"But it's always rough off Cape D'Aguilar," Mick reasoned. "It'll be fine after that."

We saw a police launch as we rounded the Cape. It, too, was making heavy going and we waved to them. The weather didn't abate after the peninsula though, it just got worse.

"We are just a bit exposed. Once we are in Mirs Bay, it'll get better," Mick reassured us. I trusted Mick. I'd been on a big yacht, he skippered one night when a typhoon was approaching. We had tacked close-hauled, sails reefed, in big seas and high winds from Stanley over to a typhoon shelter on the other side of Hong Kong harbour. The second typhoon warning was up and all the Colony's boats were making for shelters or getting out to sea to weather the storm. The radio was crackling, urgency palpable. It was a thrilling sail, hammering along, spray drenching a whole line of us sitting on the gunwale, belting out sea shanties and praying the mast could stand the excitement.

The typhoon season was over but the South China Sea could still kick up in winter, with the wind squalling round the coast. *Peta Ann* was groaning and ploughing, drifts of spume surfing over her bows when she dug in.

We told ourselves stories as we sailed, making light of each adversity. The boys were taking me to the Better 'Ole for dinner, a popular restaurant near Taipo. We wouldn't have time to change because we were running late, so we'd just find a buoy, holler for a sampan and leg it when we hit the shore.

. We assured each other that usually the wind dropped and the sea flattened as the sun sank. But it didn't happen that evening, the swell just got bigger, white caps rising. Hills and islands were tattooed jet black against stretches of a sulky red sky.

"The wind's picking up," said Jim.

We huddled in the cockpit with *Peta Ann* heaving and shuddering, making heavy weather of the storm.

Soon, big waves started breaking over the bows and knocking us off-course. Then we tacked and as we went about the jib caught on a cleat rather than passing over to the other side. Jim shouted to Twiggy who went forward to free the jib. I was hanging on for dear life and watched in horror as an enormous wave swept Twiggy off the deck, but as I screamed, the next wave deposited him back again. It was like something out of a B-grade sea-squall movie.

We were all shaken, reaching out to grab Twiggy and pull him into the cockpit as he got near, bent double and hanging on to every grab-handle.

With the rising wind, the boys shouted to each other about reefing or dropping the mainsail. They decided that as Twiggy was already drenched, he should put on a safety line and get the main in before we lost all light. With only the jib and engine we sailed on into the night.

Twiggy and I got out our sleeping bags and sat with them over our knees. We were still cold so Twiggy propped open the engine cover and siphoned the exhaust under the bags. We huddled together, only our heads cold from the salt spray whipping into the cockpit.

We were not long settled when Mick asked Twiggy for the chart. Twiggy got up and his hand reached to his back pocket, but the chart was gone, sea-snatched away when he'd gone to bring in the jib.

Without the chart, we had to change course to keep further out from the rocky coast, which meant an even rougher sea. Mick fiddled with compass and protractor and asked me to hold the next chart open. It wasn't a marine chart but an ordinance survey map, like those I'd used for the many hikes I'd done round Hong Kong.

The moon came up and raced overhead, flying past wispy clouds, a silver crescent tacking a smooth sky while we jerked through heavy swell and white caps far below.

"Dirty weather," Mick muttered.

We turned at last into the Tolo Channel, but to our surprise, it was a blind end. Just an inlet, not the channel at all. Mick peered down at a circle of torchlight on the chart. We knew we were lost, but no-one said it. "I say we stop here for the night and we'll sort ourselves out first thing in the morning. We'll get to Taipo for breakfast," said Mick.

The inlet was calm and still compared with the turmoil of our day's sailing. It was a big relief to be so sheltered and the cloud parted leaving the young moon alone. She appeared to anchor too and cast a pale streamer of light on the water that shattered as Mick dropped anchor. I dived into the broken slivers of silver light. The boys thought that was Gill again, mad about water. But I was just desperate for a pee; the water itself was uninviting, steel-cut and cold.

Twiggy threw me a towel. I pulled clothes over my damp bikini and jumped back under the pile of sleeping bags still warmed by the last puffs of engine exhaust.

Jim got the primus stove going and put the kettle on to boil. Soon the first cup of warm sweet tea hit the spot. It was so bloody cold.

"Let's brew up another cuppa, Jim, then have something quick to eat before we turn in," said Mick. "Come on, Twiggy, we'll put 'er to bed."

I dug deeper into the sleeping bags, lulled by the scuffle of their feet on the deck above, their light-hearted banter muted. It was a few moments before I heard the faint noise of a motor. I looked at Jim and saw his head was cocked, listening too. It was coming towards us, the sound swelling until we could distinguish shouting above the drubbing of a diesel engine. Jim called up. "Why are they yelling? Are we on their nets or summat? Tell 'em to go away, Mick, we're moving first thing."

Mick grunted. There was a pause before we heard him say, "Eh up, they sound bloody cross, I'll get the anchor. Twiggy, you get her going and we'll move off a bit."

I shed my warm covers to see what was going on. The solid ebony hulk of a fishing junk, without lights, was a dark silhouette against the slate hills behind. It was moving fast. Fierce bow waves surfed white and vivid in the moonlight. Jim and I jumped onto the roof of the cabin joining Twiggy – our eyes foraging into the dark. The engine throb and high-pitched, urgent shouts became clearer. Twiggy and I spoke at once, our words echoing each other.

"Funny, doesn't sound like Cantonese?"

The junk circled. Mick was crouched at the anchor about to lift it, but jumped back as the vessel turned straight for us. A searchlight blanched the blackness, blinding us. Amidst the trilling yells, familiar English words sounded cockeyed.

"Hands up or we shoot!"

My hands shot up. All our hands shot up. Seconds later the junk hit *Peta Ann* and threw us off our feet. We clawed for handholds. Through the clamour, the English was distinct, "Hands up, hands up up up; we shoot."

We scrabbled to our feet as *Peta Ann* swayed uncertainly from the hit and then bucked as men jumped on board, men with batons and guns, screaming men with little red badges. Red badges! That was it, how slow we were. Now we knew: Communist Chinese.

Pandemonium. Our captors were as confused and scared as we were. "Down, down," shouted one of the boarders and we scrambled down to the open cockpit, keeping low. Twiggy and I sat arm in arm by the tiller; Mick and Jim either side. We were all shaking – shudders of unstoppable shock rippling through us. The tea mugs had tumbled and Mick's binoculars swung fitfully from their hook. Opened maps shifted with the rocking and then slid to the deck.

"Go, go," shouted the man again. He seemed to hold the authority or maybe he was the only one with English. He waved at the hatch leading to *Peta Ann*'s cabin. We scuttled down and sat on the two bunks while a guard followed and squatted in the hatchway with an enormous gun. Half a dozen faces clustered above his shoulders, peering in. "It's a machine pistol," Mick whispered seeing me fixated on the weapon. I didn't care what the hell it was, it was bloody menacing.

We started to talk.

"Anyone got a remedy for the shakes?"

"Gill, I am so sorry."

"Yes, Gill, that goes for all of us."

They had no need to apologise but they did because I was the only civilian, the greenhorn, Capsize Gill. I had just tagged along. The idea of a sail to Taipo was not to be missed and it never occurred to me to ask questions.

"No sporking!" said the guard.

"They're some kind of militia," said Mick, and then he held up his hand, listening. "We're under tow," he hissed.

"No sporking … No sporking!" said the guard again, and this time he waved the pistol muzzle randomly and then pointed it at each one of us in turn.

My teeth chattered, my heart pounded, the shaking unstoppable; please believe me, I am not sporking.

Silenced, we listened intently to the sounds outside.

Chapter 24

We all knew that no-one came back from mainland China easily. Some American yachtsmen had disappeared six months before. I'd laughed then that anyone could be so stupid as to end up in Chinese waters. As I took in our situation, I thought, "Jesus, POD is due to leave for America on Monday. I'll be in hot water if he can't find where I put his passport." Then I thought of something even worse. "What about Mum and Dad? What will they think?"

After half an hour, we slowed. We could hear new voices shouting from a distance and the men on board *Peta Ann* shouting back. We jolted as the hull bumped something solid.

"Up up up."

The *Peta Ann* was being tied up alongside a jetty. As we stepped onto the rickety wooden planks, the structure itself was still swaying from the impact. Oh for a bigger moon! Shapes streamed towards us fractured and distorted by waving lamps. Shouts spilled over us and our captors yelled back.

When Jim saw the paintwork scoured off the hull by the collision with the junk, he was truculent and remonstrated about the damage. The boss man was very young, but securely in command. His eyes narrowed. He was not prepared for an argument right then and snapped an instruction. Jim was shoved back on board with a guard. People were crowding round us. The boss waved us to start up the pier and we felt a throng falling in behind. Ahead, a backdrop of hills held the outline of huts with windows softly lit. Hand-held lanterns sent feathery light dancing around our heels.

The shuddering had stopped once I got onto dry land. The immediate gut-clenching terror abated. Although my heart was still racing, I was focused on scanning our new surroundings and on what was ahead of us.

Twiggy and Mick linked arms with me. "We're off to see the Wizard, the Wonderful Wizard of Oz," I whispered. The boys' chuckled and we started to sing softly as we walked.

"We hear he is a whiz of a wiz, if ever a wiz there was."

At the end of the pier, a sandy path rose sharply to a flat space in front of a clutch of low stone buildings. The song had cheered and calmed us. Animated villagers flocked round and the armed militiamen answered their questions; it was taking time for everyone to hear the story and decide what best to do with this unexpected haul.

It must have been the tea, or the shock; I wanted another pee. I tried asking, but no one understood. Ten minutes later and I couldn't wait. Better dead than wet knickers. I had to find somewhere to go. So I just set off, quietly and firmly, no jerky movements. I heard shouts but kept going down a narrow laneway between low houses. I knew villagers were swarming after me but I forged on looking round desperately for something that looked like a latrine.

In no time I was right through the village with dark hills ahead and on my left, a row of ramshackle huts – outhouses for animals. I dived into a dark byre, a decrepit stable door only shoulder high with a wide gap at the bottom. Terrified squeals greeted me. I guessed it was pigs scattering. I whipped my pants down and squatted in the straw facing the door.

A rash of little faces filled the bottom gap and at the top, crammed bigger ones. Torch beams sought me out.

"I do not care, I do not care, I do not care, I have to wee," I mouthed out loud.

My enormous relief was shared by the reverberating voices of young and old who let out a collective and comprehending, "Ahh". And then the giggles started.

The crowd followed me back. News of the event had carried ahead and while the militiamen looked at me sheepishly, Mick and Twiggy grinned.

"Found the Ladies, did you?"

One of the men opened the door of a dilapidated building with a simple pitched roof and motioned for us to go in. It was an empty shed, partitioned about two-thirds of the way along by a wooden wall that did not reach the eaves, leaving a triangle of open space above. A wide wooden trestle and a bench sufficed to furnish it. We sat on the bench. The villagers filed in too and stood staring and pointing at us. Those who couldn't find standing room clambered up to peer in through the unglazed windows feebly boarded against the chill.

The chief militiaman introduced himself. "My name is Wong Tsin. Wong."

Then he took a couple of steps back, snapped up straight and shouted, "Stand up ... hands up. Down, sit, stand up ... hands up."

We did as instructed to the delight of our audience who fell about in amazement that these puppets could move with such alacrity at Wong's command.

Into the room came an older man who brought scraps of paper and asked us to write our names down.

Wong gave an order and the militia started frisking the boys. He motioned me outside, followed me out and shut the door of the shed behind him. I stood uncertain in the chill night air. Wong told the villagers to go and they evaporated, still chattering about the night's events. His back was turned on me as he talked to a couple of militia. I started to fiddle with my anorak, trying to zip up against the cold. When Wong turned back and saw my hands moving, he jumped, barking, "Hands up" and stuck the barrel of his pistol in my midriff. Our faces were almost touching. We stared in mutual shock and surprise. He pulled back the barrel and used it to direct me to another shed.

I was shaking again as Wong followed me in and closed the door. Only a faint glimmer of moonlight shone through the window to illuminate us. Wong pulled his pocket inside out and motioned to me to do the same.

I fumbled. My pounding heart was racing but my fingers wouldn't work – they were clumsy and slow. When at last I turned out my pockets a slim plastic case clattered onto the table. Wong pounced and opened it, pulling out tampons. Embarrassment galvanised me. At that time you only bought tampons from the chemist when there was a female assistant and she put them in a brown paper bag before she pushed them across the counter. I grabbed to gather them, but Wong snapped at me, knocking my hand away and said, "Hands up." He started to frisk me down. I was now furious and felt much bolder. I glared at him, standing tall with every muscle tensed. He sensed the change and stopped searching me, stepping back. I'd disconcerted him – he wasn't much older than I was. He turned on his heel, and left, slamming the door behind him. I leaned back against the ramshackle table, breathed and smiled. My heart still raced, but it spun differently – that round was mine.

Shortly afterwards the door opened and Wong brought in two girls with a kerosene lantern. They had round happy faces with long black pigtails and round padded bodies wrapped in long blue coats. They stared curiously at me and edged past the table until it was between us. Wong pushed my possessions across the tabletop, pointing at the box of tampons. They nodded. He left and they burst into nervous giggles and I started to laugh.

They mimed taking off my clothes. I took off my anorak, two jumpers, my waterproof sailing trousers and stood shivering in white shorts and my shirt. They found the sight of me in shorts hilarious and patted me down perfunctorily.

Now they opened the tampon box that I had repacked and took out a tampon. They rolled it over, discussed it, passed it between them and then the taller one started to unwrap it. They were mystified. When the shorter one snatched it and shot the two cardboard tubes together, a cotton bullet was propelled across the room. They jumped sky high and grabbed each other. They took the lantern off the table to see what had flown out and stared bewildered at the white plug. I picked it up and reassembled it for them. We fired it again and again until they tired of it. They shrugged – the question was clear. What was it for?

There was some kind of almanac or calendar hanging limply on the wall. I started there – making gestures like a shapely woman, then pointing to me – pointing to the calendar. Groaning, rubbing cramps in my groin. Then I pretended to pull down my pants and feign surprise. I'd always hated charades but my performance must have been good for they quickly turned to each other – and I could see, yes, yes, they got it. But what had that to do with the tampon?

Well, when I presented Act II, they were at first incredulous and then they fell about laughing. Tears streamed down their faces. They loved my show. It was unbelievable. It was science fiction. It was just plain weird. Did they have a story for their comrades? Yep, one that would knock their socks off. They slapped their hands together, they hugged me. They chattered to me intently, black eyes shining. I could not understand a word, but the hugs said it all. I got dressed and gathered up all the props and we went outside where Wong and the militia were waiting.

We were still laughing and although a couple of the men smiled, Wong was stern and sent the girls packing and I was ushered back to join the boys. Their heads jerked up in unison. Before Wong could say, "No sporking", Twiggy said, "Is everything OK?" with such fierce tenderness I was moved, tears of relief springing up behind my eyes, so different from tears of laughter; those roll out with ease, but tears of relief and emotion, hot and bitter, prick up from some deeper well.

"Yes, I'm fine. Everything's OK."

I breathed deeply and could not help an enigmatic smile but the boys didn't notice and I wasn't going to explain.

Old women brought in two feather eiderdowns, lumpy with worn striped covers and put them on the wooden trestle. Wong told us to go to bed. It was 3 am. He said Jim would sleep on the boat.

"Gill, we'll sleep on the floor if you'd like the bed," said Mick. That night I just wanted us all to be together. We lay down with me in the middle of the two boys. A guard sat on the bench by the door.

We heard the militia settling in on the other side of the partition. The light of their Tilley lamp filling the triangle above, the soft hiss comforting.

They were talking about us. We heard them trying to pronounce our names and laughing, then the words, "Hands up," accompanied by more laughter.

I closed my eyes but Twiggy elbowed me and pointed to the window opposite the bed. It was boarded up with an old shooting target – the hardboard head and shoulders of a man, his brain riddled with bullet holes. Twiggy rolled over and was snoring softly moments later but I couldn't get to sleep as easily. The shed door opened and shut, militia ran torches over us and let villagers look in too. As I lay there, my mind drifted back to the events of that extraordinary day. I replayed again and again the moment when Twiggy was washed off the deck and redeposited as if the sea was playing a game. I wondered if the chart had disintegrated in the sea or was made of stronger stuff and wafted across the ocean floor. Perhaps it would wash up at some beach near Taipo and be a clue for those searching for us. But who would know it was from the *Peta Ann*?

The guard opened the door, disturbing me again. The trestle bed was hard and bit into my shoulder. I pulled the eiderdown up, trying to tuck a fold of it underneath me, releasing an old pungency of duck and chicken feathers.

I rolled over. Whatever the day was going to bring, I needed to get to sleep. I watched the moonlight filtering in through cracks, etching silver threads across the eiderdown as if looking for us. It quietened me and finally I fell asleep.

Chapter 25

That first morning in captivity, Mick and I were woken rudely to the sound of a strangled brass bugle. We laughed and I put my hands over my ears while Mick shouted, "Put a sock in it. Try blowing through the other end!" The guard grinned although I'm sure he had no idea what Mick was saying.

As the sound faded, we heard people running along the pathways beside the shed and congregating in the space outside. Speeches, then chanting followed.

Twiggy slept through it all. Wong came in with villagers crowding behind him.

"Up up," he said loudly.

Twiggy roused, but took his time. We all waited with remarkable patience as he sat up, rubbed his eyes and surveyed the world with a stunned look. As if belatedly remembering the events of the previous twenty-four hours, he nodded and shook his head a little. Next he ran his hand through his spiky hair, yawned and gave a wry tight-lipped smile. For the villagers, this was pure theatre.

It smacks of holidays to arrive at night, not knowing what the darkness has concealed until the morning's revelation. That morning we stepped out of the shed and I gasped at the beauty of the scene. We were in an isolated settlement at the head of a bay. Sea and hills spread before us like an old postcard sent from some enclave along the coast of China in the days of the treaty ports. A sepia photo washed ever so gently in pastel aqua hues of tan, teal, blue-grey and indigo, blushed with fuchsia. The air we breathed was pungent and unfamiliar. We were no strangers to rank smells in Hong Kong but these earthy wafts were simpler; dried fish, paraffin, steaming rice. We stood soaking in the stillness. A whisper of smoke curled from the village and dropped down to lie gently along the sand as low soft banks of mist rolled away down the bay. Fishing nets were hanging up to dry. A basketball court, its surface beaten earth, was to the left and a small slipway to the right of the pier had a junk hauled up for repair. Other junks lay gently at anchor in the bay, while a couple of sampans floated at the end of the pier. Here, divorced from the raw voracity of Hong Kong with its neon and clamour, we had woken to a muted spot; somewhere to write, an artist's retreat, somewhere you'd come to satisfy longings for simplicity and solitude.

It was as if the village had held its breath waiting for our reaction and now breathed out, chattering and babbling. A low stone wall separated the village from the beach, and on the strand by the pier was *Peta Ann*, well and truly beached by the outgoing tide, her barnacled bottom bared, somehow indecent. I wanted to run down and cover her up, restore her dignity, reassure her. Villagers stood on the pier gawking at her, while others gathered on the wet sand and the more adventurous clambered over her.

We jumped down onto the sand ourselves, relieved to spot Jim who appeared balancing on the hull. He'd slept there with a guard and, as the boat heeled, they'd been forced to top and tail it – sleeping squashed together in the trough made by the angle of the bunk and cabin wall. The closer we got to *Peta Ann*, the sadder she seemed. She stank. Oil and muck from the bilges lapped across the decking. She had a forlorn and wasted look. We quickly collected what we felt was important; warm clothing, a jerry can of fresh drinking water, food, sleeping bags, a bottle of wine and some beer.

Once back at the shed, we didn't want to go inside so made washing an excuse; we took turns taking a little water from the jerry can, splashing our faces, brushing our teeth. The icy water elicited real gasps and shrill bluster from us. We were starting to understand that we were the visiting vaudeville. Our job was to entertain, and the villagers could not take their eyes off us. Sharp or unexpected movements scattered the throng, so we were devilish, pouncing and jumping, their bodies scooting from ours in unison with screams and shouts of gleeful terror. Yet the next moment they were pressing close in again, hands stretching to pull our clothing, touch our skin and point. Pointing, so much pointing. The militia stood around, grinning and scoffing at the villagers, forgetting that they too had been terrified of us the night before.

The boys had retrieved army ration packs from the boat. Designed for emergencies, the food was high-energy and pre-cooked. It amused the boys to see me open my "rat-pack". I had no idea what to expect and delighted in unwrapping each item; chewing gum, chocolate, baked beans and sausages, an oatmeal block, plum jam, condensed milk, and thoughtfully, toilet paper too. We'd recovered the Primus stove but it wasn't working and the militia brought us paraffin, wicks and prickers and sat on their haunches working with Jim to get it going. Jim cooked up a big breakfast. We were thawing out, less scared and allowed to talk freely. The villagers feasted too on the sight of us, pointing at our strange food, our cutlery, following every chew and swallow, twittering, giggling and gasping.

After breakfast, still the crowd stared, waiting for any movement. A nose-blow or a cough was enough. We wanted some peace. All actors need time off-stage. We ushered our audience out the door shutting it firmly and, using whatever we could find, we started to board up holes in the windows. The guards laughed and joined us, stuffing rags and finding strips of cardboard. Children pushed their fingers through the cardboard as quickly as we stuck it up, circles of bright light momentarily spilling into the room before they were sealed with a child's dark eye.

The latrines were a block of long drops set apart from the village where a strip of land was cultivated before the hills rose up. Concrete benches ran on either side, round holes equally spaced, all in a row. A set-up for very congenial and cordial ablutions. It was roofed, without walls, open to the elements, the village to one side, the hills to the other. I would take my place looking towards the countryside and sometimes

I even lingered there. For the most part, villagers scattered if they saw me coming so I felt it was the one place I could be alone. Occasionally I ended up sitting near a constipated old man who would take little notice of me. Sometimes an overly curious young girl would perch opposite, riveted by my every move.

The latrines were not unclean, but vermin infested. Big rats were bold and at night I preferred my original pigsty – it was closer and I thought that the rats might give the pigs a wide berth. Wong had designated round-faced minders to escort me each trip, but the girls would stop short on the path by the houses, leaving me alone to cross the open ground along the stepping stones that wound to the latrine block. The girls never objected if I took a different route back to our shed. The village was very small and all roads led to the bay, so it mattered little which route I took, and they allowed me to explore. Once when I started to run, just to stretch my stiffening limbs, the girls cheerfully ran with me. We raced the narrow paths together, children fleeing indoors, villagers jumping out of our way but when I collided with the shed door, startling the poor guard, it brought an admonishment from Wong. Later on, my minders didn't even bother following me and I strolled along nodding to the villagers.

An old man came to visit us in the shed. There was some pomp as he was ushered in. He had spent eight years in New York as a youth. He was now seventy-five and although he had not spoken English for forty years, he could remember a little. He was pleased to see us, and kindly. He said that as long as we were not Americans, we had no need to be afraid.

He was joined by Wong and several militia men with their little Red Books. These were a pocket-sized edition of *Quotations from Chairman Mao Tse-tung*, the text that was studied in schools, factories and collectives.

We perched on the trestle bed.

"Long Live Chairman Mao, Great Leader of the People's Republic of China," said Wong. "Do you know Chairman Mao?"

We pointed to tattered posters hanging limply on the stone walls of the room. This pleased the militia and elicited broad smiles. Wong's edition of the Red Book had an English translation on the right-hand page. He selected passages for us to read; the most anti-American, anti-imperialist he could find.

"American imperialists are paper tigers," Wong said and looked at us. "Are you Americans?"

"Oh, no, Wong," we responded in unison, "We are not Americans."

The session was repetitive and lengthy. Mick started switching or adding words to change the meaning of the quotes.

"Political power grows out of the barrel of a *British* gun," Mick intoned.

Wong had not noticed – it was very hard not to laugh.

Wong remonstrated with Twiggy who had closed his eyes, but Twiggy told him people in the West thought better that way. The old New Yorker smiled but said nothing. Wong looked unconvinced but sensing we were tiring of Red rhetoric, jumped up, pulling each one of us to our feet, pumping our hands, "London-Peking, good friends, yes! Peking-New York, noooo! New York-London, Noooo!" With that our propaganda session was over and the militia filed out leaving us alone.

Mick got up and ran his hands through his hair. "They'll have a rare old search going on by now."

Twiggy, sitting on the edge of the bed, disagreed. "They won't even have missed us. Taipo'll think we cried off because of the weather. It'll be Monday morning before Gerry comes down to the beach and sees *Peta Ann* is not on the mooring."

"But I logged our sail, they must be looking for us."

Twiggy shook his head, "Nah, it's all very well but someone would still have to say we were missing. It'll be up to Gerry."

I thought about Gerry. I'd been sorry when he said he wasn't coming. His excuse was he wanted to rub down his dinghy for the racing the following weekend, but on reflection that hadn't rung true. I wondered what they would have made of Gerry. He was no red gweilo like the four of us. I wondered if the villagers had ever seen anyone from India before. Then I thought it was unlikely they had ever seen anyone like us before. Mao had expelled all foreigners from China, even the dead – their graves levelled by Red Guards.

160

We had a sense that we were waiting for something. We were holed up in the shed and Wong was keeping an eye on us but nothing seemed to be happening.

Wong said we could have vegetables, eggs, cigarettes, anything we wanted but we must pay in Hong Kong dollars. Twiggy produced a note. Wong took it and said he would let us know when it was used up as they had no change. Whatever we asked for was delivered by dark-eyed honeyed children.

Mick pulled the trestle out and scratched a cartoon figure of a bald-headed man with a long nose on the wall. It made Twiggy and Jim laugh. "Kilroy," they said and explained to me that bored squaddies leave the same doodle on every barrack room wall.

Without books or playing cards, which had been confiscated after the first night's search, the hours dragged which gave us all time to think. None of us had been in Hong Kong for long, I had lived there for just over a year, but we'd been there long enough to be aware of China's predilection for detaining foreigners. Missionaries, journalists, yachtsmen disappeared. The length of detention seemed quite random. I only hoped that if we were to be detained in China, we could be useful. Already sitting with nothing to do was playing on my nerves. I made up a mantra to make myself brave in the hours to come, 'A life's a life no matter where it is lived'. Inside I quailed at the thought of years in China.

I tried to remember what I knew about detained foreigners. A journalist, Anthony Grey, had recently been released after two years' detention, and some American yachtsmen had been held for six months. Then there was Father Walsh, the American missionary, who was still imprisoned after a decade. I thought about his slim red book that Sister Francis had handed me at Salamat not long after my arrival. *The Man on Joss Stick Alley* was published in 1947, the year of my birth. From it I'd learned that gathering abandoned babies was the stock-in-trade of Catholic missions to China. Thousands were collected, almost all girls consigned at birth to cesspits and rubbish dumps. Already at death's door, it was too late to save their lives but if they lived to be baptised, the missionaries said their souls were saved and they went to heaven.

An ugly element of the new Communist order in China fomented wild accusations. It said that missionaries were mass murderers, the proof manifested by the graves of babies surrounding every mission. The new ideology was cleverly preached. It united the masses against an enemy, stripping the Chinese of past culpability and allowing for a new order.

Even before the Communists, it was uphill work in China. The priests' proselytising turned again and again to dust, so they focused on the needy and hoped their charity would be a beacon of light. There were breakthroughs; Walsh recorded the conversion of the barber in a market town.

"Mr Chow was an elderly gentleman who, to his attainments as a barber, added a bent towards philosophy," wrote Walsh.

I could picture Mr Chow murmuring, "Even the hairs of your head are all numbered," as he snipped off a surviving queue – the long braided plait worn by the Manchu – or teased out recalcitrant hairs from the faces of his beardless countrymen.

Barbers offered extra services in those days including cleaning ears. "Whoever has ears, let them hear," he might have exhorted as he mined an obstinate kernel of ear wax and flourished it on a long silver pick for his astonished patron.

I lay back that afternoon on a rolled up sleeping bag with my fingers interlocked behind my head. Some said that the success of Western missionaries was not in conversions but in awakening a social conscience. Some even suggested the debates they opened up on ideals paved the way for revolution.

On my next visit to the latrine block I looked around for roads. When I returned, the boys were all dozing and I lay down again thinking about how we would be moved out of the village. Maybe we were in for a long walk. My mind was still turning with the stories from Father Walsh. He had painted a colourful picture of visiting clergy unused to the long hikes that pastoral work in China necessitated; "… puffing like porpoises; their complexions went from white to red, and finally settled into mottled purple."

At least the boys and I were all quite fit, but maybe we would be taken off by sea. Walsh loved the enforced idleness of travel by junk, despite the holds that reeked of opium fumes and belched out the noisy clatter of mah-jong and profanity, "… black as night and as dense with humanity as a crowded subway train".

In Walsh's day, it was common for the privileged to travel by sedan chair carried by two bearers. Walsh preferred to walk but he mused that the sedan chair was well designed for contemplation and reflection as it was too uncomfortable for sleep, too bumpy for reading and offered no opportunity for conversation; "… in a word, a philosopher's paradise". The bearers, "the undernourished dregs of town and village", could cover an astonishing thirty miles a day. Stops were at wayside tearooms where a warm drink and tasteless congee did not restore the strength of the bearers, but opium did. The tired men would lie down to inhale and rise to carry on as if borne on the "wings of wind".

With the new order in China, opium too was gone. When the Communists took control, there were millions of opium addicts in China. With a carrot and stick combination, the new regime virtually eliminated the problem. Peasants ploughed in their poppies to plant food staples instead. A massive education program on the evils of opium and heroin was launched where addicts were not blamed but merely labelled as pawns of the British who had introduced the scourge to China. They were dried out and given useful jobs; cooperative dealers were re-educated and the obstinate executed.

I dozed off and was deeply asleep when Jim shook my arm. It was late afternoon and he said he'd brewed tea. He also said something was up. The boys sensed a change and Mick said he'd seen a stranger in fatigues.

It was not long before Wong arrived with Lei, who introduced himself as an interpreter with the Chinese People's Liberation Army, the PLA, who had come to take charge of us. Lei was tall and spare, with a slight stoop.

He was pale in comparison to the robust Wong. He said we would be interrogated.

Just the word was enough to make me feel ill at ease and when we were taken out one at a time, that feeling intensified. When it was my turn, Lei led me to a village hall. Five members of the PLA were seated behind a table and there was a single chair in the room waiting for me. All the PLA wore the same drab khaki uniform; no markings indicated anyone more senior than another. I speculated on the number of invisible stripes they'd earned. They were considerate and asked if I would like my own room and when I said I didn't want to be separated from my friends, they said they would set up another bed for me. I relaxed a little. The questioning was slow and we looked at each other with open curiosity. Name, nationality, age, place of birth, names of parents, address in Hong Kong. After about ten minutes, the PLA lost interest in questioning me and made asides, commenting to each other and laughing. I asked Lei if I could share the joke. He translated what I had said and they all laughed together, but were not forthcoming, so I just smiled and shrugged my shoulders.

I returned to our quarters and Twiggy was taken. It was nerve-racking until we were all back together. We'd been asked the same questions and everything had been very cordial so relief bubbled through us. The boys had lied and said they were civilians and the ruse was holding.

We deliberated on whether we should keep the wine and beer for Christmas which was less than ten days away, but decided to drink it while the going was good. Jim tipped cans and left-overs into a hearty goulash, Mick put a white tee-shirt over the bench as a tablecloth and we sat down to a merry meal. The boys joked about what they would tell their CO.

"I tell you Sir, you don't half look funny from the other side," quipped Mick.

With the presence of the PLA in the village, the guards were on edge. Other militia drifted in to see why we were so rowdy. To reassert control, a guard told us to finish up and go to bed. We were in high spirits and fooled around some more. I got into the single trestle bed that had been set up for me. A lamp was burning on the shelf nearby and the guards made no move to put it out. I knew I was being cheeky when I hopped up, said, "Goodnight gentlemen," and blew out the flame, but I didn't expect the reaction I got. With the room thrust into darkness, the guards galvanised, hollering. Boots thudded. Torches swept the scene. To our amazement, guns flew over the partition, slapping into the hands of aghast militia who fumbled wildly to right their weapons, clicking catches, taking aim. PLA soldiers flooded in, one with a lantern which glinted on the gunmetal and threw deep shadows. The militia and PLA stood as one, their guns levelled at us. It all happened so fast, but it was over just as quickly when Wong shouted at the guards to lower their weapons. He was clearly irritated with everyone. I felt guilty because I realised the fracas reflected badly on him. He listened to the guard, relit the lantern and called for Lei who glared at me.

"Sit up! You will not do that again."

"I am sorry," I said, managing what I hoped was a disarming smile. "In our country we sleep with the lights out."

Lei's eyes remained locked on mine while the rest of the men filed outside, leaving just the usual couple of guards.

"You will not do that again," he repeated and left, slamming the door behind him.

I rolled my eyes at the boys and pulled the covers over my head.

Chapter 26

The door flew open, crashing back and juddering. Wrenched from deep sleep, we were stiff-limbed and bewildered. Wong shouted, "Up up UP. Get up. Pack." We fumbled in the dim light, shivering with the cold. Fingers of fear bound my muscles tight. We stuffed everything into our bags and the guards shepherded us to the village hall. A Tilley lamp stood on a chair which stood on a table. I wanted to say something. My mind was briefly fixated on the odd orientation of the furniture; nothing else seemed important. A chair should not be on a table, a lamp should not be on a chair.

The log book, maps and everything else from *Peta Ann* were spread across a trestle table and a soldier tipped out our bags too. The PLA looked on somewhat disdainfully until a fat woman picked up my mascara and pretended to brush her eyelashes. Her companions were briefly jocular while we stood cold and ignored. The oldest PLA man, who seemed to be the boss, flicked through the log of *Peta Ann* and examined the maps we'd used. He nodded to Lei.

"OK, pack up. Go back to bed."

We hardly spoke, just packed, went back to the shed and back to sleep.

In another hour the door burst open again.

"Up up UP."

This time they took only Mick for questioning.

So the pattern was established, one taken, the rest almost back to sleep, the rude awakening and another of us would go.

Once again the interrogation was about identity but this time in much more detail. The questioners were polite and I sensed curiosity drove the conversation as well as official duty. Why was I in Hong Kong? Who paid for me to go to Hong Kong? Did I live with Chinese or Europeans? I was economical with my answers. I didn't go into detail on how I had reached Hong Kong on the Trans-Siberian through Russia or divulge that I lived with Japanese. I said my father was a doctor, but didn't elaborate on him either. Dad was one of the first human geneticists back in the days when new typists inevitably spelled "genes" as "jeans". He'd always been nervous of abduction by a Communist regime. He imagined himself in a laboratory with all the necessary equipment and technicians, but with no passport and no way home.

They asked about Americans. Did I see Americans around Hong Kong? Did I know any Americans? Did any Americans have connections to my firm?

Americans spilled through the streets of Hong Kong in those days, fresh from Vietnam on R&R – five-day furloughs of Rest and Recreation. In Wan Chai, Hong Kong's red-light district, servicemen fuelled ever more girlie bars. Head and heart sore, high on narcotics, they flooded along the waterfront streets. Lured in by prosaic names rendered exotic in neon – the Pink Flamingo, Blue Heaven, Oh-la-la or the inevitable Suzie Wong Bar – the young men cried into their beer, got smashed, played soulful songs on the juke box, punched each other and got lucky.

A jumbled rush of Americana rose in my throat. POD had just left for America to drum up more business. An American girlfriend had taken me on a tourist junk chartered by a lively bunch of Jews from the USA who picked up snappy fashion designs on Western catwalks, copied them in Hong Kong sweatshops and had them in-store world-wide in days. An American, Paul Ferguson, brother of my schoolfriend Oonagh, had recently wined and dined me at the Hilton's Dragon Boat Bar. Takako's good friend, an American doctor, worked at Shatin in the New Territories, running a clinic for boat people. She lived in a quaint, cosy house with pet monkeys, birds and dogs and entertained us in winter with roaring log fires and endless anecdotes. Freddie Zimmern had taken me to meet his friend, the US Navy's legal adviser to the Admiral. We toured around USS *Oklahoma City*, the flagship of the Seventh Fleet. They were especially proud of the ship's communication equipment which they couldn't use near Hong Kong as the Chinese would pick up signals and learn too much. They were a charming bunch; we spent the whole day with them and ended up at a nightclub to see the visiting Las Vegas Girls. Then there was the really cute American-Chinese guy who worked with Hannah To at the Youth Club. Greta and I regularly met American officers in the classy bar at the Peninsula Hotel who, after a few drinks, became maudlin and teary, and looked absurdly young to be in command. Or the American doctors from Saigon whom Greta had met when she went to Vietnam on holiday. They'd rescued her wandering around Saigon at night looking for accommodation, unaware of the curfew. War-weary, counting the days until they got back to their wives and children, they came to Hong Kong on R&R. Greta repaid their kindness and together we took them sightseeing and sailing.

The PLA must have known that Hong Kong swarmed with Americans. The Communists had no shortage of informers.

Did I know any Americans? I denied them all.

The questions turned to where I worked. Who did I work for? Did I work with Chinese? What was the purpose of my work?

I felt working for an advertising agency would not rate high on an ideological scoreboard. I placed no emphasis on Mrs Church. She was a high-profile figure in the colony. I thought about her anti-Communist rants and how she sniffed out "Reds", firing them on a whim. Now that was one person who'd be thrilled I had disappeared. "Good riddance," I could hear her chuckle.

My questioners pursued nothing, I divulged nothing, and I think together we were happy that I presented an uncomplicated persona. When I sensed that they were about to dismiss me, I turned to Lei and started a speech I had prepared in my head. My parents needed to know I was safe. What would happen to us? When could we go home? Why were they holding us for a navigation error? The oldest of the PLA officers held up his hand and spoke to the interpreter. Lei looked strained.

"It is not for you to ask questions, not your job, not your job. You will not ask any more questions, you will go back to bed."

The boys' interrogations were much the same. Khaki sleeping bags and rat-packs had raised the suspicion of the PLA, who didn't really believe they were civilians. The cursory body searches had not revealed the IDs the boys had hidden down their socks.

In the morning, we were all tired and on edge. I tried to reassure myself that a night's disturbed sleep was nothing. I'd partied all night from time to time in Hong Kong and turned up and done a day's work. But this was different. The alarm of being woken up each time I'd got into the rhythm of deep sleep had jarred my nerves. I sensed that even if I tried to catch up on sleep that morning, it would not come easily.

It was Monday and we knew that the alarm must be well and truly up. We expected some resolution, but nothing changed.

Lei and Wong came and chatted to us. "Do you read the *Peking Review*?" Lei asked. We knew of the Chinese government's propaganda magazine but said truthfully that it wasn't widely read by Westerners. We commiserated with them about Vietnam. Britain hadn't joined that war so we could agree on the big bad paper tigers fighting an unjust war. We nodded understandingly when Wong lamented that the Russians were forsaking true Communism and becoming more like imperialists.

"Russians are revisionist traitors," said Lei, clenching his fists.

In the afternoon, we started a sing-song. *Auld Lang Syne* brought a broad smile to Wong's face. "The friendship song," he said, opening the doors and ushering in an audience. "Sing," he enjoined us.

Our belted renditions of "Red Sails in the Sunset" and "I'd like to get you on a Slow Boat to China all to myself alone," were particularly well received even though we could only remember a few lines. It was nearly Christmas, so Wenceslas trod through the snow and shepherds gathered flocks and followed stars.

Just as he had when reciting Mao's Red Book, Mick added his own words. He subjected carols to army bastardisation; Wenceslas rhymes easily with arse and the King, had, after all, walked over sods. We moved onto safer ground and sang some Broadway musicals. But the party ended when we got to "Anything you can do, I can do better."

This brought Lei leaping to his feet.

"Oh no, Peking is better than London, Chinese better than YOU," he said angrily, "Chinese better than YOU. Better. China better," and stormed out.

We hadn't meant to upset Lei and our spirits dipped.

A little later, Wong asked us to give up our jewellery and watches. Jim started swearing and cursing; he didn't want to part with a signet ring that had sentimental value, but it wasn't our jewellery that we missed. It was our watches; it was horrid not to know the time.

With just the guards in the room, Mick said in a low voice that it was time we remembered it was a soldier's duty to escape. Mick thought he had worked out where we were. If we broke free and struck west we'd be near the border and the British Army's anti-snatch patrols would see us. Mick's murmured speech had been a monologue and no-one added to it. Lei had given us back our playing cards and the rest of the day was passed playing cards. We all thought about what Mick had said.

Mick started again. The guards had slacked off since the PLA had settled in and he felt we needed to move quickly while the moon was still new because it was getting bigger every day. He started sorting through his clothing for black gear.

His plan seemed suicidal to me so I said so. We were not immediately threatened and the situation could still resolve peaceably. We didn't need to be submissive, but we could be reasonable. Jim disagreed, he sided with Mick. It was their duty; we could be held for years. Mick rolled himself up on the bed with his back to us. Jim huddled by himself. Twiggy just dealt out cards and he and I played in silence. When Jim did come over, he said, "I'm going too," and added, "tonight."

I stared at Twiggy.

"I'm tempted," he said, looking at me, "but not without you," and carried on studying his hand.

Twiggy at twenty was the youngest in our party, eighteen months younger than me. He was steady, grounded and popular because he didn't rock boats, but held his well-mannered course.

It was a stretch of imagination to visualise all of us slinking out and taking off cross-country. I was tired and shaky, but I thought the boys had gone completely barmy.

We were questioned again in the afternoon. My interrogators wanted to establish my connection to the boys. I told them just that we were members of the same sailing club.

But for the boys, the ruse that they were civilians was over. They gave name, rank and number but their interrogators wanted figures, troop numbers, defence positions, equipment and information on armoury. The boys didn't have the answers – that was not information they possessed. Faced with irritated interrogators who wanted facts, they quickly decided to simply make up answers and keep the peace. Mick exaggerated and turned Hong Kong into an impregnable fortress.

Twiggy came back and said he'd not had to tell many lies; the truth was enough. "I said most of my time was spent sailing dinghies, so they showed me silhouettes of British ships and asked me to identify them." With his wry smile he said, "I told them I was in the Army, not the Royal Navy, and I sailed boats for fun. I told them I trained in the riot squad and practised standing and holding up a banner saying 'Disperse or we will fire teargas,' or 'Disperse or we will shoot to kill.'" He started to laugh. "They all looked at each other and asked Lei to repeat the translation."

After the round of questioning, it was evening again and Mick returned to the foetal position. Wong had been watching him all day and became alarmed. He asked if we needed a doctor. He brought bowls of hot water but Mick and Jim shunned his peace offering. I took the opportunity to wash the salt out of my hair and jokingly flicked soap suds at the guards who laughed. I went outside and rinsed off the shampoo with cold water in the blue moonlight, amusing my usual coterie of giggling villagers. I'd soaked my shirt so went back inside and whipped it off to put on a dry one. I had a bikini underneath, but I shocked the guards who spun round to face the wall, making Jim and Twiggy roar with laughter. Mick did not even turn over.

When we got into our beds that night and I called, "Goodnight," softly to Mick and Jim, they whispered "Goodbye."

"What can we do, Twiggy?" I said.

He stretched over to my camp bed, put his hand on my arm, "Only thing *to do*. Go to sleep."

I did drift off to sleep. We were well guarded that night. Several times I woke when a guard stood right beside my bed and swept a torch over my face.

Chapter 27

In the morning, we were all there. Mick had had a change of heart. They said they wouldn't have abandoned Twiggy and me.

"Whatever happens, from now on we all stick together." An intense wave of emotion passed among the four of us. We felt like the Musketeers, "All for one and one for all!"

The day stretched out and we dozed or let our minds race about far from the confines of the shed. Twiggy remembered reading a book by a wartime POW who said he kept his sanity by constructing buildings brick by brick in his head. He imagined that whenever he was disturbed, the buildings collapsed and he had to rebuild them. After a pause, Twiggy started, "My Church is nearby our house. On the left as you go in the door is the font. Up the aisle to the choir stalls ..."

He'd only "built" the main knave and was approaching the transept before Mick and I smothered him and we rolled around, with Mick yelling, "Mind out Twiggy, it's falling down; here comes the steeple."

Wong came rushing in and found us paralytic with laugher, tears of mirth running down our faces.

He called Lei and they spoke together before Lei sat us in a row and said, "You are in a very serious position, yet you laugh? What is it that makes you laugh so much?"

Laughter didn't hide the fear, but it pushed it back, gave us space to breathe. The boys were from Yorkshire; a people as warm and funny as the Irish. I had a penchant for their low-level spontaneous gags, the quick quip and ribald remark so novel to my conservative and refined upbringing.

Mick piped up to answer Lei. "It's a good place you have here; your people are happy so we are happy."

Lei's face lit up. "You mean you would like to stay in the People's Republic of China and not return to Hong Kong?" he said, one foot out the door bursting to tell his comrades.

Mick came up quickly with a diplomatic answer. "Eh up, hang on, this is your home and this is a good country for you, but we want to go home, home to our families."

The guards told us to turn-in.

We had an hour of sleep before the door flew open.

"Up up UP."

I needed sleep. I was fearful; scared I would not be able to keep my emotions under control if we had another night of interruptions. In my head I repeated my mantra, "A life's a life no matter where it is lived." But, it wasn't working. Doubt seeped into my brain. My bravado was being taken by stealth.

It was Mick they took first for questioning. He came back despondent.

"They say none of us are telling the truth; they could keep us one year or ten – it makes no difference to them."

I lay awake staring up into the rafters. Mum's voice was in my head. She told me that it is usually 3 am when the gremlins come to call. I knew that with no rhythm to the night, I couldn't hold off the gremlins until the early hours. They were gathering to snatch at moments when I could have slept, and they were invading my dreams. I listened to my own breathing, which was shallow. My body was frightened. I was very scared.

I sensed we were all pretending to sleep and I knew that none of us were smiling anymore.

An hour later the door burst open. Dear God, can they not once open it quietly, I thought.

"Up up UP. Pack up, pack up, quickly get packed."

We shuffled into the main hall. "Next stop Beijing?" Twiggy whispered to me trying to raise a smile. The Tilley lamp was standing on the chair on the table again. The PLA were lined up and we did too. The chief man made a speech in Mandarin and his comrades gave him a little clap. Then it was Lei's turn to translate. He started pedantically. "You have committed a crime by sailing into the waters of the People's Republic of China. You have made mistakes. Your case has taken up time and we have had to make a report. Tonight we have received instructions. We have received instructions to release you."

The word "release" registered imperfectly. Mick gave out a long low whistle and one of us snapped, "Shut up".

The Chinese paused for our reaction but now we stood still in a row. We trusted not them or ourselves. Was there another clause to come – released in five years or released to another jurisdiction? They scanned our faces. We were inscrutable. Lei was clearly disconcerted and he started again, "You will be released," he said with emphasis. "There are some formalities to be completed, but you will go home."

We looked at each other but did not gush or celebrate. We were formal. We thanked the PLA for our release and the militia for their hospitality.

The PLA filed out leaving us with Lei and Wong. Our relief was tempered. We couldn't quite believe there was not a catch. Some militia came in with boxes holding everything that had been confiscated. We were asked to check our belongings to make sure nothing was missing. Mick and Jim were taken down to get *Peta Ann* ready for leaving. While they were gone, Twiggy and I packed up, determined that everything be ready so we could just make one trip to the boat. The boys took an age to return but arrived beaming. "Come on, we're off, they've given us some fuel, helped us clean up and the moon's not bad."

We leapt up, grabbing our belongings. "No, no, not yet, you must wait a while," said Wong and Lei in unison.

Time dragged. It was after midnight. We were alone with a few insomniac villagers. Wong came back in with two battered copies of the *Peking Review* in English and asked us each to read an article. Mick read one about great harvests in the north and after a few paragraphs started changing the words. We had a hard job keeping our faces straight as the harvest of ice cream melted but with the help of a revolutionary agronomist, the crop was saved by being frozen on sticks. It was awfully hard to take over from Mick. The propaganda was dry and I had no wit in me and no courage.

Lei slipped back into the room. He pointed to our kit and told us to get some rest. We didn't want to sleep, we wanted to go. But Lei insisted we lie down on the concrete floor and fetched the old eiderdowns. Reluctantly, we did as we were told. I felt absolutely desperate. Had there been a change of heart? Mick sensed that I was suppressing tears and put his arm around me and I slept.

At dawn we were up, breakfasted and ready to go.

Still nothing happened. I moved to the open window and sat hunched on the sill. Women folk gathered round outside, pulling at my clothing, taking my wrist and examining my watch, my nails, teasing my hair. I smiled at them wanly, drinking in the bay view over the tops of their heads, its beauty constant.

Wong brought in a table tennis set. The locals licked the boys and everyone was laughing. I didn't join the fun. Table tennis came to an end after the boys had dented the ball. Wong shook his head; it was the only one they had. So Mick and Twiggy tried to fix it with a flame. It ballooned out on one side, so they moved the flame to the other.

"Look Wong, a new game – table rugby!"

Wong looked mildly disconcerted as the boys lunged across the table and then bowled each other over on the hard floor. The "rugby'" ball flew across the room. "Foul," shouted Jim and Twiggy yelled "Goal!"

Lei came in to see what the noise was about and I snapped at him fiercely. It was well over twelve hours since our "release". "Why did you say we can go? Why?"

Lei looked sad at my outburst. I knew he didn't want me to be upset. I turned away and stared out the window, but this time I couldn't see anything. I was biting my lip using the discomfort to keep me from bawling my eyes out.

He left and returned a short time later and addressed me directly but in a tone loud enough for everyone to hear.

"After lunch, you go after lunch."

The boys had picked up my mood. "We don't want bloody lunch. If we don't go now we will get lost again and be back. Is that what you want?" snapped Jim.

Lei sighed, shaking his head, "We have instructions to tow you back to international waters so you won't get lost."

An hour later, Lei presented us with an enormous dish of Chao Fan, fried rice cooked in a wok. He was apologetic. He had cooked it himself. Mick wouldn't eat. "How can you guys tell him you weren't hungry and now tuck in?"

After lunch, the PLA filed back in. A Statement had been prepared in English. In it we apologised for straying into Chinese waters, for the inconvenience we had caused and promised never to return. We all signed.

Lei said colloquially, "The PLA wishes you to know, the last few days have been on us." He returned Twiggy's money in grubby small denomination notes that added up to HK$100.

We waited another hour or so and sat perched on our packed bags by the door.

At last, "Come," said Lei, "We go now." His men picked up our things.

Jim was off like a shot. Mick, Twiggy and I linked arms and walked down the pier in the late afternoon sun. We knew what to sing.

"We've been and seen the Wizard, the wonderful Wizard of Oz."

Our departure was sudden in the end and not many saw us go. My pig-tailed minder was waiting in a sampan to ferry us out to *Peta Ann* moored in the bay. Lei stayed on the pier to wave us off.

"Never come back! Tell your friends to be more careful. Goodbye, safe journey."

We farewelled him with affection.

"Take care, Lei. Come and visit us!"

Chapter 28

Twiggy had been right. They had not missed us at Taipo. It was Gerry who raised the alarm. On Monday, he'd hurried down scanning the moorings, expecting to see the familiar shape of the sloop in the bay. Ah Loong was waiting for him. "No boat. Why no boat?" Gerry called Major Hoppe who came down to look for himself and Gerry said the three of them stared out to sea scanning the bay in disbelief. A search was launched that day. It was called off on Wednesday evening by which time it was determined we had either perished or were in China. The emphasis then switched to taking aerial photographs of the Mirs Bay coastline looking for the outline of the yacht.

Major Keith Hoile, Joint Services Public Relations Officer, updated listeners on Radio Hong Kong's Topics program after the 7 pm News on the Wednesday evening:

"We have had two Royal Navy minesweepers, two Royal Air Force Whirlwind helicopters and two Army Air Corp Sioux helicopters searching to south and east of the colony. This produced no results. At approximately 11.20 am today we sent out a Royal Air Force Andover of 52 Squadron which happened to be visiting Kai Tak and we are expecting that to scour an area about 200 miles south of the Colony. And we also had eight Marine Police launches out too. The search was called off when the last helicopter landed this afternoon."

It was about the time the last helicopter landed that we left Lei on the jetty. Wong was waiting on board and directed us down to the cabin where the windows were plastered over with Chinese newspapers. He was insistent on where each of us would sit; Twiggy and I on one side and Jim and Mick on the other. A guard followed us down, sliding the hatch closed above him. He squatted on the steps, his cap with its red star touching the hatch cover. We all sat quietly together, listening intently to the shouting and clamour above. We felt a tug as we started under tow, the militias' voices fading as the junk pulled away. It did not take long before we could feel the chop. "We're out of the bay now," said Twiggy and the guard nodded.

Below decks *Peta Ann* was smelly and stuffy. The motor was ticking over and the fumes that filtered down had no escape and sank to the floor. Our nostrils pinched. The motion of the boat under tow was jerky, the rope tugging and slackening from the bow. We were tired and with nothing else to do, we lay down on the bunks. Twiggy and I topped and tailed on one and Mick stretched out on the other. Jim sat with his head in his hands, lifting his face now and then, his sunburnt ruddiness draining away. Thank God for the small sink that he could stagger too, holding on, feet straddled, retching and spewing all that Chao Fan.

The guard stared ahead stoically, his eyes watering from the hideous confection of fumes in the cramped space. His capitulation came suddenly. He thrust open the hatch and disappeared out to the deck, ushering in a brief but welcome blast of sea air before the hatch slammed behind him.

Normally I would have been gagging too. But now, my reflexes were steeled. Nothing was going to affect me, fumes or motion. My head was clear. We needed to ride this out. With the guard gone, I sat up to lift the newspapers and look out. As my feet went down I saw the slick. Our bilges were full, with oily water seeping across the floor boards. Jim looked up and followed my gaze. It galvanised him. His nausea forgotten, he thrust open the hatch, hollering that we were sinking. Mick overrode the panic in Jim's scream, shouting to Wong not to worry, we'd be right. I didn't know who to believe, but when Wong slammed the hatch closed again, terror grabbed me; I didn't want to drown in that stinking, swilling cabin.

Jim and Mick shouted furiously at each other, but their altercation was short-lived, for the hatch flew open. Wong's face was briefly silhouetted against a square of fading daylight. He yelled something and disappeared. Mick reacted quickest and was out and onto the tiller in one bound. The junk, as it swept past to collect Wong and the last remaining militia, hit *Peta Ann*, just as it had that first night. This time we did not tumble like nine-pins, but the impact ripped off a hand rail with a horrible splintering noise. Wong yelled, "Very sorry!" Then he pointed one way, "Hong Kong," and the other, "Taipo".

We waved and started to belt out a verse of *Auld Lange Syne*. That delighted them and they hung over the gunwales, waving too, laughing, calling farewells as they turned at full tilt back into Chinese waters.

We hugged each other, grins splitting our faces, and immediately got to work. The boys divided their attention between a hapless bilge pump and rigging the sails. Mick told me to make sure the life-jackets were still on board. From each locker I opened sprung rubbish, our rubbish. The boat was stuffed; every single rat-pack wrapping, discarded tin, tube, and scrap of paper was there. The Chinese wanted to make a point. They took nothing from us, not even our dignity – just some sleep – that was all they took.

"Right," said Mick. "Eyes skinned for police launches; they'll be looking for us."

I'd fancifully imagined a reception committee once back in Hong Kong waters, maybe even a formal hand-over. But here we were, rather heavy about the keel, uncertainly bobbing around in the late afternoon in an empty seascape. Hong Kong that way – Taipo that way. Which way?

We settled down to a long haul home, tossing up whether to go round to St Stephen's Bay or to the Hong Kong Yacht Club in the harbour.

Jim, still green gilled, went below to sleep. Mick and Twiggy started to discuss whether we should head for Taipo, which might be closer. Moreover, we didn't have a full tank of diesel. If we chose Taipo, we could still make the Better 'Ole for dinner after we'd phoned Stanley to let them know we were OK.

Twiggy went and checked with Jim. We were all agreed so Mick swung the tiller towards Taipo. The sun was low, ready to drop below the horizon.

The boys thought we would soon see the light for the Taipo Channel.

Jesus Christ, I thought, lost again, they don't have a bloody clue where we are.

"Better get the flares out Twiggy," said Mick. "Just so we have them ready."

Darkness fell, the sea blackening. The yacht's moonlit wash tracing our peripatetic journey was quickly swallowed by the following sea. A comfortable silence fell among the three of us. We sat side by side, each, I suspect, thinking back to the village and the people we had befriended; our brief encounter with a soft cog in a totalitarian regime.

"Look, a red light over there," Twiggy pointed.

"What the hell can that be," questioned Mick. "That's not a channel light?"

"Maybe it's one of those marker buoys in shipping lanes."

"Shall we head for it?"

"Yeah, even if it's a buoy, maybe the best thing would be to tie up to it until the morning."

We headed on in silence, all peering ahead.

"It's not a buoy, it's a ship!" shouted Twiggy.

Mick opened up the engine, thoughts of saving diesel forgotten.

"It's the bloody Navy! Get Jim up!"

The ship was quietly at anchor. There were a couple of seamen hanging over the rails chatting who took no particular notice of our approach. Mick shouted out, "We're the *Peta Ann*, just released from Communist China!"

"You what?" came the laconic response.

"We're the *Peta Ann*, just released!"

This time the name registered and with a whoop of delight, their arms flew up.

"We are on our way to Taipo, but we'd like some more diesel," called Mick, throttling back, the swell with us, pushing us up to the grey ship's hull.

"Come on board first," the sailor yelled, a rope ladder already snaking down the side of the ship. I was first up. Acrophobic and no gymnast, I scaled that ladder like a marine. Strong arms reached down lifting me bodily onto the deck. The boys followed me up. The Captain and his Number Two arrived and two seamen scuttled down the ladder to take over the yacht.

It was sheer unmitigated joy. The Captain's welcome was so warm. I got hugs, the boys had their hands pumped. It was as if we had achieved some great feat, won the Taipo Regatta and more; we were welcomed as heroes. Captain Leyman ushered us into the Wardroom, pouring a toast the first priority. Conversations collided, sentences unfinished, we were all talking at once.

The ship we'd found was a minesweeper, HMS *Hubberston* that had been part of the search. Once the search was abandoned, the ship had anchored awaiting further orders. Tuesday's edition of the *South China Morning Post* lay on the table and there on the front page were the headlines "Yacht Missing with Four on Board."

"You must be famished!" said the Captain. "Get down to the Radio Room, I've let Hong Kong know, but you need to get something off to your families."

We crowded round the Radio Officer, working out what to say.

"Safe and sound." How prosaic, but what else?

Even the boys, so full of quips, were stumped for once to think of something original.

We felt so elated and excited – it wasn't until I looked in the mirror that I realised why the Captain had sent a message along for us to clean up before dinner. I was pale, red-eyed and absolutely filthy, my face streaked with dirt. After a shower I broke out the spare clothes I'd kept for dinner at the Better 'Ole or for meeting Chairman Mao. Clean hair, a hint of lipstick and I was a new woman. Over dinner, officers came in and chatted as we tucked in to eat steak and chips. Jim's sea-sickness had vanished.

We had an invitation to the Petty Officers' Mess for more drinks after dinner. The radio was playing and someone turned it off, saying, "We heard on the radio that the search had been called off before we got it from the bloody Bridge."

We toured the ship, greeted warmly by each crew member, and finally we were taken up to the Bridge.

The Captain turned to me. "Marine Police were all for coming and collecting you right away. But these hills are funny; radio contact is easily lost or breaks up badly. Just happens tonight's one of those nights," and with a big wink he said, "thought you'd prefer a night on board rather than in a police station."

The Captain gave up his cabin for me and the boys disappeared down to the crews' quarters. An orderly had been in to prepare the cabin. The sheets were starched and pristine, my bedraggled belongings neatly arrayed on the bedspread. The loudspeaker had been left on in the cabin and I could hear the communications between the Bridge and the officer who'd joined the two seamen on *Peta Ann*. First they pumped her out and in the early hours, the minesweeper lifted anchor and took the yacht in tow. Despite the long rope and slow pace, the crew on the yacht were having a rough ride. That night, it wasn't the intermittent crackling of the radio conversation but the static crackling of my emotions that kept me awake.

I went up on deck, and the odd seaman who noticed me nodded and smiled. I stood watching *Peta Ann*'s progress tethered behind the *Hubberston*. She was reluctant and yawed as if this was a final insult at the end of a difficult few days for the old lady.

I felt someone behind me and turned to find Twiggy. We smiled but didn't need to talk. We just stood together in the moonlight watching *Peta Ann* for a while until Twiggy put his hand on my shoulder, "Come on, turn in, time for sleep," he said, ever the pragmatist.

I woke when the engines slowed. In the cool grey softening of dawn, the stars receded and familiar hills and a shoreline took shape. HMS *Hubberston* had brought us home. The seamen had already put *Peta Ann* on a buoy in St Stephens Bay below Stanley Fort.

The Captain had instructions to take us to HMS *Tamar*, the naval base in Hong Kong harbour, for a press conference.

Major Hoile, and a very tired looking Major Hoppe, came on board the minesweeper at *Tamar*. Their initial greeting was restrained, with a curt reprimand for the trouble we had caused and a warning to watch what we said at the press conference. The ticking-off made scant dent in our high spirits. A well-timed and poorly stifled chuckle from the *Hubberston*'s Captain made both army officers glance at him. He started to laugh out loud and the other two officers relented and welcomed us properly.

It was brilliant sunshine when we left the *Hubberston* and walked down the gangplank at 9.30 am. I was barefoot; my filthy, smelly sandshoes consigned to a rubbish bin on the *Hubberston*.

A barrage of photographers and TV cameras greeted us. The press reported we looked well and happy. They were right; we were the happiest people alive. We all told truthfully how well we had been treated. I hoped Wong and Lei got to hear that. A couple of US TV stations had private interviews with us and then there was a final round of photographs on board the *Hubberston*. My bare feet were a highlight; photographs appeared in the Chinese press. "Red Chinese stole her shoes," or even better, "Girl loses shoes in swim for freedom."

The boys disappeared with Army Intelligence and Major Hoile drove me home. He turned into MacDonnell Road and parked outside my block. "Well, it'll be bedlam for a couple of days, but today's newspapers wrap tomorrow's fish and chips. Call Greta. Major Hoppe has invited you both to stay up at the Fort for a couple of nights. Take up the offer; it's a good idea to lie low. The Gate Guards at the Fort know to expect you." He put his hand on my arm and added, "You are a very lucky girl. My phone never stopped ringing with calls from your family and friends and Greta certainly wasn't one to give up on you. Count yourself privileged to have such good people in your corner."

I put my key in the lock and our amah flung the door open with a gushing torrent of Cantonese, "Missy Gill" being the only words I could make out. She patted me, took my bag and put it down to pat me again as if making really sure I was no apparition. I stood there; home was so familiar and so strange. A pile of mail was waiting for me but I could not settle to read it.

I called the telephone exchange and started to explain why I wanted an immediate call to UK. They knew who I was and put a line straight through. I got Dad out of bed at 4 am. He said he went from deep sleep to standing in seconds. We all cried and Mum said, "What on earth did you do with your shoes?"

In the days to come I was sometimes to wonder if the mystery of my shoes wouldn't eclipse our whole adventure.

I phoned Greta and cried again.

Major and Mrs Hoppe had one of the original Victorian houses in the Fort grounds. Mrs Hoppe had furnished it with a comfortable chintzy elegance. I felt strangely clumsy and unkempt in the surroundings, but Greta could bridge any gap and we settled down to tea and gin and tonic in rapid succession while I told the story all over again.

A few days later Intelligence asked if I wouldn't mind a word. I knew by that time they had grilled the boys.

"The Chinese were pussy cats compared with our lot!" Twiggy had told me, so I went in with some trepidation. However, I was a civilian, so they had out the tea and biscuits and were exceedingly patient and polite. They showed me charts and asked if I could work out where we were held. I didn't have a bloody clue. Intelligence felt Wong's insistence on seating the older boys on the starboard side when we got on board *Peta Ann*, together with the papered windows and late afternoon release, were significant clues. It suggested we were towed past a Chinese-owned island of strategic importance that they didn't want us to see.

Intelligence marvelled that the Chinese let us go so quickly. Their assessment had been that if the Communists had us, we'd be there for months at the very least. There were about forty Europeans detained in China at that time, including yachtsmen.

The simplest explanation is that after the riots in Hong Kong two years before, the Chinese were building a new accord. Our quick release demonstrated their goodwill. It also avoided a confrontation with the British Government who might have taken a firmer stand on the detainment of British Army personnel than of civilians. But it could equally have gone the other way according to Intelligence and the Chinese could have made tremendous mileage out of our incursion.

The Casualty Section of the War Office had rung Dad's office before word of our disappearance broke. A lady asked to speak to a senior member of staff. It was Martin, one of the other doctors, who had to tell Dad his only daughter was missing at sea, presumed drowned. That evening it was all over the news. Mum and Dad sat in shock with my brother David who was home at the time. Then Greta rang them from Hong Kong. "Blessed Greta" as Dad called her – as close as he could get to canonisation. Greta knew some of the pilots on the search who had told her there was no sign of wreckage. No wreckage confirmed what local sailors thought; we must be in China. Greta was the first person who'd suggested we could be alive; she sounded assured and practical and she was Scots. She gave them hope.

The national and local press gathered outside our Oxfordshire house and were waiting for Dad at his research unit in the city. It was the press, not the War Office, that was first to ring. "Good news, Dr Stevenson. Your daughter has been handed to British authorities." Dad shouted the news to Mum and David. As soon as he put the phone down, it rang again and it went crazy for hours. The BBC rang and had a little more information – we were on a minesweeper – and then called back and said they had recorded the call and could they broadcast it. Dad was so slap happy, he'd have said yes to anything and so his voice went out with subsequent broadcasts much to the amusement of family, friends and colleagues.

"Well, that must be a marvellous Christmas present for you, Dr Stevenson."

"By golly, it is!" said Dad.

Jim Lowth, Paul (Twiggy) Hutchinson, Mick Darcy and Gill on board HMS *Hubberston*, the British Royal Navy minesweeper that took the yacht, Peta Ann, in tow in Mirs Bay after the yacht and crew were released from Communist China. This photo was taken after a night on board the minesweeper, just before the press conference.

Press Conference for the crew of the yacht Peta Ann at HMS *Tamar*, the British Royal Navy's Hong Kong shore base, on 18 December 1969. Seated: Mick Darcy, Gill, Paul (Twiggy) Hutchinson and Jim Lowth. Behind Mike stands Major Keith Hoile, Joint Services Public Relations Officer.

Chapter 29

It was difficult to settle down at first. A plethora of telegrams, cards and letters streamed in and the phone rang constantly. I was back at work the following Monday when I was surprised to discover hand-over notes that had been penned in my absence. Connie told me they had got in a temp, an Australian. I shook my head but let it go.

I found it hard to concentrate on anything anyway and, after a day or two, rather than working through lunch as I often did, I walked out of the office and down to the harbour. I was feeling on top of the world, peaceful, fortunate and content when a strange thing happened. I stepped into another dimension, a vibrant wonderful dimension where even the squalid and unlovely aspects of Hong Kong were beatified, the asphalt I walked on extraordinary, the unlit neon newly radiant. The people were all exquisite, their movements fluid, their clothes yielding in harmony, every colour better than Kodacolor. Although it only lasted a few moments until the newsreel of daily life snapped back, I had experienced something singular and extraordinary.

It defied explanation. And it wasn't just a visual anomaly but a feeling of effortlessness that wasn't selfish or wanton, just fulfilled, complete and sublime. I held the experience – I still do. How could I convey the feeling that I'd been ambushed by a moment's euphoria? I had no idea who to share it with. I didn't want anyone to dismiss my experience because I felt if I'd had to argue for it, there was the risk of tarnishing its brilliance. Perhaps I could have told Takako. She would, I am sure, have deliberated that it was a moment of being present, but I kept quiet. Instead I tried, unsuccessfully, to replicate the encounter and walked the same route for a few days, but I couldn't find the way in again.

I thought back to the faltering words of my father. We had capacities within us for heaven. What was elusive was not paradise itself but rather our ability to keep the connection to it.

In the New Year, Greta asked me to go with her to a party at the Ghurkha Mess in the New Territories. It was a new crowd. It was cold and in the Mess a big log fire was burning. A couple of guys asked Greta and me for a dance. As Greta moved past on the floor, her partner said loudly to my guy, "Hope you know who you're dancing with!"

My dance partner scrutinised my face. "Do I know you?"

"No, we've never met."

"But you are familiar."

"Of course she's familiar," said his friend passing us again. "Her photograph is on your desk!"

Paul was left red-faced. Over a drink he explained that he was in Intelligence and writing a report on our detention. I was intrigued and so when he rang the next week and asked me out to dinner, I accepted. I went out with him a second time and it was then he told me that our two dinners had been sanctioned out of his unit's petty cash. Our escapade was unusual, our navigational ineptitude too shocking to believe, our release too quick, so Intelligence decided it needed to look closer at the participants. The boys were in the clear so that left me. For some reason my entry into Hong Kong had not been recorded and neither had my address been registered. Was I a Communist sympathiser? They established I had come via Russia. Were they missing something in this bizarre little tale? The genuineness of my naivety did not take long to establish – I was no Mata Hari.

Paul asked me out for a *real* dinner. He said this time he would pay the bill, but I was still smarting a little at his deception. I sensed he was looking for a relationship, and anything that smacked of settling down made me cringe. I wanted the freedom for adventure. I declined.

A week or so later Paul turned up at the office. He was just passing and thought he'd ask me to join him for lunch. I was closeted with POD who was in a foul mood and had given instructions that we were not to be disturbed, so Pauline the receptionist went and got Pierre to ask what to do. Eventually Pierre stuck his head in the door and asked POD if he would like lunch.

"Why Pierre? Do I look as if I want lunch?" growled POD.

"No, Sir, you might not but I think Gill would."

After that it became a regular thing that Paul would find himself *just passing*. Often the poor man sat in the Reception area for some time before I was free. I think he knew that if he rang and asked me it was unlikely I would say yes.

Paul told me he enjoyed sitting in Reception watching the message boys rushing out to meet deadlines; ferrying print-blocks, proofs, share scripts and betting slips. The hum was rudely disrupted one day when David stomped through in a shocking temper. The hot meal he'd ordered for lunch had arrived twenty minutes before the start of the firm's official lunch hour and one of the Chinese staff had put it in the fridge as Mrs Church had hated anyone knocking off early. David's melodrama subsided when he saw Paul and he'd broken out some cold beer. Pierre had come out to see what the ruckus was about and joined them. In truth, I think it was probably the office girls, in their gorgeous cheongsams, that held Paul's attention.

I didn't mind lunch. It was a safe meal and I usually chatted to Paul about sailing with Greta.

I suppose it was inevitable that he'd turn up at Stanley Beach one Saturday. He said he realised the only way to see me at weekends was to learn to sail. I rolled my eyes at Greta who laughed and said she'd teach Paul. There were many obstacles when pulling away by sail from Stanley beach; moored boats, sampans and the pier. Like parking a car, once it went wrong, it just went from bad to worse. I'd be mute and hope no-one noticed but Greta never did bungles quietly. Shrieks and screams for help ensured a riveted audience and a feverishly animated crew. She never actually needed rescue for defying all laws of probability; she'd sail clear and soon be happily picking up speed across the bay. We were all watching and marvelled at the view when, on one of these occasions, Paul, a hefty bloke who like all amateur crew bounced around, split his pants. Greta's reaction was a hearty slap across his bare backside as she roared with laughter and admonished him for such a sight. A heavier crew is a decided advantage in bad weather so Greta took Paul out even on rough and windy days. Inevitably he'd return wounded and joked he might be a *Green Beret*, but crewing for Greta was an equally hazardous occupation.

The boys were wary of Paul, an officer, joining us. They didn't want to let anyone else into our circle, especially an officer.

It was about a month later when Paul revealed his own discomfort. He said it had never occurred to him that Greta and I sailed with other ranks. On the first day he came down to the beach at Stanley and discovered us with a bunch of privates and lance-corporals, he had little alternative but to join in.

"I'm telling you now because I'm so impressed. I want you to know that I think your friends are just such a great bunch of guys. It's been a good lesson for me."

I was dismayed and irritated by the entrenched attitudes of the armed service, so it was good to talk to Paul and get my views off my chest.

The snobbery of young officers could be suffocating. They failed to recognise that only opportunity separated them from the men they commanded. It was not intellect or capacity but education and privilege that elevated them. "Lions led by donkeys" – a phrase that described the British infantry of World War I – made perfect sense to me.

Paul, to his great credit, gained the respect of the boys by being modest and unassuming.

That I sailed with *other ranks* came up again when I met young officers off the *Hubberston*. I kept bumping into them socially and as soon as they felt just a little at ease with me, they would question why I chose to sail at Stanley instead of at clubs that officers frequented. Each time words failed me. I wanted to quip with something cutting: "Funny you should ask. *Other ranks* are so much more cosmopolitan, they don't mind who they sail with; even officers at a pinch."

I felt protective of the army boys. The wonderful camaraderie that I enjoyed at the Sailing Club was intensified after the experience in China, and for me it was the officers who had to prove their worth and I was hypercritical of them.

After the trip to China, I decided I didn't want to share a room any more. I wanted some space and time to myself and as I felt more comfortable down at the beach with the boys than anywhere else, I choose to move over to Stanley which was on the far side of the island from the CBD. I was sad to leave Takako but I would still see her because she lived so near Greta. I found a tiny place on the corner of a big house. It had its own entrance and with the door open, I looked out to a scrubby hillside and could hear waves landing on a curve of sand far below.

The apartment was a white and spotless canvas for me to colour. I staggered to the local tailor, my arms brimming with fabrics of turquoise, gold, emerald green and rust and in a day he'd squared them away to curtains, a bedspread and cushions galore. A vegetable seller in Stanley market was happy to part with a huge green-glass carboy that was languishing near his stall. The bottle neck took a lamp fitting – all I had to do was to buy a big lampshade. I bought cane chairs and an antique Chinese blackwood coffee table.

Each morning I drove along the coast, up over the prettiest road on the island, then through the Gap. Sprawled below me was the city, the harbour and Kowloon. I'd take a deep breath and then the Mini and I would plunge down, rejoining the thrusting traffic and frenetic activity.

It was easier to entertain, too, when I didn't have other flatmates to fit in with. I repaid hospitality and told my China story over and over again, inviting Leon and Takako, Pierre and his girlfriend Liz, a niece of Freddie Zimmern, David and Anne, and the Gibsons down to my tiny but perfect home. I saw just as much of Greta. She'd sleep over with me at weekends and if we were partying late together in the city, I'd sleep at hers.

Gerry said he'd had a letter from John who queried why no-one had been looking out for me. "I agree," I said jokingly. "Why didn't you come to China with us?"

"Because I was looking out for you. None of them had enough experience for that sail," said Gerry. "I spoke to Major Hoppe but he wouldn't listen – even when I told him Mick didn't have charts. I spoke to Norman too." Norman was an experienced sailor who'd been coaching the boys, and he had agreed with Gerry. "I thought if I pulled out you'd get the message, but you were so mad keen to go you wouldn't listen ..."

The army held a brief enquiry into the Peta Ann incident. The blame was laid squarely on my late arrival which had delayed the departure by an hour. The adverse weather report which had been ignored, the lack of marine charts and absence of navigational skill were not regarded as material. I was fuming. Norman laughed out loud and Major Hoppe said it didn't really matter whose fault it was as no harm came of it.

Norman encouraged Major Hoppe to improve the army club by starting weekend races and persuaded him to put up money for new sails. Hoppe agreed only if the boys contributed to the cost. Once the boys had helped pay for their own sails, they argued that each boat was assigned to them personally and drew up rules about how the boats were to be treated by casual sailors. Soon the rather sad-looking dinghies shed their uniform red paint and were resplendent in a rainbow of colours with bright blue sails. The boys took great pride in renovating their boats, completely revitalising the club.

At Easter, we wanted to compete in a friendly competition with the sailing club at Little Sai Wan. Our club had made a poor showing previously and Major Hoppe was hesitant to let us compete again. It was a question of time and money for no return. But Norman spoke up. He said it wasn't surprising Little Sai Wan had beaten us because their club was so much better resourced. He said that the new sails and his coaching had made a difference to our chances.

We took the first seven places.

"How could you guys have improved so much?" asked the Commodore at Little Sai Wan.

Major Hoppe was tickled pink.

The next sailing event at Little Sai Wan several months later was part of Hong Kong's Festival of Sport.

It was gusty and spitting rain when I arrived early, excited at the prospect of the day ahead. We were to sail an Olympic course for the first time. Little Sai Wan was a high security area and it took time to be cleared at the gate. (It later transpired that while the gate guards assiduously checked all visitors and patrolled the perimeters, Chinese cleaners were taking secrets out of the waste-paper bins and flogging them.) The club was in a lovely old house with a veranda overlooking a wide lawn that sloped down to the beach. I found Major Hoppe already there, sitting on a cane chair surveying the wind-blown spume racing across grey seas. "What do you think of the weather?" he said.

"Great," I thoughtlessly replied, "Exciting sailing coming up!"

He looked gloomily back out to sea and said, "Gill, sometimes I think you are quite mad."

An hour or so later, we were all on the beach rigging the boats in driving rain and I was beginning to feel it wasn't so great after all. I was petrified. Eventually the Royal Hong Kong Yacht Club crash boat came into sight bouncing over the waves. The officials were in wet suits, sleek in the rain like black seals. Through a loud-hailer they shouted, "Racing cancelled. Too rough – survival weather." I heaved a sigh of relief. We started packing up, soaked and cold. I noticed the Commodore of the Little Sai Wan club talking to Major Hoppe and suddenly, Hoppe was striding up, shouting, "Little Sai Wan say the beating they took from us at Easter deserves a return match."

Norman, our coach, shook his head, "No way. It's too dangerous and the best we'll get is damaged boats with no time to fix them before next weekend's races."

Hoppe said, "I've said I'll race and anyone who doesn't is a chicken."

Norman looked stunned. "I don't need to prove my endurance skills," he said and walked off.

Now it was time for me to think Hoppe was quite mad.

The boys had no choice. Gerry tried to dissuade me from crewing but

I insisted. Tide, wind and currents were fighting each other, rain and sea spray indistinguishable. Getting the dinghies off the shore was a challenge, the language as foul as the weather; the wind tore at the sails, everything was shaking and snapping and as soon as we were afloat, the dinghy quivered like a thoroughbred and took off like one too. My job was to balance the boat and in those conditions, Gerry and I were at a disadvantage as we were too light. I had to constantly come inboard as I could not breathe for the surf that lashed my face. Other times, the bow plunged into green waters and I gasped, questioning if it would ever come up. In the end, we made it and came second to Twiggy. Mick was third and Hoppe fifth. Only one Little Sai Wan boat made it and came fourth. The other five capsized and two ended up on the rocks on the wrong side of the high security perimeter fence with a long walk home. It was a rout again.

Gerry and I only spoke to each other twice during the entire race; that's how we were when we were racing together. It took teamwork to get the dinghies beached. We had to stand chest-deep in the water waiting for help to walk each boat in through the breakers. The cold was penetrating and the wind biting. Once we were all in though, the idiot Major was forgiven, and joined us as we whooped and danced the drowned rat victory tango on the sodden strand.

Little Sai Wan didn't invite us to their Junk Island Race that season. The Major inquired and their Club Secretary blushed and admitted, "Well it's an individual trophy and we like to keep it within the club; Stanley didn't used to be much competition."

POD had returned to Hong Kong just after Chinese New Year. He'd seen Edward in the UK. Edward had recovered well from his breakdown and wanted to get back to Hong Kong. Instead POD found him a job in London, "I told him that returning immediately to the temptations of the flesh in Hong Kong wasn't a good idea." A few days later, David announced he could not settle. The side-line idea he and POD had had of creating a sound and vision studio had not taken off and David wanted to go back to Africa.

Pierre was upset when he learned that Edward was not returning and David was leaving. When we took on a new trainee Chinese account manager, Harry, Pierre detested him on first sight. Harry was twenty-six and had a Degree in Economics from Glasgow University. His father spoke no English and ran a tiny factory in Kowloon. Why Pierre felt so threatened I never knew and I was sad as I liked them both. They were the same age yet very different; Harry was good fun. He was astute, with local knowledge, connections and the confidence of a top-rate education, while Pierre was a colonial boy, a kind-hearted and creative soul. Pierre was a Director and Harry an intern. Harry didn't give Pierre the respect that Pierre thought was his due and POD didn't care a damn because he knew Harry was smart and represented the future. POD was disillusioned that none of the young expatriate men he had recruited had matched expectations and told me he should have recruited more Harrys in the first place.

A month after POD got back it was St Patrick's Day, March 17. He was churlish because I didn't present him with a green rosette and irritated that I didn't get round to finding him a bit of green ribbon for his button-hole until mid-afternoon.

His mood did not improve when he asked me for his medals which he would wear that night to the St Patrick's Ball at the Hilton Hotel. I said I'd never had them. He didn't believe me but rooted in his drawer and came out with his second set. However, there was a problem because the second set had an emblem missing and the ribbons were dirty. I dashed out to a bespoke tailor's shop which had someone who knew about medals. He was Portuguese and a delightful man. Together we poured over reference books looking up illustrations of the medals. He shook his head. He could replace the ribbons but would have to order in a Battle of Britain Bar.

"We don't have time for that," I agonised.

"Wait," he said and disappeared. He came back brushing dust off an old wooden box and tipped out onto the table hundreds and hundreds of bars, rosettes, fiddly bits and bobs. We scratched around, trying to find a match to the photograph in the book. We shattered the dignified air of the establishment with our delight when we found it.

The Ball Room at the Hilton was resplendent in green, huge paper shamrocks, wreaths of green balloons and heraldic shields. POD was determined that everyone was going to enjoy themselves at the Ball.

As soon as I arrived with Pierre and his girlfriend Liz, POD detached one of the paper shamrocks and insisted that I wear it. He was not happy until I had pushed the stalk into the waistband of my long evening skirt and wrapped the leaves around my torso. POD had ordered champagne and several silver ice buckets were wheeled up to our table. Then he ordered whiskey and cocktails. Pierre and I secured a bottle of Smirnoff vodka and said that we might just stick to that between us. POD rolled off innumerable toasts before anyone else had smoothed their linen napkins for Murphy's Chicken and O'Brien's potatoes. When the Green Soufflé arrived, POD drowned it in John Jamieson Irish Whiskey. In between courses, POD circled the ball room, bursting green balloons on the candles and from other tables he gathered pretty girls and brought them over to us, introducing them with names, jobs and identities he thought suited them. He was oblivious to their discomfort.

Pierre noticed that Mrs Church was also there, fighting fit, and eyeing POD, so he went and whispered in POD's ear. POD proclaimed loudly, "Oh Gawd, Betty's here and I'll have to kiss her – give me some stiff ones first."

Mrs Church glared at Pierre and disappeared back to her own table.

It was a good band and the dance floor was packed. Before the ball I was worried that despite the efforts of my parents, I'd never mastered ballroom dancing, but by the time POD asked me for the first dance, we were ready to improvise and had enormous fun. He claimed exhaustion and Pierre stepped up and we slayed the *Gay Gordons*.

I left with Pierre and Liz before the end. I heard that POD and David finished up in the fountain outside the hotel where David told his wife's best friend he thought her a "Silly Moo". Anne refused to have David home so he lurched back to POD's hotel room.

Chapter 30

The St Patrick's Ball was POD's swan song. A final letting go. When he'd recovered from an almighty hangover, he took himself off to Macau for the weekend with a new book he'd acquired on gambling. He told me he was going to test a system to beat the roulette wheel. He arrived back on Monday, pockets bursting with money, saying the system was good but he'd got a better one and told me I was having lunch with him.

"Gill, I'm pulling out. I was going to put a consortium together with the boys but I hesitated because I doubted I'd ever recover my investment with them running the business, and now, with David and Edward gone, the decision is made for me, so I'm selling, but it's going to take time. I'll have to stick around in Hong Kong for another six months or so. As long as I'm here I don't think Betty will start up another business but I need to keep her at bay. I've decided to spend that time writing a book."

The book was to be a manual for beating the wheel at roulette.

"Clear the decks, cancel your weekends and make ready for the longest roulette game ever played. We are going to play for a month non-stop."

"I don't know anything about roulette, Sir," I protested weakly.

"Time you learnt then."

The rest of lunch POD devoted to recounting his own gambling history. He didn't often talk about his past so I was surprised. When little more than a youth, he'd seen a man blow his brains out on the steps of the casino at Monte Carlo. Although he made light of it, the experience bloodied him; the empty crumpled corpse and red trickle down the steps, vivid after more than forty years past. What game had the power to drive a man to that?

POD called the waiter for another round of cocktails. He wanted to enthuse me. "The wheel's a work of art, beautiful to look at; the chips sensual to feel; the whole ceremony aristocratic," he said, pausing to light another cigarette. He drew in deeply and then continued. "There's the low hum of the spin, the clatter of the ivory ball as it hesitates, wriggles, bounces and drops." He expanded on the ambiance of casinos. "The solid luxury of casinos, the comfortable chairs … caviar … Dom Pérignon champagne …" He revelled being the centre of attention when he was winning and likened it to business. "The strong get stronger and the weak get weaker," he said, bringing out another PODism.

"In any case," he added, "roulette helps keep a man elegantly young." His conviction that on the whole he beat the wheel was a lacuna in POD's perceptions. He didn't hang onto failure, he simply erased it. He focused on his successes. "No matter how you play the game of roulette or life, you will have both success and failure. Don't let failure live on or it will impact on your future successes," he cautioned me. "I look for ways to make luck my servant and not my master," he said, but it was only bad luck that he relegated to servitude.

Apart from horse racing, gambling was prohibited in Hong Kong, but in Macau, casinos had been operating for over a hundred years.

I had been over to the Portuguese colony, first with Takako and then in boat parties with Mickey Mok. Macau wasn't a member of the International Monetary Fund and in the post-war era had become the black-market centre of the world's gold trade. For the savvy, Hong Kong's adherence to economic rules and Macau's informal approach made a perfect combination.

Macau had a habit of surviving – just. Its down-at-heel subservience belied its real usefulness through centuries of trade. It was a place where everyone had always looked the other way.

Macau even survived when Hong Kong fell during World War II. The Macanese could hear the conflict across the water. Their windows rattled and local wireless stations one by one went off the air and gave way to, "cackling Nips". The fall was so sudden that the wife and daughter of Macau's British Consul, who were over in Hong Kong doing their Christmas shopping, ended up interned there. The British and hangers-on in Macau maintained a stiff upper lip with stoicism and humour. The Consulate announced that sherry would be served to visitors from 11 am daily for the duration of conflict, and a round of cocktail parties and festivities ensured that the Japanese and Macanese would have no doubt that the British might be down on their luck but were certainly not out. It so happened that the British and Japanese Consulate buildings were side by side. Soon, the Union Jack flying on the Consulate's flagpole was the only one left between India and Australia, and beside it flew the white flag of Japan with its red circle, symbol of the land of the rising sun.

With a garrison of only five hundred men, Macau was indefensible and there was little argument as to who really held control. Japanese *advisers* forced the Portuguese Governor to walk a sloppy tightrope of neutrality. Japanese agents simply assassinated troublesome citizens and did their best to trap escapees from Hong Kong who moved through Macao cautiously with the help of allied sympathisers into Japanese-occupied China and beyond to freedom.

Gambling continued in Macau as did restaurants, opium dens and brothels. Business boomed with gangsters, wealthy refugees and the Japanese, all of whom were in high spirits at finding themselves in a safe enclave while the world scrapped around them.

Macau did see action near the end of the war, when American airmen said they mistook it for Japanese-occupied territory and emptied a bomb-load on its oil storage tanks. The US paid compensation after the war; it had been worth the "error" to starve the Japanese war effort of fuel.

POD decided that we would get Harry and Miriam to join the permanent roulette team with back-up from a couple of the other girls in the office, and that we would train in Macau.

When POD started our training, I could see he was in his element and thoroughly enjoying himself. He extolled the virtues of roulette systems; patterns, dominance, pre-sets, dozens, columns and sleepers, Neighbours, the Paroli, Martingale, Alembert and the Cuban. I had always resisted absorbing what I thought was futile information as my school marks for Latin testified, so while my time with POD had greatly increased my mental confidence, lessons in the art of roulette left me cold. It was gruelling work. Miriam, the glamourous graduate who'd joined the APB to run our PR, was soon side-lined from the team after POD glanced at her at 4 am and decided she did not look cheerful and needed worming. Harry and I made an excellent team. We had struck up an easy rapport. We laughed at the same things. We'd kick each other under the table or nudge an elbow and whisper, "Look cheerful." POD tried employing temps to sit the night through at the tables, but they were decidedly not cheerful and much of the burden to keep on playing fell directly on him.

The idea that Harry and I would be bitten by the gambling bug and tempted to use our own money was a very real concern for the boss. We assured him, tremendous fun though it was of course, we would steel ourselves against addiction. Privately, both of us doubted if we'd ever want to set foot in a casino again.

Over the next six weeks, I divided my time between Macau, Stanley and the office in that order. When I drove over to Stanley from the ferry, I'd scan the bay for the red-and-white striped sail of the *Sailfish*, a second-hand sailing dinghy – dubbed the "ironing board of the ocean" – that Greta and I had bought together.

Greta figured out that with the mainsheet between her toes and a shoulder against the tiller, she could stretch out and read a magazine or paperback. Reading matter had to be expendable as the boys were incorrigible and would swoop in with the ski boat, showering her with sea spray or deliberately orchestrating a capsize.

If I couldn't find her, I had a key and could just go to Greta's flat. She'd come home from teaching or an evening out and find me asleep in her bed or in her bath and we'd sit and exchange news. Then she'd fashion impromptu meals, give me solace and share laughter. I tended to focus on the melodrama of the moment. Greta was the painter of bigger pictures. She pulled me through with her into places where hypocrisy and histrionics had no part to play.

I also took time out to have lunch with Takako. Leon had given her a ring. She was radiant and in love, but still not completely relaxed. Takako wanted the deal sealed so she could direct her bustling energy towards organising her new life. "He gets cold feet very easily," she said. Takako might have studied philosophy, but at heart she was a sorceress. The spells she needed were complex. Leon was an enigma; a scholar one moment, a philosopher the next.

Each visit to Hong Kong was brief and I'd drag my heels going down to the wharf to board the hydrofoil back to Macau. Yet, despite my lack of enthusiasm for roulette, once I was aboard and speeding over the sea again, I was fine and never tired of the view out the window. We flew past islands of all shapes and sizes and rocked the prawn fishers, junks that sprouted long poles from all angles that made them look even more ungainly than their fishing fleet counterparts.

Because we kept such irregular and unsociable hours, the afternoons sometimes dragged. I explored on my own or with Harry and POD. POD loved to seek out the simplest restaurants with bare wooden floorboards and get Harry to order, "Whatever the locals eat," before dispatching him to find some Mateus Rosé. Just for me, Harry kindly removed the heads of pigeons, assured me the lumpy mess of pottage presented one day was only potato soup, grinned across the table when I tackled webbed duck's feet and celebrated with me when the worst that came was steamed crabs, a local delicacy with which I was at least familiar.

There were roulette sessions where we had fun and made money and others where I thought the clock had stopped until dawn delivered me from hell. POD was good on the theory and psychology of gambling but in practice he was a disaster. He couldn't stop if he was winning and wouldn't stop if he was losing. He supervised us and when we hit a streak of bum luck, his impatience overrode the systems he'd allocated. "Bet on your birthday Gill, and Harry, you must have a lucky number." We didn't mind; anything to break the monotony.

POD told Harry and I to look out for interesting people. "The book will be too dry without some characters to populate the pages." While Harry and I enjoyed ourselves, conjuring up exotic lives for the gamblers, we knew we were out of our depth. POD was a master raconteur, his stories richly laced with anecdotes drawn from conversations with the quirky, rich and famous. Aged twenty-one, POD had taken a sea voyage. His fellow passengers included Bernard Shaw, Charlie Chaplin, Barbara Hutton and the Aga Khan. Hobnobbing with the famous set a pattern he would continue all his life. His direction certainly made us more aware of our fellow gamblers. This was not the casino of movie sets. Many of the gamblers were not wealthy and looked far from happy. There were some who made us feel ill by venting their wealth wantonly ... And each night we hoped we wouldn't hear a gunshot out on the steps.

At first, the management was most cooperative. POD was a big gambler with important friends. The second week, POD and I had long interesting conversations. I asked him about his early days in China as a cigarette salesman. His mentor had been Carl Crow from Missouri, a famous old China hand. Crow had started the first Western-style advertising agency in China and had taught POD how to get the maximum bang for his buck when advertising Rothmans cigarettes. POD told me what had drawn him to China was the opportunity to pitch to the biggest cigarette market in the world. The way he said it reminded me of Father Walsh and his countless potential souls to save. But POD was not forthcoming about his time in China or his early life, so I asked instead about his war decorations. He dismissed bravery. "It depends on the day, which side of bed you get out of, as to whether you are a deserter or get decorated." Snap decisions were taken under enormous pressure, on the spur of the moment. His, he said, could have gone either way. "You don't consider the consequences, Gill." He looked weary. "Impetuous youth is fun at the time, but there are consequences."

By week three, POD was clearly exhausted. Although he was adamant that we were breaking even, I was not so sure. I was the cash courier. It was curiouser and curiouser; like the White Rabbit, the funds disappeared into a hole. Paranoia joined the tea party. POD felt he was being watched. Casino management was certainly watching and clearly alarmed. They suggested Mr O'Neil-Dunne return to Hong Kong. They proposed that each day they would send him records of the spins from the roulette wheel of Table 14, our gaming table. In hindsight, the proposition showed genuine concern for a VIP gambler unravelling before their eyes, but at the time, in POD's head, it was proof that they needed him out of the way.

When I arrived back in Macau one afternoon I had difficulty in getting POD to open the hotel room door. His suite was dark, the curtains drawn and POD was wild-eyed and dishevelled, most unlike his debonair self.

He snatched me in the door and asked if I had been followed.

"The manager's avoiding me. The croupiers won't look me in the eye," he said by way of explanation.

"Why, what's happened, Sir?" I asked, alarmed.

"I think the casino is laundering money; in fact I have evidence. I've been watching the gamblers at the other tables; they keep them away from Table 14."

He paused to listen with his ear to the door and his finger to his lips.

"Come," and he tiptoed to the bathroom and turned on a tap to mask our voices.

He whispered, "The next time you see me, it may be my corpse floating in the Pearl River. I don't think they'll wait much longer."

"Well let's get out of here ..." I urged.

"It's too late, they won't let me leave. You have to go straight back to Hong Kong. They won't realise you're here yet. I've got a letter – it's got to be kept safe – to be opened in the event of my death."

"What?"

"Shush. Here, put this inside your jacket and go straight to the ferry terminal. Stagger your route, don't get a taxi until you are well away from the hotel. Stay near other people, be alert."

He opened the hotel room door, looked up and down the corridor and beckoned me out. It had none of the glamour of a James Bond movie and everything outside POD's room was disappointingly normal. Nevertheless, his fear was contagious and I fled back to Greta, far away from Table 14 and a deranged POD.

I went to see Freddie, POD's lawyer, delivered the letter for his safekeeping and told him I'd suggested a doctor, but POD was convinced they'd be agents-of-death in the pay of the casino. Freddie caught the ferry over, put the poor man to bed with a whisky and a sleeping draught and told Harry to keep him there for at least forty-eight hours before he went back to the tables. When I went over to Macau mid-week, POD was a new man.

All he had needed was some uninterrupted sleep. I thought back to China. It had only taken a couple of nights before I started to feel I was coming apart at the seams.

Although the marathon of 31 days' play took its toll on all of us, once back in Hong Kong we were elated. I typed the first draft of POD's book non-stop until he disappeared home to his beloved Brantwych and arranged publication of *Roulette for the Millions*. He had the game listed by the Guinness Book of Records as the world's longest roulette game ever played, with 20,000 consecutive spins.

Chapter 31

Gerry did up his *Enterprise*. Bit by bit he stripped layer after layer of old paint off the hull. I joined him in the evenings and we continued working long after the other boys had gone back up to the Fort. We'd be oblivious to the night creeping in until Ah Loong came and hung an oil lamp. A magnet for moths, their bodies beat a soft drum against the crescendo of cicadas. The lamp brought shadows that kept us company long into the night.

The paint tin said "Dolphin Gold". Gerry chose it; a deep daring yellow. He also had badges made in black shiny Bakelite. His surname "Knight" inspired his choice of image: the silhouette of a Roman knight's battle helmet, plumed on the crest, jutting cheek plates meeting a pointed visor. No-one else had badges on their boats; the ferocity of the shiny black Gladiator against the burnished gold of the hull said it all. He meant to make a mark.

We both bought yellow sailing anoraks and toyed with the idea of buying a monkey that would live with me when it wasn't up the mast sailing with us. We spent a day in Kowloon talking to private sellers and owners and returned chastened. Romantic as the idea had seemed of a monkey swinging from our burgee, the reality would have been a bad-tempered primate biting our bums on a capsize.

Gerry waited until I came down after work before the maiden sail of the finished dinghy. The sun had lost its glare and St Stephen's Beach was suffused in warm maize and saffron. The loveliness caught me out and I stood staring out at the bay with my heart in my mouth. My reverie was broken by Cliff, who hailed me from the jetty. "What are you gawking at? Have you forgotten you've booked a ski?"

Gerry waved and shouted, "Get Cliff to leave you in the water after your ski and I'll pick you." When he sailed out, he turned the dinghy into the wind so he could help me in over the transom because my arms were tired and weak from skiing. We laughed as I slithered into the dinghy, ungainly and water-logged. The wind was light so we headed out of the bay looking for more. There we met a whole fleet of motorised wooden junks heading back to Aberdeen Harbour from their fishing grounds. They were stretched out in lines on either side as far as the eye could see, winding through islands sprinkled like green droplets on an azure weave. They had to give way to sail. Our light bark scudded between the junks pounding on every side. They avoided us, the crews laughing, shouting and pointing at our red burgee. Chinese sailors love red; it pleases the dragon that lives in the clouds who, when angry, sends typhoons and storms.

The sun was setting gold and red in the west yet when we turned and tacked for home, the sky before us was delicate lavender holed by a pale round moon. The stars came to life one by one as we did one reach across the bay and then another. At last we turned for the shore. As we got close in, I spotted someone sitting on the pier. It was Twiggy; when he stood up, his silhouette was unmistakable.

The local police had phoned the Fort's guardhouse to say there was a little boat sailing in the moonlight that might require assistance. The guardhouse called Twiggy.

"What colour is the hull?"

"It's a yellow boat."

"Don't worry about it, they'll be OK." Nonetheless, Twiggy came down just to be sure.

As we packed up, a sprinkle of fresh rain showered us and when it passed, there in the moonlight, a dim rainbow arced the bay – the pot of gold by the end of the pier. "Blow me ... that's just where I was sitting," said Twiggy.

The first occasion Gerry had to really trial the yellow dinghy was at the Spring Regatta at Gordon Hard, a dot on the western shore of the New Territories. It was a well-appointed army sailing club with a wide concrete slipway.

I'd been there before for an earlier regatta and that time we had all booked into a small hotel, simple but absolutely spotless, though we learnt the hard way to check their toilets for frogs before sitting. (I have travelled far and wide since my stay at the Dragon Inn and gained a wider than normal experience of ablutions, but those loo-leaping frogs have never been beaten for surprise value.)

This time Greta and I had a party to go to on the Friday night of the Regatta weekend. It was at Sham Shui Po, halfway to Gordon Hard, so after work we donned our cocktail dresses and finery, loaded Greta's car and took off for the Intelligence Officers' Mess. We arrived late, in high spirits. Paul was waiting for us and we were danced and dined out at a local restaurant before going back to the mess for coffee. We left about 2.30 am and, out of sight, we pulled to the side of the road to change into jeans and ditch our high-heels. We'd decided beforehand we would just sleep in the car for the rest of that night. We didn't want to be too isolated and yet we didn't want to be too prominent either. We agreed we would pull in quietly to a layby. The very idea of Greta and I being able to do anything quietly was an anathema. The interior light switch broke off with the light on, the mosquito coils went out and we lost the matches. Greta insisted we both went to sleep with a can of hairspray in our hands. It was her patent protection against rogues and rascals. She assured me that one blast and they would flee. For backup she had her diving knife stuck into the dashboard.

When Greta finally got to sleep in the front, I was wide awake in the back, the noise of the traffic unsettling me. I climbed over, pushed her comatose body off the gear stick and drove to the carpark of the Castle

Peak Hotel. A gardener woke me at sun-up when he touched my foot which was stretched out the car window. I roused Greta cautiously. She was notoriously cantankerous on waking, and I wanted to avoid a blast of the hair spray.

Once down at the beach, we borrowed a dinghy and rowed slowly out to *Peta Ann*. The sun was just caressing the still water that seemed to stretch and breathe in the dawn. The oars stirred the silky sea, lifting to shed limpid droplets that coiled on the surface. Cliff and Gerry had spent the night on board and we woke them when we arrived alongside. They insisted we sit in a sunny spot while they cooked us a hearty army breakfast.

Stanley won the Army Inter-Unit race, the Cup that 50-Command always won. Gerry and I won the Novices and we did well in every race. By the end of the day Stanley was no longer a laughing stock.

When I was standing at the notice board that afternoon checking where we were in the series, I overheard someone say, "Who the hell is the dark guy who helms that bright yellow boat? Where did he spring from?"

"He's called Gerry Knight."

"Never heard of him. He's bloody good."

Paul came to the regatta on the Sunday and joined in helping to lift boats up the beach, and when that was all done he went to speak to Major Hoppe. "Are you pleased with the results, Sir?"

"Good God yes, I've phoned the Colonel and the Sergeant Major's sent his compliments … says he can't believe we actually won something!"

At the end of the weekend, Paul drove Greta's car back so that she and I could sail home with the boys on the *Peta Ann*. It was dark when we left with several hours of sailing ahead. Our thermos flasks had been topped up with black coffee and we had a bottle of Scotch. *Peta Ann* took wings, straining every muscle like Pegasus racing through the sea and spray under a full moon. It was so thrilling that we all protested when we reached Stanley Bay. We just wanted to sail on into the night.

I was on cloud nine at the office and subjected POD to a blow-by-blow account of the rounding of every buoy. POD insisted on using our win as an excuse for taking David, Pierre, Harry and me out to celebrate. He took us to Kowloon-side to a restaurant recommended by Han Suyin. Walking through the night markets, POD saw socks. "Where in the world could you buy socks for that price?" He bought everyone a pair and when the others insisted they didn't need socks and refused his gifts, I took them, not wanting to spoil his fun. The Chinese hawkers, seeing POD haggling, offered socks at lower and lower prices until I had my arms full and had to beg him to stop.

The next day at the office, POD was still fixated on socks and said he had a new business idea. He wanted to set up a company that sourced incentive goods for European clients. I was trying to suggest that not everyone would see socks as so highly prized when word came that Mrs Church was in hospital and seriously ill.

POD said he would go immediately.

"That might finish her off altogether, Sir," I said with acid on my tongue, surprised at his concern.

"Gill, old friendships are difficult things and it's all water under the bridge."

He came back and said it had been worth his while going. She was quite lucid and they had talked about old times and parted friends.

"Really? Friends?" I said.

"I doubt I will ever see her again, Gill. Actually, I never want to see her again, so let it be like that. We parted friends. It's important not to burn your bridges. A lesson to learn, Gill."

He never saw her again and neither did I, but she recovered and left hospital. Boadicea reigned at Castle Salamat for another decade. She became a JP and involved herself in various committees and good works. She saw us all off as she had predicted.

I regret that I did not ever say goodbye to Mrs Church. I owed her that. At worst, she would have risen from her sickbed to admonish me or else thrown her alarm clock at my head. But then again, she might have welcomed me warmly, asked after my parents, patted my hand and told me I was her bright little Scottish girl from England. I like to think that our last goodbye would have been like that.

Not long after the Gordon Hard Regatta, Paul rang one evening with a question. "Gill, do I come down to the beach to see you or to sail?"

"Oh, to sail," I replied without hesitation.

I told Greta about Paul asking me such a funny question. Greta laughed with tears in her eyes and hugged me. "He is so cute and cuddly, Gill. He's like a bear and I so want you to meet someone special. Why can't you like him? Don't you realise how much he likes you?"

"He's OK but he's just not my type."

I told Greta about working late one night and finding Paul skulking in a doorway. I was surprised to see him. I thought perhaps he wanted to take me to dinner. I said, "Hi, Paul, what …"

But he cut me short and hissed, "I'm working, please go."

Later, he told me he was out on surveillance and if I ever met him in the street I was not to acknowledge him unless he acknowledged me first.

"Greta, I couldn't handle that. God knows what he gets up to – he's a commando. Can't talk about his job and probably goes round bumping people off before breakfast."

A month or so later, Paul got a transfer to the UK. He came to Greta's flat to say goodbye to us with a pretty nurse on his arm. They were engaged. It was a genuinely happy farewell. When the door shut behind them, Greta said, "I still think he's cute and I still wish you'd liked him."

Soon after I heard Paul had ditched the nurse, went home and married the girl next door whom he'd known since school and, I hope, lived happily ever after.

Paul's departure was the end of another thread from the *Peta Ann*'s short sojourn in China. The incident still sat with me. I'd find myself wondering about Wong. Where was Lei stationed? How were my pig-tailed minders? Each time I felt a smile on my lips and a stir of affection. They were good people trying to do the right thing in shifting circumstances. I shook my head – that was Leon's voice still resonating.

It was the height of the Cultural Revolution and every doomsayer about Communism in China had their vindication. The voices of forbearance, like Han Suyin, finally quietened in light of reports coming out of China of wilful persecution and torture of "class enemies." We had indeed been fortunate to have washed up at such a tiny village far from Red Guards and power struggles, a spot where Mao's ideology was put into practice as a code of good conduct. We had laughed and made fun of our captors without any idea of the tensions, paybacks and contradictory directives that were sweeping China.

I was driving home one afternoon when I heard on the car radio that James Walsh, the last foreign missionary to be expelled from China, had crossed the border into Hong Kong at Lo Wu Bridge. There was no warning of Walsh's release and British soldiers on the Hong Kong side were startled to observe a gaunt white-haired old man dressed in crumpled khaki trousers and a faded checked shirt walking alone across the bridge towards them. The newsreader went on to say Walsh was the first foreign national to be expelled since the crew of the *Peta Ann* had been released, just as unexpectedly, six months before.

Father Walsh, the author of the slim red volume *The Man on Joss Stick Alley*, was free after twelve years' imprisonment on trumped-up charges of spying for the Vatican and the USA. He'd found the monotony of years of solitary confinement hard to bear, but insisted he held no bitterness towards those who had condemned him.

Pundits later saw Father Walsh's release as the first important signal from Beijing that China was ready for a thawing of relations with the West – the start of a rapprochement that would lead to President Nixon's historic visit to China two years later. I like to think the thaw started earlier, when they released the *Peta Ann*.

Chapter 32

The Round Lamma Water Ski Race was an annual event. Gerry was competing for the army using a new speedboat the Club had recently acquired. When I asked Major Hoppe if I could compete using the old boat, he was surprised but agreed, probably because I'd caught him off-guard and he could not think of a reasonable excuse to deny me. "OK, but you'll have to pay your own entrance fee," he said sternly. I nodded and asked if that meant I could get free skiing for training like Gerry. He laughed and said only if I did the training at the same time as Gerry, using double ropes from the ski boat. All the training had to be after hours so it didn't interfere with the ski-boat generating revenue for the Club, so that suited me. We needed stamina for the distance. It wasn't so much about finesse as the ability to hang on doggedly and stay upright even in stormy weather.

When we wanted to train in rough seas, it was difficult to find a volunteer boat crew. It was much more punishing being in the boat, which easily became airborne and thumped across the waves than being on skis. But on evenings when the water was as smooth as silk and the sky like honey, there was no shortage of crews to take us on long trips round the islands. Once on such a night, a huge cloud erupted and we knew that a freak storm was building fast so we took shelter at Repulse Bay. We sat at a beach café until the storm passed as suddenly as it had come. We waited until the sea levelled out to a smooth swell, watching spellbound as the sun set behind the storm clouds, lacing the edges of the leaden thunderheads in molten gold. We debated what to do as we had no navigation lights and two police launches were anchored in the bay. Eventually we decided to explain our predicament. The police were all having dinner and the coxswain paused his chopsticks and said, "Your boat very fast … we never see you, go – don't stop." We took off round the point, but did pause out of sight to drop Gerry and me into the water to ski. Distant fissures of lightning flickered and flared as the dark closed around us and we followed the white wake home.

On a hot day when there was very little wind, Gerry and I took the dinghy out but it was hopeless sailing weather. We were becalmed and idly debated with each other whether or not to go for a swim. I settled it impulsively by somersaulting backwards into the water and caught Gerry unawares. When I surfaced I was startled to see the dinghy slowly capsizing. He fell backwards, hitting the sea, shouting and laughing. Once the dinghy was righted, we bailed out, throwing as much water at each other as into the sea, splashing a haze of fleeting diamonds into the sunshine.

I don't see how I could have avoided falling in love with Gerry. We spent every spare moment together sailing, swimming, or skiing. We worked on the boat; we climbed up the cliffs near Stanley on ropes that the fishermen left dangling; we hired bicycles and flew screaming down the steep hillsides in Pokfulam. We were so comfortable with each other, an ease that never bored us. He was gentle, with long limbs, beautiful brown skin, white teeth, a shock of black hair that the army had not tamed, and eyes that melted my soul.

We were putting things away in the boatshed when he took me in his arms and kissed me. At first I thought this can't be, but it was.

We didn't broadcast the change, but it swept through our little community like wildfire. A friend of Greta's saw me holding hands with Gerry in the speedboat, and the boys at the beach had already sensed it. No one was happy for us. I didn't care.

Greta wasted no time in speaking plainly as she saw it. It was Gerry who would get hurt and he didn't deserve that. I would leave Hong Kong and Gerry. She said I had stepped over a line in the sand which was there for a reason. She didn't need to elaborate. I knew the British social codes – constraints that spelt constancy and stability. I didn't see myself as a rebel, but nor could I understand why anyone needed such rules.

In any case, I had no answers. I was quite helpless. And happy.

POD was adamant he didn't want me to stay on at the APB even though in the negotiations the prospective new owners were quick to offer me a position. I'd been thinking about what I would do after Hong Kong. Casual conversations with visitors passing through had fuelled my desire to travel; the Khyber Pass and Afghanistan, Africa from coast to cape, the Panama Canal, South America. It was Africa that kept coming up. It wasn't just that David had filled my head with his Africana; my Dad had been in the RAMC in West Africa during the war. He'd photographed Arab forts from the air and flown the length and breadth of the continent in a sea plane, landing on Lake Naivasha and Lake Nyasa. His descriptions had fired my imagination. Greta, too, was an African romantic for she had taught in Zambia before Hong Kong. She spoke wistfully of the smell of the earth when it rained, of sunsets on the Copper Belt, and of camping in the bush under the stars.

I'd chatted with POD about the future in a casual way and knew that he thought I should focus on my career path rather than on my romantic notions of nomadic wandering.

It was mid-morning when POD called me into his office and said he had something for me. He handed me an envelope. It was a letter from his friend Anton Rupert inviting me to join his personal staff in Johannesburg. I was aghast.

"Well, you said you wanted to go to Africa," said POD.

"But not to *South Africa*!" I stammered. "Not to apartheid".

"Gill, Anton is South Africa's premier industrialist. He doesn't want apartheid either. This is a stunning opportunity. He is fabulously wealthy, a philanthropist, a brilliant man. He is going to employ you not just as a minion, but in his personal office. He will mentor you."

I looked at dear POD. It seemed he didn't know me. I felt deflated. With a flash of clarity, I saw that he'd regarded my dissenting moments as bumps on a learning curve that left me on his original trajectory.

I could see he was exasperated and incredulous that I was not delighted. "You will hobnob with billionaires, meet top society, get all the travel you can possibly imagine – first class at that. I have given a glowing report of you and he will take you under his wing."

I went to the Board Room, poured two gin and tonics and knocked on David's door.

"Jesus," he said. "Anton Rupert."

I waited but David was not forthcoming. I pushed him and he just said, "Christ Gill, I don't know. It's an incredible opportunity. POD thinks the world of you. You'd never look back." And then he started to tell me about the cricket scores.

I drove home and took myself off to the beach below my house, sat on a rock and hurled my confusion at the waves, bawling into the wind. How could life have become so complicated all at once?

Of course, South Africa with its apartheid regime was out of the question. It was embarrassing enough in Hong Kong where echoes of past bigotry still scarred the present.

Yet POD's offer had unleashed fresh introspection. What did I want? I wanted to travel. But when POD emphasised "first-class travel", I knew I didn't want that. In Hong Kong, I'd frequented world-class hotels. The private boats and banquets, clubs and boxes at the races had become commonplace. I'd felt wealth's seduction and seen, with its adoption, an indefensible assumption of power. In my head I likened sidling up to wealth like membership of an exclusive club with a whole set of rules that I found stultifying.

I recognised that POD was trying to do his very best by me, but had I followed his previous advice and stuck with people of *my own kind*, I'd have still been on bacon and eggs at the Helena May and would have missed out on watching Takako take a whole afternoon to prepare sukiyaki. Now POD was trying to get me to stick with people of *his own kind*.

I also knew that if I refused the offer, I'd not risk failure. Anton Rupert could never write to POD and say, "Can't see what you saw in the girl," echoing Mrs Church's words: "Can't see what Mrs Wentworth saw in the girl." Just as Miss Moller, my old headmistress, couldn't see what was in the girl at all.

And what about Gerry? What were the consequences of unintentionally falling in love? Gerry had fixed goals – to get out of the army and settle down near his family. My goal was only to emulate the journey of the last traveller I'd spoken too. The posts were too far apart.

The evening sun mellowed, the waves were less insistent, and the tide was going out. The ocean had listened long enough.

I walked for a while along the beach picking up handfuls of warm sand that trickled through my fingers like the reckoning of an hourglass. I thought about Jimmy. His future had been laid out before him from the moment he was born. He would follow his father into the family firm. He'd enjoyed his travels but there was, he said, no place like home. Nevertheless, there was a line in his correspondence from India. He wrote, "I have seen so many interesting types of people and wonderful buildings that my mind at present is all of a muddle although I have no doubt that it will all come back to my memory and be a lasting pleasure and education in the years to come."

And while I hadn't shaken off all my insecurities, I did know there was something in *the girl* – and that, more importantly, there was something in everybody. I wasn't ready for a career, or for a relationship, or for *home*.

I just wanted more travel. And if that was a path that promised … *lasting pleasure and education* … how could I resist?

I stood up and looked at the scrubby hillside, its gullies now in deep shadow. It would be harder to scramble up than it had been to slide down, I thought.

Finally, POD sold the APB. Pierre would stay on but POD remained adamant he wanted me out. "I don't like the new owners. I don't even want you here during the handover and I want you on your way before I go."

When I told Irene I was leaving APB and Hong Kong, a big tear rolled down her lovely serious face and she said, "Never, you're never coming back?"

We had weathered so many dramas together and had both cultivated oily wings. She, too, had chosen POD over Mrs Church and suffered the wrath of the tiger-dragon-fire.

Irene told Connie before I had time to, but Connie knew. Her ears were always open. And when word spread round the office, I went and saw Lao so he would not have to make the awkward journey through the office. Mr Yi, the Art Director, the one who hated David, had championed Lao and encouraged others in the office to accept him for what he was; a good artist.

Back at my desk, I spent the rest of the day with a box of tissues close at hand. POD came in and I think he wanted to cry too. Instead, he broke the mood of gloom and said, "Gill, do you remember the name of the feng shui guys we had in the office when we did the renovations?"

"I can look them up, Sir. Did you want them off your Christmas list?"

"No, I thought I'd recommend them to the new lot."

Irene and Connie looked puzzled but POD and I laughed out loud.

The yellow boat saw Gerry and me together at Gordon Hard once more before I left. It was the Colony Championships which gave the whole show an extra spit and polish. It was held the weekend David and Anne Dunlop left for Africa. I took them to the airport and drove on feeling bereft and sad until, at Gordon Hard, I was immediately swept into all the activity.

When we were not sailing, Gerry didn't want to sit around with the others in the easy companionship we had all enjoyed together. He wanted to spend the last few days alone with me. So at dawn and in the late afternoon, we took off exploring. We watched the sun set over Deep Bay. The border between Hong Kong and mainland China ran through the bay. It wasn't marked so the oyster beds of the fishermen at Lau Fau Shan, the small fishing village on the Hong Kong side, merged with the Chinese beds that stretched from the other shore. Disputes about where the beds separated fuelled an unease that suited the waterline, jagged with shells.

We were out again at dawn at Lok Ma Chau where Hong Kong's land border with China was well marked. Bright green wetlands spawned duck ponds stretching out on both sides of the boundary. The fresh morning air vibrated with the quacks and squeaks of innumerable squads of fluffy ducklings obediently marching after their mothers.

From the border, we set off to look at some walled and moated villages. The hinterland was once wild and the villages fortified themselves not only against the pirates but to ward off rival clans and tigers. Few tourists visited these neglects of time and certainly not at dawn or dusk. In one village, Gerry and I dodged pigs, buffalo and poultry to squeeze our way through high-walled laneways. We disturbed old crones dressed in black who gathered crowing for money. They pulled and tugged at my pockets. Their cackle disturbed a man who appeared in a doorway. He was terribly deformed, his utterances so ghastly that I grabbed Gerry's arm. He flew past us leaping with a crabbed gait, bowling the women ahead of him who disappeared into laneways and melted through walls, shrieking with laughter. He turned, beckoning with his twisted arm to show us a decrepit notice board which asked for donations for the upkeep of the village and had a slit for money. We thanked him but I had already given away all my coins, so I went back to the car to see if I could find some spare change, and when I returned Gerry and he were old friends, engrossed in animated conversation without a word in common.

We'd glimpsed old China where, sadly, only the old and infirm were left. The young had long gone – scattered through America and Europe. We stopped in a village on the way back to Gordon Hard for breakfast. Gerry went off to look for bananas on which he survived day in and day out. I sat watching the street scene watching me.

The wind picked up strongly at the end of the second day. "Giving us a send-off," said Gerry. It was our last race together. I was exhausted and Gerry could hardly hold the main sheet by the end of it. It wasn't just the physical exertion. It was the end of a youthful epoch.

Gerry took the Gladiator badges off the bows when we got back to

Stanley. He would find another crew but it would never be quite the same, so he decided we should have one each. He gave me the Starboard and he took the Port.

I didn't sell my scuba gear. Instead I asked Greta to look after it and said that I would be back some day. I just could not bring myself to believe that our time together would ever end.

I confounded POD by politely refusing Anton Rupert's offer.

And Gerry? I walked away. Love was not enough, even a love so tender and so exquisite. By its very nature, it was fragile. I knew I had to set us both free because I would have demanded too much of Gerry and he would not have demanded enough of me. So young and so in love, yet I had a knowing we had separate paths to walk. The shy, determined and graceful Gerry was not yet forged, not complete and neither was I. We both needed more time to find out who we were.

I wrote from Africa two years later and told Gerry I had met my soulmate. He wrote and quoted Tennyson, "Tis better to have loved and lost than never to have loved at all." He also called after I was married to congratulate Mike and wish us both well.

I never spoke to anyone about how I'd felt about Gerry. I never wanted to have to explain or justify our love. After we parted, he had his own unassuming and imperishable space in my heart. He shared an August birthday with my mother, so when I remembered her each year, I would smile, sending him happiness and light wherever he was.

I kept the Gladiator. I have it still, brittle and split. When I look at it I shiver with delight, remembering the mercurial ride Gerry and I took from being the worst sailors in the worst boat to among the top in our class in the Colony. I'm back too to softer days when we sailed at sunset side by side with ancient fishing junks from Red China. Huge and weathered, caulked and battered softwood hulls, seasoned with Tung oil, pushed through the South China Sea on square-rigged sails laced with battens; a patina of russet weathered by winds, bled by storms, bleached by sun, patched by men and achingly beautiful.

Two gorgeous years. It was out of this world.

Chapter 33

The untying of the green ribbon on my Hong Kong letters in 2012 brought a cavalcade of characters back to life and begged the question, where were they now? I had moved so much that most people had given up accommodating me in their address books by the time Facebook and the internet came along. Only Greta never left my life. We've met up on three continents and whenever we do, the years roll away. It's not all nostalgia, for she is Greta. Time is still not to be wasted and so there is always a fresh dimension to explore. After she left Hong Kong, she took a contract in Kuwait and from there she wrote enthusiastically of trips into the wilderness of the Arabian Desert, camping and birdwatching. Then she married Peter, an old beau. They'd returned to live in Hong Kong until Peter retired shortly after the hand-over in 1997. After travelling for a year or so, they settled in Norwich with a boat on the Norfolk broads within striking distance of Covent Garden so that Greta could indulge her passion for the opera.

I knew that Takako and Leon had married and stayed on in Hong Kong and that after 1997 they too had moved and were in Australia. I found their daughter, who is a doctor, through Facebook. It was extraordinary to catch up with Takako and Leon in Melbourne in 2015. Leon, now in his nineties, still writing, still working, and Takako as modest and cheerful as ever, still with a laugh that rippled around the walls of their sitting room.

Leon talked about Han Suyin. I reminded him that when I first met him in 1968 he didn't want to talk about her. Leon laughed softly and said it was a story that was never going to go away. He got to his feet and pulled a book from the shelves that lined the room; a 2013 commemorative edition of *And the Rain My Drink*, the book that Han Suyin wrote in Malaya that effectively ended Leon's career in the Police. Leon had written the Foreword and read it out loud to me.

We sat and talked about Han Suyin and Takako. Both of them, for different reasons, hadn't fitted easily into the lands of their birth. Han Suyin, restless with life and men, kept searching for a homeland. Takako embraced wherever she landed as her present land with acceptance and curiosity. She had kept her man. Takako's a very unusual woman, I said.

"I like that," said Leon, "Yes, Takako is a very unusual woman."

I knew, of course, that David, the artist and Sound and Vision Manager of the APB, who had dried my tears many times, had returned to his beloved Africa. In the early 1980s, I was living with my family in Zimbabwe. My kids sailed on Lake McIlwaine near Harare and one day I overheard a conversation that mentioned the local National Park warden, a guy named David Dunlop. The following weekend, I drove into the park's workshop area, passing a large notice which said, "ONLY AUTHORISED VEHICLES".

That evening, I laughed out loud as I listened to my daughter, Kim, telling the tale.

"Daddy, we were down at Lake Mac and a very angry man with a hairy red face put his head right in the car window and shouted at Mummy, "Can't you read?" Mummy just laughed and the man opened the door and pulled Mummy right out of the car and we thought he was eating her and we all started to cry."

"What was that all about?" asked Mike.

"I found David from Hong Kong. He's a game warden at the lake. He didn't recognise me at first but then I guess he was very pleased to see me. He and Anne have asked us down to visit."

We left Zimbabwe and my letters to David went unanswered. I now know that David eventually went back to the UK and ran a guest house in Norfolk, not far from Greta. But I was too slow. David died a few years before I untied my letters and started my quest.

I'd last seen POD at the wedding of his daughter Sally to her Playboy croupier in 1972, the same year I was married. He wrote to me years later to say he found great peace in being at home in his garden and accepted it was worth paying the tax man instead of trying to avoid him in exile. Forty years on I found a tribute to POD on the internet by his son Timothy dated 1 December 2008. It read:

> I would be remiss if I did not recognize that today would have been my father's 100th Birthday.
>
> A visionary, some called him a genius. Reviled by some, admired by many, never one to leave you feeling ambivalent, in the more than 20 years since his death, there have been few days when I have not been eternally grateful for his guidance and even some of his bloody mindedness.
>
> As the old joke goes, "When I was 15," said the young man, "I thought my father was an idiot ... When I was 25, I was amazed at how much he had learned in ten years."
>
> So here's to my father, POD. Fighter, inventor, gambler, storyteller, man.

I got in touch with Timothy and for a few months he would message me, always in the sky, travelling for his business. Eventually, he came down to earth in Sydney and we met as he came off the ferry at Milson's Point. I had no trouble recognising him. He looked so like his father. POD, I learned, had gone back to his love, teaching marketing to young men in industry. He died in 1988, too soon to know that the speech he made in 1958 – acknowledging that smoking could cause cancer – would be back in the news in the new millennium, used as evidence by lawyers in a landmark tobacco class action in the Montreal Tobacco trials that started in 2012 and finished almost three years later.

POD's wife, Biddy, lived on at Brantwych until she was a very old lady. His daughter's marriage to the Playboy Club croupier had, predictably, run a short course and sadly both she and her oldest brother Jarlath, had died from cancer. Timothy and Pik-Yuk remained close and both live in America.

Timothy recalled a letter he had received as a schoolboy from POD in Hong Kong. At the bottom it said, "Dictated by Patrick O'Neil-Dunne and signed in his absence by Miss Gill Stevenson, Secretary." Timothy responded by dictating a letter to a school friend who at the bottom wrote a similar signature line. POD was incensed at Timothy's impudence and phoned his head-master who rather sided with his pupil.

Pierre married his girlfriend Liz, Freddie Zimmern's niece, and stayed on in Hong Kong. I had imagined that he lived a charmed life, but his marriage had not lasted. And Timothy told me that he too was dead, leaving behind two sons on the brink of adult life. I was very sad. I would have loved to have talked to him again and had hoped that he might have been able to put me in touch with my Chinese friends from the APB whom I had not had any success in tracing. In 2017, on holiday with my daughter Dale, we caught up with Andre, Pierre's son. It was strange to be back at the Hong Kong Country Club where I'd so often lunched with Mickey Mok. Extraordinary as it sounds to say it now, even in the 1960s membership of several Hong Kong social clubs was restricted to Europeans. The Country Club was created to overcome that and provide an up-market club where all were welcomed equally. I smiled to myself as I watched Andre and Dale chatting together. I hoped Pierre could time-travel and know it was so. I also thought how much of the present flows from the past.

Timothy was able to connect me to Mrs Church's great-granddaughter and she forwarded me Mrs Church's obituary. The obituary revealed that Betty was not born in 1906, the year of the dreadful typhoon but in 1902, a year not noted for stormy weather. But the 1906 story suited her and shaved a few years off her age. She had died in 1979 aged 77 and enjoyed a daily glass of champagne right to the end. Wendy Barnes, a good friend of Mrs Church's on secondment to Hong Kong Radio from the BBC, did a series on famous people called *A Time to Remember*. She interviewed Mrs Church when I was there and the recording is archived and accessible. It was quite extraordinary to hear her gravelly voice taking me back to her living room and the stories she told me so long ago.

I recalled a conversation I'd had with Mrs Church about a run-in she had had with the Hong Kong Club. Women were not allowed to be members but could enjoy the club's privileges through their husband's membership. "I made a tremendous fuss and in the end they made me their first woman member, even before they got round to changing the regulations."

I wondered if that was true and it also occurred to me that if the old visitors' books at the Hong Kong Club still existed, they would reveal who had entertained my grandfather, Jimmy, in 1908.

I wrote to the Club but the Secretary replied that, sadly, when the majestic building was demolished in 1981 and the Club moved to prosaic quarters in an office block, out went all the records, generations of visitors' books and memorabilia, so they could not help me.

Now I am older than Mrs Church was when we first met. I can understand how irritating I must have been at times. She insisted on having a secretary from the old country who could share her love of Empire-past, but my generation was renouncing Empire without a backward glance. Had it not been for the intervention of POD I would only have lasted a few months.

Recently I came across the Julia Cameron's description of a "crazy-maker" in her book *The Artist's Way*. Charismatic, inventive, persuasive and destructive ... Cameron also has a theory that crazy-makers attract fixers. I realised a little ruefully that Mrs Church was the first, but not the last, crazy-maker I'd been drawn to and failed to "fix" during my working life. I give her the accolade of being the most entertaining of them all. I also know it was a privilege to share the stage, however briefly, with such an extraordinary character.

I had no idea where any of my sailing gang had gone. I thought fondly of them all from time to time, but I'd lost touch with every one, even Gerry.

When I was going through my letters, I found an old newspaper cutting from 1973. That was the year after Mike and I were married.

We were in England driving north up the M1 when we pulled off for a break. Lying on the café table was a newspaper with a headline about a young Army corporal who was being recommended for a bravery award for stopping a double-suicide attempt. I was startled to realise that the hero of the story was John, my old friend from Hong Kong, who'd taught me to water-ski. A few days later I phoned his Regiment, the Dukes, and got him on the phone. He brushed off the whole incident. "The police were there when I went to the pub and when I came out they were still talking to these blokes. I thought, everyone wants to go home, I'll just go up to the roof and get them, so I did."

Forty years on it seemed like a good idea to start with the Regiment again. The officer I eventually got hold of was polite. He couldn't help because of privacy issues but suggested I might find a lead in the Regimental magazine. And there, in a back issue, I found a photo of an army sailing event. I didn't recognise anyone in the picture but a name sprung off the page. A line in italics said that John Cockshot wasn't present as he had already left for the Azores.

It didn't take long to find a photo of John on the internet, owner of a diving business in Ponta Delgada on Sao Miguel, the largest island in the Portuguese archipelago. I stared at the image, big nose, all beard, a man's body, I wasn't sure. Was it him? Where was the boy I knew? I put a photo of the young John next to the old and held my hand below the eyes. And then I saw it. He was so stunned to get my email, he questioned me, thought it was some hoax, until he accepted I was real, and then the questions flew back and forward. Twiggy was in Alicante in Spain. He'd lost touch with Gerry who'd left the army as soon as he could, unlike John and Twiggy who'd stayed on.

Eighteen months later I arrived in Portugal en route to the Azores. I strolled in Lisbon's wide elegant squares and admired the baroque facades of muted pinks, blues and palest citrus laced with a filigree of black iron balconies. I then walked the city behind the grandeur; simple houses fronted onto cobbled lanes with washing strung across the street, a little the worse for wear, stonework crumbling. It made so much sense that the men who grew up here and sailed the oceans to faraway Cathay built the same simple houses in Macau out of habit and nostalgia.

The next day I was at the airport early to catch my flight to Sao Miquel, the largest of Azores nine islands. The islands sit out in the Atlantic a third of the way across to the Americas from Portugal. It is the furthest landfall you can make from Sydney. I had come half way round the world to meet up with John again.

The isolation of Sao Miquel is palpable; it is an isle bared, adrift. Low and green, denying its volcanic heritage, it flattens itself to avoid the weather which is capricious, dashing unhindered over the Atlantic. To the trade winds unfurling and hurling across the sea, the islands are of little consequence. From John's house I could see weather queuing up, blue sky and billowing white clouds gracing the day while grey overcast waited to scud in. Mare's tails on one side and pea soup on another.

All in all it was the perfect place for John, who had come to Sao Miquel to set up a diving company. He blew in and the locals embraced him as one of their own. The homeless boy had found a home. Jane, his wife, was swept up with him. She was a musician and taught the oboe at the Conservatorio Regional de Ponta Delgada School of Music. Their friends were an eclectic mix of nationalities.

When John changed his surname to that of his house parents in the boys' home where he grew up, his initials became JC. Before long, he just about lost rank and number; everyone knew who JC was. He'd steered his career where he wanted. He and Twiggy had worked together in Joint Services Army Adventurous Training; Twiggy concentrated on sailing and John on diving.

John looked after his adopted parents until they both died and when he settled in Sao Miquel, he continued doing good turns big and small; helping improve diving in the Azores, campaigning for a decompression chamber, and occasionally called in for rescue operations. He ran the BBQ at fetes, decorated churches with flowers on saint's days and gave lifts. "If you get lost walking home, just ask for John's house," he said, "They'll know."

John's damaged leg had not stopped him hauling air tanks and scuba equipment on and off slippery rocks for tens of years, but now it was painful and he had stopped diving. He was resilient still; bearded, a briar wood pipe clutched permanently in his teeth and a well-pronounced limp. A pickled old mariner home from the sea, yet I could see the boy so clearly.

Sitting on their veranda, John flamed the local sausages in brandy and Jane poured us cucumber gin. The sky was settling for the night, and so were we, when John said, "Do you remember you asked your father to visit me in hospital?"

"Of course I do," I said.

"That's right," said John. "Well, when I got back to the UK, the doctors didn't like the look of my leg at all; told me I'd never be able to walk properly and I'd be invalided out of the army." He broke off, saying he had to flame the sausages again, and stood for a moment with his back to me. When he sat down he said, "It was tough leaving Hong Kong, but it got worse when they told me that. Like I was all finished up. Then your Dad came to visit me and he said, 'You're young, you're fit and you've got the right attitude. Your bones will heal and there's nothing to stop you from a full recovery. You're going to be OK, your leg is going to be OK, so don't let anyone tell you otherwise.'"

Shivers ran up and down my spine. "Oh God, John, Dad was entirely in research by that time. I wonder if he knew anything about your broken bones."

"Well, he spoke with a lot of conviction and I believed him, since he was your Dad 'n all and, Gill, I never looked back."

We all raised our glasses to Dad. There wasn't a dry eye in the little house on the hill.

As the plane lifted off from Ponta Delgada, I felt content, so happy to see John but a little sad too. John had lost touch with Gerry. Gerry had gone a bit weird, he said, taken up with religion. I looked out over the patchwork quilt of green fields fast disappearing. Did I want to find him again if he was weird and religious? Maybe I'd prefer to have him as I remembered.

Next stop was Alicante. Twiggy and his wife Patsy lived only a few stops away by train. When I stepped onto the platform, I recognised Twiggy immediately, no longer quite so skinny, but the same spiky hair, the same wide smile. He took my backpack – manners the same too.

We drove to their villa, and settled into the comfortable chairs on their patio. Twiggy selected a cold white Albarino wine and filled our glasses.

He said, "No one's called me Twiggy for a very long time."

Patsy chipped in. "Just after we were married some of his friends came to the door and asked for Twiggy. I'd never heard him called that so I said he didn't live in the house anymore. Caused a bit of a stir."

We talked about the beach, sailing, our lives, but as a compass seeks north, our conversation turned to our foray into China.

"The funniest thing I remember," Twiggy said, "was on the Monday afternoon, when Lei came in and stated quite calmly, "You British soldiers.""

"No way, we're civilians, friends, sailors," we replied.

"Then Wong came in holding a transistor radio and tuned the crackling to Radio Hong Kong. It was news time:

'An intensive air and sea search has failed to find any trace of the missing yacht *Peta Ann* and its crew of four. The four, three British soldiers and a European girl, were reported missing while on a sailing trip from Stanley to Taipo'."

Twiggy broke into a wide smile. "Lei and Wong couldn't keep their faces straight and we all fell about laughing."

Twiggy looked at me and we laughed all over again. "I made two promises after that trip and I kept them both," Twiggy said. "I would write home to my parents every week and I would learn to bloody navigate."

Twiggy became a sailing instructor at the Joint Services Adventurous Sail Training Centre in Gosport near Portsmouth in the south of England and skippered large sailing yachts all over the world.

Patsy said, "When we were first married and used to go over to Twiggy's parents, he got away with blue murder. Never had to do the washing up or lift a finger. I got cross about it, but his Mum said 'Oh, we nearly lost him that time. We thought he was gone you know.' And that was it; she spoilt him rotten for the rest of her life!"

Twiggy poured another glass of wine. "I think we should drink a toast to our parents wherever they are now." So we did and we all sat quietly, the sun warm on our shoulders alone for a few moments with our own thoughts.

Nine months later, back in Sydney, in August 2014, it was Mum's birthday, her 101st had she still been alive. I took a walk round the block and sent her love and gratitude. My mother, living in Hampshire, had died suddenly and unexpectedly in 1989. It was the wrong way round – my Dad had been the invalid. Each time I'd said goodbye to him, he'd hugged me for the last time. Mum was much more cavalier. Resilient and strong, it hadn't occurred to me that she could die. I was heartbroken; irrationally angry that she had left me so suddenly. It was many years before I let go of the anguish that there was no good-bye, no last message. And with that, Mum returned to form a timeless, comforting liaison. Now simple things catch my eye – a flower, a painting, or some composition – and suddenly, I'm not alone. She is there to surprise and delight me and captivates the moment. I cannot summon her company at will or make more of it, but each visit leaves me comforted.

Gerry's birthday fell on the same day as my mother's, so all through the years I had remembered him with affection. But that year, as I did, I got a smack in the head with such force I stood stock still. Gerry hadn't gone religious; he'd gone back to his beginnings – spiritual, not religious, sane, not weird.

Back home, I emailed John. "I need to track Gerry down, where did you last hear of him?" He emailed, "Last heard of in Northern Ireland." It took about three minutes before I turned up a website, just the back of a person sitting meditating. He lived in Ballymoney. Within a few hours we were speaking on Skype.

Our life's journeys had taken us in such different directions and yet we had ended up on the same page. If he was weird, so was I. We found we shared the common ground; spiritual beliefs, green politics and alternative ideas on medicine and healing. There was no awkward getting to know each other again – the years disappeared. He'd carried on sailing and he and his wife had won trophies all over Ireland. Gerry had been Commodore of the Coleraine Sailing Club. He had three sons and taken pride in teaching them to sail too. Now Gerry lived on his own and taught meditation all over Ulster.

"I never doubted we would speak again, Gill. I've tried to track you down but couldn't remember your married name. I never gave up hope that somehow I'd find you again."

We spoke of sailing together at Stanley. "Oh Gill, if I'd known then what I know about sailing now, we'd have been Hong Kong champions … in fact, I think we might have conquered the world!"

I was overjoyed to talk with Gerry again and I felt content. We would have compromised each other, not complemented one another. I knew I would have interfered with Gerry's journey on his spiritual path. Initially I would have been too conservative and tried to hold him back. He might have given it away to please me. Separately we had reached the same place albeit we had walked such different paths.

There was one more loose end I wanted to tie up. I could not remember the name of the Captain in command of HMS *Hubberston,* the minesweeper that had taken me and my friends on board in Mirs Bay in 1969. I contacted the Mine Warfare Association in UK. They answered that it had been Lt Cdr Christopher "Kit" Layman and told me he'd gone on to a distinguished naval career and retired as a Rear Admiral. I'd never forgotten the wonderful warmth and humour of the man. I looked him up on the internet and found he was also the Gentleman Usher of the Green Rod. A ceremonial office of the Order of the Thistle, a Scottish order of chivalry founded by King James VII of Scotland. I still didn't have an address for him and I contacted Raymond, a friend in Scotland who I knew would know about these things. He replied, "Write to your Admiral care-of St James's Palace. That usually works." Raymond's response did make me wonder how many other people went looking for lost Admirals; nevertheless, it did work. After some weeks a most delightful email arrived from Kit

Layman. He indeed remembered the China incident. Serendipitously, he lived a stone's throw from my brother Robert in the South of England. In 2018, we met again. Kit had out his scrap books with press cuttings of the incident. I realised he was only ten years older that I was; from my perspective at the time, I'd put him in a middle-aged bracket. I reminded him about the loss of radio contact that gave us a night's rest. He laughed, "You could do that kind of thing in Hong Kong in those days!"

When I got home, I hunted for the Gladiator, the badge from the dingy I had sailed with Gerry. It was split into pieces, brittle with age. I pieced it back together, put it with the bundle of letters and tied them all together with the narrow green ribbon. Dad had been quite right. When he had insisted I cherish the letters, he'd added, "I think there's a book in there."

Select Bibliography

Cameron, Julia. *The Artist's Way.* TarcherPerigee, 1992.

Han, Suyin. *A Many-Splendoured Thing.* Jonathan Cape, 1952.

Han, Suyin. *And the Rain My Drink.* Jonathan Cape, 1956.

Han, Suyin. *The Crippled Tree.* Jonathan Cape, 1965.

Luard, Tim. *Escape from Hong Kong: Admiral Chan Chak's Christmas Day Dash, 1941.* Hong Kong University Press, 2012.

Mason, Richard. *The World of Suzie Wong.* William Collins, 1957.

Sacklyn, Raymonde. *A Short History of the Hong Kong Stock Exchange.* John Wiley & Sons, 2016.

Walsh, Fr. James Edward. *The Man on Joss Stick Alley.* Longmans, Green & Co, 1947.

Acknowledgements

At first writing a memoir is a lonely journey; travelling solo back in time. Then the fun starts as the past elbows up to join the present.

It has been a delight to track down old friends to ask for their recollections and comments. My thanks go particularly to Greta Solly, Takako and Leon Comber for their input. And of course, to all my sailing friends, Gerry Knight, John Cockshot, Paul (Twiggy) Hutchison and Len Hepworth. I failed to trace Mick Darcy and Jim Lowth who shared the China adventure. Perhaps my book will find them for me.

I am grateful for input from Patrick O'Neil-Dunne's son, Timothy, who filled in the blanks on what had happened to members of his family and put me in touch with Pierre's son, Andre Morkel, and Mrs Church's great-granddaughter, Charlotte Davison.

I dearly wish I could find Irene Chan, Connie Tang, Harry and Lao from the Advertising and Publicity Bureau's staff in Hong Kong. I keep hoping.

I wish too that I could identify the village where we were held on mainland China in 1969. While I am sure it is now under tons of concrete, I am disappointed that to this day, I don't know exactly where we were held.

Ann McDonald, who revealed on Boxing Day that our paths had crossed so long ago, did not live to see the publication of the book. However, it meant a great deal to me that during her last illness in hospital she read the manuscript.

My thanks go to friends Darren Cronian and Rosamund Burton for their practical advice on promotion and to Kathleen Sumpter for her last minute proofreading.

Revisiting Hong Kong in 2017 with my daughter Dale would not have been nearly as much fun without Roy Chan to guide us to places where I could recapture the vibrant colour and sense of enterprise I so remembered

For the confidence to write, I thank my husband and soulmate, Mike, who led me on many new adventures after Hong Kong and always told me that I could do whatever I put my mind to. And for encouragement, I thank my daughters, Kim, Dale, Emily and Alice who discussed amongst themselves how they should give me space to write but made sure I never felt lonely!

I am forever in the debt of author Claire Scobie. I attended a Travel Memoir Course at the Australian Writers' Centre that she delivered. Her initial encouragement was decisive for me and afterwards, when I floundered, she mentored me and pulled me through.

My daughter Dale was my first editor and trod a merciful line, holding together her mother's fragile ego while proposing changes. Katie Lavers and Jon Burtt, deep in their own manuscripts, took time out to add suggestions as did my dear friend, Stephanie Chiu.

Many thanks go to Camille Scarf. When I was tired and dispirited, she stepped in with a new perspective and put a great deal of time and thought into a meticulous edit.

I am deeply grateful to my agent, Irina Dunn, who worked so diligently to find me a publisher. (By a delicious quirk of fate, Irina is the niece of Patrick O'Neil-Dunne, POD, my old Hong Kong mentor!)

And finally, to Australian Scholarly Publishing and especially, Nick Walker, Anastasia Buryak, Amelia Walker for her gorgeous cover design, and all the ASP team – thank you!

Lightning Source UK Ltd.
Milton Keynes UK
UKHW040624181019
351846UK00002B/476/P